The Handbook of
Hypnotic Phenomena
in Psychotherapy

The Handbook of Hypnotic Phenomena in Psychotherapy

by

John H. Edgette, Psy.D.

and

Janet Sasson Edgette, Psy.D., M.P.H.

BRUNNER/MAZEL *Publishers* • NEW YORK

To our son, Casey Alexander, a phenomenon in and of himself...

Library of Congress Cataloging-in-Publication Data

Edgette, John H.
  The handbook of hypnotic phenomena in psychotherapy / by
John H. Edgette and Janet Sasson Edgette.
      p.   cm.
  Includes bibliographical references and indexes.
  ISBN 0-87630-750-0
  1. Hypnotism—Therapeutic use.   2. Psychotherapy. I.
Edgette. Janet Sasson. II. Title.
RC495.E34   1995
616.89' 162—dc20   94-35103
                                                        CIP

Published by
BRUNNER/MAZEL, INC.
19 Union Square West
New York, New York 10003

Manufactured in the United States of America

10   9   8   7   6   5   4   3   2   1

CONTENTS

FOREWORD

I am not the only practitioner of hypnosis who has been waiting avidly for this book. There has been need for a fresh perspective on the importance of hypnotic phenomena in psychotherapy. Fortunately, the Edgettes recognized this lacuna and responded admirably. *The Handbook of Hypnotic Phenomena in Psychotherapy* is a comprehensive, scholarly exposition that is eminently practical and is sure to empower hypnotherapists of all persuasions.

The Edgettes stress the approach of the late Milton H. Erickson, M.D., whose pioneering work propelled an unparalleled resurgence in twentieth-century hypnosis. Erickson's use of hypnotic phenomena has never been systematically studied, yet hypnotic phenomena were integral to Erickson's approach.

In hypnosis, patients can delete, modify, and create experiences that are seemingly uncharacteristic of normal consciousness. People can be elastic in their ability to perceive the duration of subjective time; hypnotic time can be perceived as extremely long or short. Hypnotic subjects can distort their body image, change peripheral blood flow, ablate sensations of pain, dissociatively perceive themselves in other realities, convincingly regress to childhood, respond to suggestions with pinpoint specificity, and communicate cryptically with automatic drawings, while unimpedely carrying on a conversation. In summary, through hypnosis, subjects can alter their relationship with time, change sensory experiences, respond automatically, and modify memory.

Erickson saw latent potentials in such subject abilities, and he researched and utilized hypnotic phenomena clinically. His hypnotic inductions were predicated on their use and his therapies harnessed them. In each induction, Erickson suggested and used a wide variety of hypnotic phenomena—customarily indirectly. For example, he might seed "regression" within an induction. In subsequent therapy, patients might hypnotically regress to discover unrealized potentials. Further, the intense reality of hypnosis might be subjectively deepened and convincingly demonstrated as the patient carried out the regression instructions.

Want to know how to identify and use hypnotic phenomena expertly? Then, read this book. The Edgettes present and define hypnotic phenomena. They cite pertinent studies; they provide model techniques so that beginning and expert hypnotherapists can learn new perspectives easily. Importantly, they present a map through which clinicians can negotiate these previously uncharted territories and discover methods of immediate benefit to patients.

I have known John and Janet Edgette for many years and have watched their professional growth and development with keen interest. They are sure to become leading figures in the field of clinical hypnosis. With this book, they establish their expertise. They have a gift for presenting the depth of their wisdom with clarity. My wait for this book has been rewarded with a text of singular value. I look forward to learning from the Edgettes' future work, as well.

> JEFFREY K. ZEIG, PH.D.
> *Director*
> *The Milton H. Erickson Foundation*
> *Phoenix, Arizona*

ACKNOWLEDGMENTS

We would like to gratefully acknowledge the help of numerous people who participated in the development of this book. Our thanks to: Natalie Gilman, our editor, for her interest, dedication, and support; Jeffrey K. Zeig, whose ideas about hypnotic phenomena were seminal in the creation of this book; Carol Paca, our secretary-cum-friend, for her herculean efforts to type and retype the mounds of manuscript that unrelentingly came her way; Leon Sasson, my (JSE) father, who shared with me his love of learning and of words; Sarah Sasson, my mother, for her never-ending faith in my abilities; Tehsin Khokhar, for her unfailing support; George H. Morris, who taught us both about the courage to command a body of knowledge unapologetically; and Harry Aponte, who helped us believe in ourselves and own what we know.

INTRODUCTION

Many therapists attend workshop after workshop on hypnosis, read innumerable books, and still find themselves limited in their ability to use hypnosis as more than a means to relax a client or to offer basic suggestions. *The Handbook of Hypnotic Phenomena in Psychotherapy* takes the therapist beyond these basic applications toward a broader, more sophisticated scope of practice. By describing in detail the different hypnotic phenomena and how they can be widely used as **vehicles of intervention**, this book hopes to take the therapist to newer and more effective levels of clinical competence.

The Handbook of Hypnotic Phenomena in Psychotherapy discusses the selection, elicitation, and therapeutic use of the variety of hypnotic phenomena that are natural outgrowths of trance. Despite their clinical utility, we have found that hypnotic phenomena are vastly underutilized by therapists in their work with clients. They will often see workshop leaders elicit arm levitations and other forms of ideomotor movement and catalepsy in demonstration subjects or observe a client on video-tape describing an experience of positive hallucination, but they don't choose to evoke these phenomena in their own practices. We have come to realize that sometimes it is because there is uncertainty about **how to use** these experiences constructively—toward therapeutic goals. Or, sometimes a therapist is uncertain about **how to elicit** the phenomena under consideration.

Another reason for the underutilization of hypnotic phenomena is that the prospect of targeting a specific trance experience with a client is anxiety-provoking—the therapist feels solely responsible for its manifestation and worries that the client will feel disappointed if the results are not those sought. Therefore, many therapists are more comfortable simply doing generic, nonspecific trances. These allow for some relaxation and a hope that the "unconscious" will spontaneously (and benevolently) take advantage of the experience and, almost of its own accord, "do something (anything!) therapeutic."

The Handbook of Hypnotic Phenomena in Psychotherapy presents step-by-step instructions on how to elicit hypnotic phenomena such as age progression, hypnotic dreaming, hypnotic deafness, anesthesia, negative and positive hallucinations, hypermnesia, catalepsy, and others. It furthermore provides specific instruction on how to use the phenomena manifested in trance in the service of treatment. Numerous case examples* address intervention in a wide range of clinical situations including anxiety disorders, trauma and abuse, dissociative disorders, depression, marital and family problems, sports and creative performance, pain, hypersensitivity to sound, psychotic symptomalogy, and more. The book should be of interest to clinicians looking to expand their conceptualization of hypnosis as a clinical tool and to those seeking a wider repertoire of skills with which they can treat clients.

---

*All identifying characteristics have been changed to protect client confidentiality.

PART I

Preludes

Chapter 1

AN OVERVIEW OF ERICKSONIAN HYPNOSIS

Over the last decade, the popularity of Ericksonian clinical hypnosis has grown tremendously among clinicians. This approach to hypnosis and treatment is based upon the therapeutic insights and interventions of Milton H. Erickson, M.D. (1901–1980). Since the time of his death there have been six International Congresses on Ericksonian Approaches to Hypnosis and Psychotherapy, each drawing about 2,000 attendees. Any one of these meetings would constitute the largest collection of individuals in history learning about hypnosis (Zeig, 1988a). Furthermore, each year hundreds of workshops are given around the world, training thousands of professionals.

This chapter is designed to give an overview of Ericksonian hypnosis—what it is, how it works, how it is different from more classical hypnosis styles, and what its clinical uses are. It provides the foundation for the rest of the book, which deals more specifically with hypnotic phenomena, one of several vehicles of intervention in psychotherapies in which hypnosis plays a part.

HYPNOSIS

In basic terms, hypnosis refers to an altered psychological state generally characterized by certain physiological attributes (e.g., relaxed muscle tone, reduced blood pressure, slowed breath rate), by an enhanced receptivity to suggestion, and by an increased access to unconscious feelings, ideas, and memories (Erickson, 1989). It is not a stereotypical ritual involving pendulums, watches, or crystal balls, nor is it a static, fixed internal state. Rather, it is an interchange or form of communication between two (or more) people that results in the accessing and subsequent utilization of latent or underdeveloped resources. These resources may consist of past experiences, affects, or forgotten skills, and their renewed experience or application can result in changes in one's memory, perception, sensation, and/or emotion so that new behaviors and attitudes manifest (Zeig, 1987).

Trance is understood as an experience that allows for the creation of a new phenomenal world for the client. New behaviors and attitudes are able to evolve and manifest because old, limiting, rigid, or maladaptive ones are modified, dissipated, or shifted to more innocuous areas of emotional or social functioning. An example of the latter is where one's compulsive need to worry about meeting work deadlines can be channeled into worrying about when changes in one's worry pattern will first be noticed, or into worrying about how one will best use newly found recreation time.

DIRECT AND INDIRECT SUGGESTION

Suggestions made by the therapist during trancework can be either direct or indirect. Direct suggestion refers to a proposal made in a straightforward, recognizable way. Thus, a client may be told to remember vividly (hypermnesia) an earlier experience (age regression) that had filled him or her with feelings of mastery and confidence. Alternately, a client may be encouraged to have a dream (hypnotic dreaming) that will offer an insight, a partial solution, or an idea for a new direction of exploration.

On the other hand, one would use indirect suggestion to allude to a proposed action instead of suggesting it outright. For instance, a burn victim may be told stories of how firefighters put out fires and how they protect themselves from, and cope with, the experience of heat. Similarly, it can be recounted to an insomniac how she once learned to float effortlessly in water, hinting at the processes of relaxing and letting go that are requisite for sleep. In describing the process of floating, the therapist importantly avoids saying "you can go to sleep right away by relaxing and letting go, Leslie, but don't try hard to make those things happen because then they won't; instead let them happen naturally."

Indirect suggestion is always useful when conscious effort on a person's part to remedy the situation serves only to exacerbate the problem. Among those in the Ericksonian community these ideas regarding the merits of indirect suggestion are widely and strongly endorsed. The ideas seem to pan out consistently in clinical work and seem sensible. A cautionary note, however, is that experimentalists have been unable to demonstrate consistently any advantage to employing indirect suggestion (Lynn, Neufeld & Maré, 1993). Here what seems obvious in clinical work needs to be reconciled with what is being found in the research.

Among the general population exists the misconception that the effectiveness of hypnosis is largely derived from a direct suggestion on the therapist's part for the client to give up the symptom (e.g., "You will no longer feel depressed" or "You will not desire cigarettes"). Hypnosis, and particularly Ericksonian hypnosis, is better suited to and more effective when used as a means of setting in motion a constructive psychological **process** that moves clients in the direction of change. Thus, suggestions during trance may be either direct or indirect (or both), but they often do not target the symptom as the immediate site of intervention; instead they target the psychological infrastructure of the cognition, affect, or memory supporting it. Certainly, there are many exceptions to this. Cases where direct suggestion to give up the symptom is the most prudent intervention include those with hypervigilant, controlling clients who will accept therapy only if every step of the way is immediately decipherable and logical to them and those involving response-ready clients who offer negligible resistance to change. An example of the latter would be a traumatized woman psychologically ready to put behind her the disturbing, ruminative memories of a brutal assault. It could be suggested that she *"...let go of, forget those thoughts, and allow the space left open by their leaving be usurped by better ones, more joyous ones, ones of warmth and succor...even touches of humor once again, perhaps...."* An anxious test-taker can be encouraged to *"...become aware of ever-increasing degrees of relaxation, now...and then...there, seated for the exam...taking note(s)...of how easy it is to become relaxed, composed, assured...."*

The internal psychological process leading clients toward desired change can take many different forms. For some, it will be a train of relevant thoughts and associations (Zeig, 1988) that mobilize new perspectives, feelings, or behaviors. For others, change comes from the mobilization of an individual's association processes and mental skills in certain, healthier directions (Erickson & Rossi, 1981). An example is an individual who has allowed work considerations to dominate his personal life to great detriment and who is guided in trance toward such concepts as balance and perspective and then led to recall prior occasions in life where a shift in priorities reaped great reward. For yet another, it will be a change in the meaning of the symptom, as in the case of an acting-out teenager who begins to experience his behavior as *out of control* rather than as *controlling of others* as previously construed. And for a different one still, it will be plainly and simply a behavioral response to an idea or concept introduced at an unconscious level of thought by the therapist. My (JSE) most poignant recognition of the power of the latter was my utterly inadvertent making of decaffeinated, rather than caffeinated, tea right after doing a hypnosis workshop demonstration with a subject who had wanted to decrease her caffeine consumption.

Clinicians new to hypnosis often harbor one other misconception about the use of hypnosis in psychotherapy: that its effects are superficial and short-lived. Hypnosis involves changing the client's phenomenal world, the way that individual experiences his or her own self and that self in relation to the world. It is a dynamic and active form of therapy, and the effects of new experiences inside one's head often are very powerful, resonating at many levels of emotional functioning.

PERMISSIVENESS

The excitement about the Ericksonian approach to hypnosis has much to do with the revolutionary philosophy underlying its use. Erickson departed from the traditional use of hypnosis in a number of important ways. We have already described his pioneering use of indirect suggestion. Another significant departure was his conception of the hypnotherapist as permissive rather than authoritarian in the induction of the hypnotic trance (O'Hanlon, 1987). Thus, rather than definitively telling the clients what they will or will not do or experience during the trance, the therapist offers up any number of possibilities for change.

The approach uses permissive verbs such as "can" and "may," in contrast to the classical hypnotherapist's more frequent use of authoritarian verbs such as "will" and "must." This changes hypnosis from being somewhat dictatorial to being more of a democratic and cooperative endeavor. This permissive stance on the part of the therapist is especially useful when working with the more oppositional or rebellious client for whom an authoritative suggestion provides prized opportunities to resist the therapist's effort to help.

THERAPY CLIENTS AS ACTIVE AND RESOURCEFUL

Another aspect of the Ericksonian approach to hypnosis and psychotherapy that distinguishes it from the more classical approach is a change in the conceptualization of the client. Traditional hypnotherapists tend to see themselves as putting something *into* the client *from outside*. However, Ericksonian hypnotherapists emphasize the resourcefulness within clients and their inherent capacities for productive change. They therefore gear their hypnotic suggestions to these heretofore undeveloped or latent abilities. Once these unconscious or even conscious resources, are mobilized, they can be applied to the presenting problem or problems (Zeig, 1987). An example would be the parent who has difficulty allowing a college-bound child to separate and leave home; this parent's therapy would be organized around resources used previously that successfully allowed him or her to separate from the child earlier in life, such as for kindergarten or summer camp. The hypnosis thus becomes an *evocative* process, geared toward *evoking* and *utilizing* existing mental and physiological functions rather than programming or suggesting a specific course of action *for* a client (Rossi, 1980c).

TAILORING

A third important distinction between traditional hypnosis and Ericksonian hypnosis is the degree to which hypnotic inductions and suggestions are tailored to the individual needs, values, and personality structure of the client (Zeig, 1987). In the traditional approach, the clients (and experimental subjects) are often recited a standard script of a hypnotic induction and then proffered generic suggestions for symptomatic change. The change agent is thus seen as being something or someone extrinsic to the client, a perception that mitigates his or her feelings of empowerment and leaves the person feeling dependent on the therapist for the maintenance or generalization of change. Semitraditional and especially Ericksonian approaches emphasize the tailoring of induction formats and suggestions to fit each client. This not only enhances receptivity and responsivity to interventions, but expands the range of clients for whom hypnosis would work. It has been our clinical experience that hypnotizability is directly proportional to the degree to which the hypnosis is custom-fitted to the client.

To us, and most others of an Ericksonian bent, it seems axiomatic that the macro- and microtailoring of trancework is the key to effectiveness. No other technique of psychotherapy assumes a standardization of interventions, in particular of verbal injunctions; why would or should hypnosis be so limited in its conceptualization and/or application? Consider the hypnotic treatment of a cigarette smoker who needs to remove all memory and evidence of smoking from his or her life in order to successfully quit, compared to a different smoker who needs to actively mourn the loss of cigarettes by vividly remembering the last smoking experience, the smell, the feeling of exhalation, and so on. Or consider someone who overeats. A treatment approach consistent with Ericksonian tenets of individualizing the therapy would include a thorough assessment of the presenting problem and of that person's personality style. This would guide the therapist's development and delivery of the therapy. Therefore, it could be possible that for one client, issues of passivity, boredom, or depression reign prominently in relation to the problem and need to be addressed either directly or indirectly; for another client, maladaptive pleasure in the kinesthetic feeling of fullness or even "stuffed-ness" becomes the primary psychological site of intervention.

Directing interventions to the most relevant symptom-maintaining aspects of a problem, or, alternately, where you believe you will find the most plasticity in the symptom complex, are but two of innumerable ways to individualize this kind of therapy. Decisions are based upon the therapist's clinical judgment regarding the most fruitful and expedient path of intervention. Method of intervention, degree of directness or indirectness, language patterns, word choice, and story settings pose other means by which a therapist can tailor the hypnotic work.

MULTILEVEL COMMUNICATION

Ericksonian approaches to psychotherapy stamp the hypnosis done by Ericksonian practitioners with other characteristics that distinguish it from classical hypnosis. Multilevel influence communication is one such characteristic. It is a way of talking to people at multiple levels of meaning and influence, with the goal of indirectly causing some change in behavior, feeling, or attitude. These indirect, "psychological level" communications are not apparent in the overt content of the communication and are designed to effect responses without the subject being fully aware (Zeig, 1985b). This is how anecdotes, metaphors, word plays, and seemingly irrelevant (and irrational!) task assignments find their way into therapy.

A wonderful illustration of the role and power of multilevel influence communication is Erickson's work (Haley, 1973) with a very conservative couple who had never sexually consummated their marriage. The treatment consisted wholly of Erickson talking at length about the proper and most luxurious way to eat a fancy dinner, all the while emphasizing sensory and mucous membrane stimulation. The unconscious transfer of sensory stimulation to the sexual realm was evident in the follow-up letter sent by the couple a short time after the consultation!

UTILIZATION

Utilization of client attributes previously thought irrelevant or even troublesome is another essential aspect of Ericksonian hypnosis (Zeig, 1985b; Zeig & Rennick, 1991). This is apparent, for instance, in the therapeutic use of amnesia (i.e., forgetting about overeating, forgetting about chronic pain) for someone who forgets frequently. The utilization concept of Ericksonian therapy dovetails with another fundamental principle of this approach, that of the therapy being *naturalistic*. This means that it is the client's naturally occurring behavior in the here and now that is used to absorb attention, redirect it inward, and induce trance. No external devices or stimuli are needed to facilitate the development of trance; rather, those natural facets of internal experiences (images, memories, affects, experiences in the body) are the basis of treatment (Erickson & Rossi, 1980a).

Whereas a more rigidly traditional hypnotherapist might find a client's obsessional self-vigilance during a first hypnosis experience to be a hindrance to developing trance, a utilization approach would allow for the use of that client's self-consciousness *as the very means by which he or she enters into a trance.* By suggesting that the client become *more and more absorbed by* self-consciousness, the therapist can help the client become inwardly focused without "fighting" against his or her natural tendency to be obsessionally self-aware. Such a client *could have been* labeled "resistant" or a "low-hypnotizable"; however, in this therapeutic framework, utilization of the client's presenting behavior without trying to change, eradicate, or suppress it affords a smoother and more efficient therapy, as well as the application of hypnosis to a wider population than traditionally thought possible (see Edgette, 1988, for a more extensive discussion of this point and for examples with psychotics). Attention to motivational factors, a future and solutions focus rather than a past and problems orientation, and confidence in their clients' resourcefulness—once the therapist creates a context to propel adaptive change—are other important distinguishing features of this type of therapy.

CLINICAL APPLICATIONS OF HYPNOSIS

There are many applications of clinical hypnosis and there is no psychological disorder in and of itself that could not be treated with it. Some conditions, however, do require an advanced amount of knowledge of hypnosis and special parameters because of the risk of severe regression, the emergence of overwhelming affect states, or personality disorganization. Treating psychotics or severely character-disordered clients would be included in this category (Edgette, 1988). Sometimes hypnosis is contraindicated because of *what it means* to a client; one example of this is the client who insists on seeing hypnosis as a way of giving up responsibility for solving a problem. Another example is the client with a very eroticized transference who insists on construing the hypnotic session in sexualized terms. Apart from intense and idiosyncratic interpretations of the meaning of hypnosis, all types of clients and disorders are potentially treatable.

There are, though, some important and unique indications for hypnosis. These are areas where other psychological and psychosocial treatment approaches are ineffective or irrelevant. One such application of hypnosis is in the field of forensics, where the clinician helps a witness to remember things related to a crime (Alexander & Brady, 1985). Hypnosis is also especially useful in the treatment of multiple personality disorders and other dissociative states or in cases of trauma where severe repression exists (Millette, 1988). Hypnosis is also highly effective for pain control and can obviate or reduce a need for narcotics or other types of medication (Erickson, 1980d).

Severe burns, headaches, and phantom limb pain are other examples where hypnosis is particularly helpful. It can also be used to treat such diverse conditions as tinnitus, hemophilia (Cheek, 1982; Corley, 1982; Mon, 1982) and the negative side effects of cancer treatment, such as nausea or vomiting or even the fears that develop around the treatment regimen itself (Rosen, 1985). Furthermore, hypnosis is quite effective with dermatological conditions such as eczema, excessive blushing, alopecia ariota (disorder of the autoimmune system resulting in hair falling out in clumps), and even warts (Cheek, 1982; Corley, 1982; Mon, 1982).

In addition to the above, there are particular pediatric applications. Asthmatic conditions (Baumann, 1982) can be treated with hypnosis, as can encopresis and enuresis (Mills & Crowley, 1988). Children who are hyperactive or who have attention-deficit related problems can be taught to relax and focus, helping them to reduce or even eliminate the use of medication (Baumann, 1982; Rigler, 1982). Hypnosis can be used to help students compensate for various learning disabilities by using other senses and psychological capacities (Mills & Crowley, 1986). For instance, a youngster with poor visual processing can be taught to enhance and rely more strongly on auditory capacities.

Recently, Ericksonian hypnosis has been applied and extended to new clinical situations that had been ignored or considered untreatable by classical hypnotic means. For example, special populations now seen as treatable using Ericksonian clinical hypnosis include agoraphobics (Edgette, 1985), psychotics (Edgette, 1988), and uncooperative and severely disturbed teenagers (Edgette, 1990). Advances in areas such as these are born of the creativity and flexibility of hypnotic design afforded by the Ericksonian approach, in contrast to the more standardized approaches to induction characteristic of traditional hypnosis.

We have spoken about the characteristics of an Ericksonian approach to psychotherapy and hypnosis and indications for its clinical use. The next two chapters continue to provide a foundation for the subsequent chapters on specific hypnotic phenomena. Chapter 2 provides a brief definition and description of the different hypnotic phenomena, while Chapter 3 discusses the selection process by which a therapist can measure the relative usefulness of the various phenomena and likelihood of successful elicitation. Following this, the reader can examine the remaining chapters in any order guided by interest, curiosity, or clinical need.

Chapter 2

WHAT ARE HYPNOTIC PHENOMENA?

Hypnotic phenomena can be described as natural behavioral and experiential manifestations of the trance state. They include both subjectively experienced psychological events, such as remembering, forgetting, distortions in one's sense of time, and alterations in perception, as well as observable events, such as the levitation of an arm or the automatic, unconsciously driven scribbling of words across a pad.

Hypnotic phenomena have been reported in all cultures across the world and throughout all periods of recorded history (Wickramasekera, 1988). They typically manifest in either religious or healing/medical contexts. Wickramasekera also notes that the discovery of hypnotic phenomena did not begin with Anton Mesmer (1734–1815) as is commonly believed; he was simply the first to propose an (arguably) naturalistic, rather than magical or demonic, explanation. Mesmer's theory of hypnosis was based on the idea of "animal magnetism" radiating from one's own person.

Lankton (1982) describes how trance phenomena are not elicited solely during courses of psychotherapies where formal hypnosis is being used but are often found in other therapies as well. He notes that such phenomena occur as a result of trance-eliciting communication patterns and concentrated internal attention, and not from physical differences between normal waking states and trance. He wisely points out that what might be called an "age regression" in one therapy would readily appear as a "child ego state" or as a "transference reaction" in another, and he uses verbatim transcript material to illustrate the presentation of a variety of hypnotic phenomena, such as hypermnesia, positive and negative hallucination, and age regression, in one session of a therapy conducted without formal trance.

CHARACTERISTICS OF THE TRANCE STATE

Erickson (Erickson, 1934/1980; 1939/1980; 1944b/1980; 1952/1980) described several mental/somatic features of trance he considered characteristic of most hypnotic states. These include suggestibility; literalness; and the phenomena of catalepsy, amnesia, sensory changes, and posthypnotic suggestibility. There are other regular features of hypnotic trance, too: the physiological concomitants of trance such as depressions in respiratory and pulse rates, ocular changes, and decreases in orienting movements (Zeig, 1984) or the experiences of enhanced rapport and trance logic (Erickson, 1944b/1980; Gilligan, 1987; Orne, 1959; Zeig, 1984). We prefer to view these as manifestations of trance that are categorically different from the hypnotic phenomena discussed in this book, which rise out of the hypnotic experience and are usable for therapeutic gain. The distinction is between mental mechanisms that are best used for therapeutic change and those physiological and mental indicators of trance. The latter are excluded here from consideration.

VARIETIES OF HYPNOTIC PHENOMENA

Catalepsy is a special state of muscle tone and balance that permits the subject to sustain postures and positions for unusually long periods of time without appreciable fatigue. It is accompanied by a slowing of all psychomotor activity and is the basis for other phenomena such as arm levitation (Erickson, 1941/1980).

An alteration in one's sense of time is another hypnotic phenomenon that is commonly experienced by subjects even under conditions of light trance. Time becomes very subjective and dissociated from standard measures (Erickson, 1959/1980). A person in trance for 25 minutes who thinks the trance has been only 10 minutes long is experiencing **time contraction**. Someone who feels a 10-minute trance to be a half hour in duration experiences **time expansion**.

Dissociation is one of the more widely recognized and experienced hypnotic phenomena. O'Hanlon (1987) describes it as a separation of psychological states into conscious and unconscious or as a separation of emotions from thoughts, behaviors, and feelings. Gilligan (1987), citing Hilgard (1977), writes that dissociation may be defined as "a mental process in which systems of ideas are split off from the normal personality and operate independently" (p. 35). Gilligan adds that dissociation, apart from being a vehicle of intervention in its own right, is also the process by which the development of other hypnotic phenomena—such as age regression, automatic writing, pain control, and therapeutic hallucinations—take place. After all, it is the suspension of logical, rational, intellectualized thought that allows these other, seemingly irrational or regressive, experiences to be brought forth into consciousness.

Amnesia refers to a functional loss of the ability to recall or identify past experiences. Erickson described amnesia as constituting "...a form of dynamic behavior quite different from ordinary forgetting" (Erickson, 1980b, p. 53) manifested in its ability to have subjects forget things generally considered impossible to forget, such as one's name and age. Amnesia can be induced in hypnosis either to ablate memories (of experience, affect, cognition) that occurred prior to trance or ablate those being created during the trance experience itself. This is important in those instances where the therapeutic work would be compromised if the client were to become consciously aware of the hypnotic learnings before being able to integrate them into a more conscious awareness comfortably (Gilligan, 1987).

Hypermnesia refers to an enhanced memory ability that transcends everyday recollection. This hypnotic phenomenon allows subjects to remember vividly earlier memories in all their sensory detail (Erickson, 1944b/1980).

The phenomenon of **age regression** is partly based upon the mechanisms of amnesia and hypermnesia. In the context of hypnosis, age regression allows one to reexperience memories of an earlier period. Age regressions differ from simple hypermnesia in that the subject *relives* rather than just remembers past events and, at times, experiences a return to the psychological state as it existed then (Weitzenhoffer, 1989a). Thus, an adult can respond to suggestions to have amnesia for his or her adult years and return to the cognitive, affective, and behavioral experience of being a teenager. True age regressions like that, where there is a demonstrable suspension of adult faculties and motor responses, are more difficult to elicit than regressions where the subject retains adult faculties and behaviors and simply reexperiences an earlier time/memory. In fact, the validity of these types of experiences has been vigorously debated in the journal literature (see Chapter 8 on Age Regression). Nonetheless, there are reports of subjects evidencing childlike intellectual functioning, handwriting changes, altered vocabulary, and other objective manifestations of those types of regressions (Erickson, 1980c; Kroger, 1963).

Future progression (also referred to as **age progression, future orientation**, and **pseudo-orientation** in time) is the hypnotic phenomenon that disorients the subject away from the present and into the future. The experience can be one of seeing the future self, talking to the future self, or being the future self, with access to the imagined thoughts and feelings of the older self.

Negative and **positive hallucinations** refer to alterations in the subject's experience of sensory stimuli. Hallucinations can involve any of the sensory systems of vision, hearing, taste, touch, and smell. Negative hallucinations refer to the person's *not* perceiving a stimulus that actually does exist in the immediate environment. For instance, a person who is sensitive to cigarette odor and who works in an environment where smoking is present may be helped to reduce her perception of cigarette smoke in the air via negative olfactory hallucinations. A teenager taunted at school can learn to effect negative auditory hallucinations for the comments of his pesty or cruel peers. A sales manager anxious about giving an oral report to a roomful of supervisors can use negative visual hallucinations to blur the clarity with which she recognizes their faces. **Hypnotic blindness, color blindness,** and **deafness** (extremes of the phenomenon of negative hallucination) have been reported in the literature even (Erickson, 1939/1980; Kroger, 1963). This ability of the body to ignore the perception of specific sensory stimuli is one of the bases for using anesthesia and analgesia for pain control.

Positive hallucinations refer to a person's experience of a sensory stimulus that is not actually present. Thus, a person can use the positive olfactory hallucination of liniment as a posthypnotic cue to gear up for an athletic competition. Positive auditory hallucinations can help a self-doubting, novice therapist recall the encouraging words of a respected supervisor or the positive feedback from a satisfied client. That same sales manager, anxious about her oral report, can alternately be helped to created a positive visual hallucination vis-à-vis her audience of supervisors, wherein she experiences the room filled instead with family and friends or even strangers.

Automatic writing is a hypnotic phenomenon that is an outgrowth of a dissociation between conscious and unconscious mental functioning. The subject, in response to direct or indirect suggestions to write, does in fact write with pen and paper but without conscious awareness, vigilance, or interference. The material may include previously repressed ideas or memories useful in propelling the client toward health. It may give rise to associations that the client then applies toward problem resolution, or it may provide a new perspective on the problem or a solution. Also, the process of uncensored writing may actually turn out to be the most important aspect of the experience, allowing for reengagement with a more liberated, creative, and disinhibited part of the self. **Automatic drawing** or **painting** would be, of course, the artistic correlates to automatic writing.

Posthypnotic suggestion refers to the execution, at some later (posttrance) time or date, of instructions or suggestions given during trance (Erickson, 1941/1980). A couple using hypnosis for childbirth can be told together in trance that their first sighting of the hospital when they drive up during labor will automatically begin the upper/lower body dissociation and anesthesia sensations practiced previously in session.

Analgesia refers to a dulling in one's awareness of pain whereas **anesthesia** refers to a complete lack of awareness of pain (Kroger, 1963). These hypnotic phenomena are especially useful in pain control cases where medication is contraindicated (i.e., risk of allergic reaction, history of drug addiction or abuse) or is unavailable.

Hyperesthesia refers to an enhanced sensitivity to physical sensations such as touch, warmth, or coolness. Kroger (1963), noting differences in responsivity to hyperesthesia among different psychiatric populations, hypothesizes that pain is not a fixed response to a painful stimulus but rather a sensation, the perception of which is modified by past experiences, expectation, and cultural attitudes. This idea provides the essential underpinnings for the viability and applicability of pain control measures such as analgesia, anesthesia, and hyperesthesia.

Hypnotic dreaming entails the subject's capacity to have, either in session or at home during sleep, a directed therapeutic dream that is an immediate by-product of the suggestion given in session.

Ideomotor movement involves the body's motor system reacting and acting as if directed by the unconscious mind, with the result that the person feels the movement to be avolitional, that is, that the conscious mind is a passive observer. **Arm levitation** is one example of ideomotor movement.

Many practitioners of hypnosis have remarked upon the similarities between clinical symptoms and trance phenomena (Gilligan, 1988b, 1990; Kershaw, 1992; Kihlstrom, 1979; Yapko, 1990). Beahrs (1982) reframed symptoms as "misused hypnotic skill." In fact, in the nineteenth century it was the ability to induce hypnotic phenomena phenotypically similar to the symptoms of hysteria that led investigators to propose theories of psychological causation as alternatives to the somatogenic viewpoint prevailing at that time (Kihlstrom, 1979). The experimental study of the phenomena of hypnosis for purposes of better understanding basic psychological processes involved in psychopathology continued throughout the next century (Kihlstrom, 1979).

Gilligan (1988b) describes symptom phenomena as being everyday versions of classical trance phenomena. Shared characteristics include an increased experiential involvement, whether it be a sense of detachment (symptom) or dissociation (trance phenomenon); temporal variability, such as a depressed person stuck in the seeming hopelessness of the present (symptom), or time expansion (trance phenomenon); and sustained attention, for instance, feeling in a rut (symptom) versus feeling in a groove (trance); among others. We frequently refer to symptom expression as hypnotic phenomena run amuck.

Kershaw (1992) expands the concept of symptoms as hypnotic phenomena to include their manifestations in couples' relationships. She describes how one partner will often "see" or "hear" the other partner behave in a way that is not perceptually accurate (positive hallucination) or, in other instances, *not* perceive behavior that is present (negative hallucination). An extreme example of the latter is when one partner doesn't see rather obvious evidence of the other partner having an affair. Another example from Kershaw is the arguing couple, in which one partner excessively remembers each little detail of a previous interaction (hypermnesia) while the other has largely forgotten the entire episode (amnesia).

Gilligan (1988b) writes that the task of the therapist using hypnosis in psychotherapy is to validate the symptom phenomena and pave the way for their transformation into a more psychologically adaptive solution. This involves deframing the client's perceptual orientation so that the phenomena can be observed independently of their previously ascribed value. The client then shapes the symptom phenomena into *hypnotic skill*, which then become part of the solution. The critical variable in making this transformation from a devalued, deficit-oriented experience to a valued, resource-oriented one is the relationship context between therapist and client. This provides an opportunity for a different phenomena *content* (i.e., to remember/reexperience/relive times of mastery and confidence instead of times of disempowerment and despair), a different level of trust in one's own self and resourcefulness, and a different self-valuation.

Hypnotic phenomena can also be understood apart from either a symptomatic or clinical context. Erickson (Erickson & Rossi, 1980a) viewed them as coming out of the repertoire of experiential ("latent") learnings that a person collects and stores over a lifetime. They are said also to spring from the innumerable overlearned, automatic behavioral responses that become part of one's ordinary psychological experience of the world. Thus, hypnotic phenomena can be seen as being borne of familiar aspects of one's day-to-day mental and physical functioning; their significance in hypnotic work is that the experiences transcend—in richness, pervasiveness, and pliability—the normal experience of the phenomena in question and can be used to effect therapeutic change.

INDIVIDUAL MANIFESTATIONS OF HYPNOTIC PHENOMENA AND HYPNOSIS SUGGESTIBILITY TESTS

The hypnotic phenomena that manifest in trance vary both in their degrees and varieties for each individual, depending upon the person's innate personality style and native endowment. They manifest differently even within an individual depending upon the type and depth of trance or as a function of personality needs. Therefore, a client's need to be solicitous and dependent vis-à-vis the therapist on a particular day will likely result in a different trance experience than one elicited on a day where the client's need is to be aggressive and covertly uncooperative. Thus, the interpersonal dynamics of the psychotherapy setting are clearly very important and very relevant. Certainly, different affective states will affect the hypnotic phenomena experienced; for example, a depression may make it either more or less difficult to summon forth the sensory details and nuances of a deep age regression or to appreciate the whimsy of an arm levitation.

This is quite a different emphasis from how hypnotic phenomena are typically treated by traditionalists and experimentalists. They often view them as more fixed entities and examine them primarily by way of hypnosis suggestibility tests. These hypnosis suggestibility tests provide standardized measurements of hypnotic responsivity or suggestibility based on a standardized induction and presentation of the material.

Traditionalists value these tests mainly as research instruments to control for level of hypnotizability and to isolate high hypnotizables for experimental groups and low hypnotizables for control groups. Traditionalists sometimes also value these scales (and their modified versions) for clinical use; with their classical emphasis on standard inductions and direct suggestions, many of them believe that hypnosis should be offered primarily as a treatment to those for whom it is deemed appropriate—that is, moderate to high hypnotizables. Scales then become useful in determining treatment or possible treatments of choice.

In and of themselves, the scales are not of much interest to us; we emphasize helping each client to become a "good enough" hypnotic subject, either through his or her practice of certain hypnotic techniques or through our modifications in the hypnotic setting and/or induction.

Furthermore, we consider the onus to be on us—the therapist—to figure out and to provide the context and means by which a client can go comfortably into a hypnotic trance, experience a variety of hypnotic phenomena, and put them to use in constructive ways.

For the purposes of this book, these scales are important because they are composed entirely of items that test a subject's ability to produce hypnotic phenomena. Unfortunately, none of the scales reveal a connection between a given hypnotic phenomenon and how the phenomenon can be used in treatment. The hypnotic phenomena are merely a means to an end, test items to be passed or failed en route to an overall score, which is usually the additive sum of the items passed. Nonetheless, these hypnosis rating scales then become of some interest to us; as standardized tests, they provide well-researched information on how difficult one hypnotic phenomenon is to achieve compared to another.

The end result is that by examining these scales we can get a general idea of how the general public responds to various hypnotic phenomena. As Bowers (1976) points out, the general finding is that the easier items tend to involve ideomotor responses requiring eye closure and hand lowering (such as "your hand will get heavy and fall"), while the more difficult items tend to be those requiring profound perceptual-cognitive distortions, such as posthypnotic amnesia and hallucinations. (For example, one item, rated very difficult, may suggest that the subject will be unable to smell household ammonia placed right under the nose.)

For more specific information, we have reprinted a chart from Bowers (1993) listing each test item from the newly developed Waterloo-Stanford Group C Scale of Hypnotic Susceptibility (WSGC) (see Table 2.1). Listed are the percentage of subjects passing each item in the test. Also listed, to the right, are the percentage that passed the corresponding item on the better-known and more widely used Stanford Hypnotic Susceptibility Scale, Form C (SHSS:C). It is important for practitioners unaccustomed to referring to these scales to note that although there are general tendencies for some items to be much easier for average subjects to pass compared to other items, many of the percentages are close enough to each other to indicate that for a given subject, one item generally considered difficult may be passed, while another generally considered easier is failed.

This observation is also reflected in the item-total correlations listed, which show how the score on each item correlates to the overall score. Basically, the correlations show that although each test item is responded to distinctly and differently by subjects, each item also has enough in common and enough overlap with other test items that there will be distinct individual patterning apart from the averaging of individual statistics into group norms. The upshot for us as clinicians who deal with different types of clients is that although it is important to have an awareness of which hypnotic phenomena are generally easier or more difficult to elicit, we should always be tuned into individual preferences and the responsivity of a given client who may depart radically from what can be expected given group norms.

Why not give a hypnotic susceptibility test to determine individual patterns of responsivity? Some people might consider doing this, but traditionally the length of time it takes to administer these tests plus the formality associated with them have precluded their common use in everyday clinical practice (Spiegel & Spiegel, 1978). Most tests take

TABLE 2.1*

Item Data From Normative WSGC Sample and for Comparable SHSS:C Items

	WSGC		SHSS:C	
	% passing (n = 259)	Item-total correlation (biserial rs)[a] (n = 259)	% passing (n = 203)[b]	Item-total correlation (biserial rs) (n = 203)
Hand lowering	90	.47	90	.60
Hands moving together	70	.50	88	.49
Age regression	61	.73	43	.68
Arm rigidity	60	.71	45	.76
Arm immobilization	56	.57	36	.81
Taste hallucination	55	.58	46	.75
Dream	44	.46	44	.57
Posthypnotic drawing	41	.46	19[c]	.65[c]
Mosquito hallucination	38	.65	48	.80
Amnesia	25 (35)[d]	.74 (.67)	27	.85
Negative visual hallucination	24	.67	9	.87
Hallucinated music	15	.49	9[e]	.63[e]

[a] Calculated by correlating each item with the entire scale minus the item.
[b] The *n* here is based on a subset of the normative sample (*n* = 307).
[c] SHSS:C values refer to the anosmia item, which the posthypnotic drawing replaces.
[d] Values in parentheses refer to the amnesia item when scored using the classic criterion of remembering three or fewer items.
[e] SHSS:C values refer to the hallucinated voice, which the hallucinated music replaces in the WSGC.
Note. SHSS:C data from Hilgard (1965, p. 238).

*Reprinted with permission from K. S. Bowers (1993), "The Waterloo-Stanford Group C (WSCG) Scale of Hypnotic Susceptibility: Normative and comparative data." *The International Journal of Clinical and Experimental Hypnosis, 41* (1), p. 41.

at least an hour or an hour and a half to administer. For research purposes the total time that has to be put into giving these tests has been reduced by the development of susceptibility scales that can be given to entire groups at once, such as the WSGC and the well-known and often-used Harvard Group Scale of Hypnotic Susceptibility (Shor & Orne, 1962). However, these tests don't help the clinician who is looking to get some information about the client of the hour.

The problem of the length of these scales has been solved by Hilgard and Hilgard (1975, 1983, 1994) with their development of the Stanford Hypnotic Clinical Scale (SHCS), which considerably shortens the time for administration and scoring, though still not sufficiently for many clinicians (Spiegel & Spiegel, 1978). Herbert and David Spiegel (1978), in the development of their Hypnotic Induction Profile (HIP), shortened the time of administration and scoring even further, making their susceptibility test the most user-friendly in clinical circumstances. But even with administration times down to 10 or 20 minutes or so, these abbreviated tests designed for clinical use have one major drawback for those of us interested in using hypnotic phenomena in treatment: they have been abbreviated to the point where they only measure two or three hypnotic phenomena. Therefore, by using them, you may get a sense of how hypnotizable your subject is vis-à-vis the general population, but you're not going to get the information that we consider valuable, which is a profile of the pattern of hypnotic responsivity across the variety of hypnotic phenomena.

We strongly feel that one good way to get a working profile is for the clinician to learn to do informal assessments based on well-honed observational abilities supported by a broad knowledge base for how hypnotic phenomena appear in everyday life. Once a therapist is aware of how hypnotic phenomena pop up in everyday life and interactions, it's easy to make good informal assessments. A second good way is to induce hypnosis and observe and ask about what phenomena are produced naturally (without items being suggested). This will be discussed in greater depth later.

If the clinician wishes to log the time necessary to administer one of the longer and research-oriented hypnosis scales, he or she might be best off utilizing the Stanford Profile Scales, 1 and 2 (SPS: 1 & 2) (Weizenhoffer & Hilgard, 1967). According to Bowers (1976), these were developed for the purpose of identifying "specific areas of hypnotic skills in a person—to determine his or her hypnotic profile, so to speak" (p. 65). Hilgard (1987), however, currently downplays this use of the test and mainly discusses it in the same way that people discuss the Stanford Hypnotic Susceptibility Scale, Form C—as an upward extension of the earlier Stanford Hypnotic Susceptibility Scales Forms A and B (Weitzenhoffer & Hilgard, 1959), which are much easier since they are loaded with a preponderance of motor items and only have a few items that call for profound perceptual-cognitive distortions.

Hypnotic susceptibility is just one aspect to measure in the production of hypnotic phenomena. Hypnotic depth, which can fluctuate more rapidly, is also a consideration. Tart (1978/1979) found that when clinicians get a hypnotic depth report before each item on the SHSS:C, the mean depth report across all subjects item by item was always greater for SHSS:C items subsequently passed than for the items subsequently failed. This difference was statistically significant for almost all items. Further, the more difficult an item (in terms of fewer people passing it for population norms), the greater the average difference in mean depth report between those subjects subsequently passing versus those failing. For clinicians not familiar with how to rapidly assess hypnotic depth, we refer you to Tart's excellent article (1978/1979), "Quick and Convenient Assessment of Hypnotic Depth: Self Report Scales," which was published in the *American Journal of Clinical Hypnosis.*

Tart's findings on the significance of trance depth are at odds with what Erickson said about the matter (Erickson, 1952/1980). It was Erickson's belief that no hypnotic phenomenon belonged to one particular level of hypnotic trance; some subjects will develop phenomena in a light trance that others will only get during deep trance states and vice versa. Equivocal findings notwithstanding, clinicians who use hypnotic phenomena in their practices will want to be alert to all relevant variables of a client's experience. Knowing how to accomplish an assessment of depth will enable the astute clinician to garner even more information with regard to the likelihood of a given client being able to produce a particular hypnotic phenomenon, in session or out, given the clinician's suggestion. If the production of a hypnotic phenomenon is based in part on subject depth, it is prudent for therapists to take this into account.

Erickson himself wasn't so interested in conducting research based on group comparisons. He was more interested in individuals and how each one could respond to therapeutic intervention optimally. He was also interested in exploring the outermost limits of responsivity for a hypnotic phenomenon in a given subject. In fact, Erickson would often train his research subjects for hours, to the point where they could go into very deep trance states. He would then see what kind of hypnotic experiences could be produced. We posit that if you take low and medium hypnotizables and work with them on developing their hypnotic responsivity in ways that are appealing and make sense for them as individuals, there would be significant increases in their responsivity to hypnotic suggestion and therapeutic intervention.

Murray-Jobsis (1991) provides an interesting piece of clinical research that contributes to the notion that tailoring hypnotic procedures to an individual client and developing the therapeutic relationship enables clients to elicit hypnotic phenomena better than they would have under standard and impersonal conditions. In her research, Murray-Jobsis found that her borderline and schizophrenic patients consistently performed better than the schizophrenic and borderline patients in prior studies, which were experimental in nature. Her clients achieved much higher scores on various measures of hypnotizability, such as on the Stanford Scales and the Hypnotic Induction Profile of Spiegel. In observations made during the standardized administration of these scales, and then especially on post-test interview, it became clear to Murray-Jobsis that because there was a good therapeutic relationship, coupled with attention given to control and trust issues, clients were able to manifest catalepsy, arm levitation, and positive hallucinations. The clients clearly indicated that were they not familiar with Dr. Murray-Jobsis and trusting of her, they would not have been able to perform these hypnotic phenomena.

Although Murray-Jobsis works from a very different theoretical framework (psychoanalytic), she concurs with an Ericksonian viewpoint when she says that performance on hypnotic susceptibility scales and hence the manifestation of hypnotic phenomena are "relationship dependent," and that key patient issues need to be accommodated and meaningfully addressed in order for maximal performance to be evident. This lends credence to the notion that individuals do not necessarily do the easier hypnotic phenomena ahead of the more difficult hypnotic phenomena and that performance can vary greatly depending on conditions.

Interestingly, one of the issues that these patients found most difficult about the test was that it was so direct and seemingly forceful; their difficulty was attenuated however by their having relationships with Dr. Murray-Jobsis. This makes an interesting case for the value of using indirection in hypnosis.

Protinsky is one of the few clinicians currently writing in the journal literature about using hypnotic phenomena in therapy. His pioneering article in the *Journal of Strategic and Systemic Therapies* (1988) describes not only the use of a variety of hypnotic phenomena in therapy but makes a breakthrough by showing how hypnotic phenomena can be used in marital and family therapy. He points out that individual hypnotic experiences can be elicited and utilized *to change the system*, be it marital or family.

For example, in his section on negative hallucination, Protinsky describes how a husband who says he cannot stop himself from being angry at his wife when she has a "disgusted look on her face" can be given a negative hallucination for that look so that the pattern is interrupted. He also talks about using age regression with partners to take them to earlier times in their relationship, times when they may have felt closeness and intimacy so that they can rekindle it in their present relationship. Linking, or connecting, the retrieved hypnotic resource to the current situation is discussed as an important part of the therapy. The couple who are age regressed and discover their feelings of affection are encouraged, for example, to come out of trance, look at each other, experience the retrieved affection in the present, and then sustain the affection as they solve current arguments.

Interestingly, Protinsky discusses the use of dissociation as an antidotal symbol for an undifferentiated couple or family. For example, he might have an enmeshed couple experience the dissociation inherent in an arm levitation and then have them *really notice how their arms feel apart*, suggesting to them that just as their arms can be experienced as being separate from them, they can create a firm boundary between the two of them. We can add that it might be additionally useful in such situations to point out to the couple that they can feel the dissociated separateness of the arms from their bodies while also knowing at a different level that the connectedness remains—the arm can feel at once apart and connected. This would be an excellent intervention for people who feel that when they are away from their partners, the relationship ceases to exist. At those times they wind up feeling very alone and abandoned and often go back to their enmeshed ways.

Later sections of the book will describe the different hypnotic phenomena defined in this chapter in even further detail, discuss clinical indications and contraindications, and most significantly, explain how to facilitate their development in session. First, however, the next chapter will show how a therapist goes about deciding which hypnotic phenomena are most appropriate to apply in different clinical situations.

Chapter 3

WITH A BUFFET SPREAD LIKE THAT, HOW DO I KNOW WHAT TO EAT?: SELECTING APPROPRIATE HYPNOTIC PHENOMENA

Although the chapters that follow largely deal with *how to elicit* the hypnotic phenomenon in question, this chapter will elucidate the major principles regarding *how to choose* amongst the different phenomena and apply the correct one for intervention. These guidelines will aid you greatly in making your choice.

PANNING FOR GOLD IN
THE RIVERBED OF PERSONALITY

The first principle is to use the hypnotic phenomenon that the person does best. By virtue of their personality and psychological resources, people come to life and come to therapy sessions "prepackaged" to perform some phenomena and not others. How do we discern which these are? One way is simply to start off a session with a "neutral" trance, a trance experience involving relaxation and the other aspects of hypnosis, but without any clinical intervention per se. When the person comes out of this "neutral" trance and together you process the experience, he or she will quite likely say to you that one or another hypnotic phenomenon was experienced, although of course the client won't know to call it that.

For example, one person might come out of trance and say that he felt as if his mind was divided in half, with one part observing and the other part experiencing, and that it was a very interesting and odd experience (dissociation). Another person may come out of trance and say that she forgot most of what was said (amnesia). Still, a third person may come out of trance and say that she was quite struck by the numb, warm, heavy feeling that developed in her arms (catalepsy and anesthesia). Another way to discern which hypnotic phenomena a person does best is to conduct trial probes, experimenting with the elicitation of different ones to see which come forth for the person most easily and are experienced most richly and pleasurably.

Often, a sensitive clinician can respond to minimal cues and discern which hypnotic phenomena the person might be good at prior to even the first therapy session. For example, I (JHE) got a call from a new client who wished to set up an appointment time. She did not mention what the presenting problem was. When she came into the office, she sat down and an alarm clock in her pocketbook went off. She proceeded to apologize profusely while pulling out some vitamins to ingest. She explained to me that she had to set the timer and then take the vitamins whenever the timer went off or else she would forget to take them. This woman was a natural for the use of amnesia, and I found myself thinking how ironic it was that I knew what the intervention would be even before I had a sense of the presenting problem!

Other clients might take an appointment time and not need to write it down on a card or in an appointment book (hypermnesia). Another client might write it down in two places and yet still call to confirm an appointment (amnesia again). Still another client might come a half hour early for the session saying that he thought it would take much longer to get to the office, even though he knew the route (time distortion). When you have a mind set oriented toward panning for the gold of hypnotic phenomena, you can see them most easily, even in everyday life. Whatever hypnotic phenomena the person does best and most naturally can become a resource for accomplishing the therapy (Zeig, 1988a).

The hypnotic phenomenon to be considered in treatment should be determined not by the wishes and hypnotic aptitudes of the therapist but by the client's innate tendencies. Furthermore, it is important to keep in mind that whichever phenomena actually manifest are largely determined by the client's (conscious and unconscious) interpretation and acceptance of the therapist's suggestions. Situations—either clinical or experimental—where subjects respond to an operator's suggestions for anesthesia with dissociation or catalepsy should not be considered failures! Accepting, utilizing, pacing, and leading clients' behaviors in the direction of constructive change is the name of the game.

IF IT'S PART OF THE PROBLEM, IT CAN BE PART OF THE SOLUTION

The second principle of using hypnotic phenomena, and one that often overlaps with the first, harkens back to the principle of utilization. It involves the therapeutic use of the very phenomena that have been a part of the problem (Erickson, 1965; Gilligan, 1987, 1988 a, b; Zeig, 1988a). Thus, if hypnotic phenomena are involved in the manifestation of the pathology or the symptom, they could be involved in the treatment of that condition. The classic example of this occurs with people who have a dissociative disorder secondary to having experienced a trauma. These people often dissociate involuntarily and it becomes problematic for them in many life situations. Yet, one method of working hypnotically with such individuals is by enabling them, if clinically indicated and timely (see Chapter 8 on Age Regression for parameters of treatment), to work through some of the trauma while maintaining some degree of dissociation. This way, experiences that were once overwhelming, be they abuse, war, accident, or some type of disaster, are not *re*-experienced in full—painfully.

Likewise, every obsessive unwittingly uses hypermnesia to get "radar lock" on his or her obsession of choice. One can intervene by having the person develop hypermnesia instead for the idea or thought that would assuage the relevant worry. For instance, a man ruminating about an awkward social encounter with a prospective date can instead remember over and over the many times people have experienced his shyness as endearing. Gilligan's (1990) examples of utilizing a client's shaky hands for ideomotor signaling, or a client's stomach nausea as a source of *warmth* that can spread throughout the body, also illustrate this concept of changing problems into solutions.

OPPOSITES NEUTRALIZE

Another principle for selecting the most appropriate hypnotic phenomena is to use that which is the *opposite* of the one generating the problem. Hypnotic phenomena frequently come in complements; that is, phenomena are sometimes like one side of a coin with its "matching opposite" constituting the other side. Here is a list of common pairings of phenomena:

amnesia	—	hypermnesia
time contraction	—	time expansion
age regression	—	future progression
anesthesia	—	hyperesthesia
negative hallucinations	—	positive hallucinations

Most depressed people, as a part of their formula for engendering depression, are very past-oriented. Moreover, they usually take themselves back to past example after past example of their failings. One therapeutic tack then could be to use future progression, moving them forward in time to imagined circumstances of success. This might be a challenge for the person so lacking in esteem or so devoted to the position of helplessness or hopelessness that he or she cannot imagine any positive future scenario. For some, the notion of competence and/or success might be too psychologically frightening and thus engender anxiety. These points are said to underscore the multidimensional nature of symptoms and diagnoses and to orient therapists toward developing overarching, conceptually integrated plans for the therapy in which the use of hypnotic phenomena is systematically employed, rather than being "applied" to the client in a haphazard and isolated fashion. Therapy is a process and not an event or intervention.

Another example of using complementary phenomena is with a client who has the habit of chewing her cheek inside the mouth. That person does not feel pain when most people would and so could be said to be using anesthesia to create the problem. Using the complement would entail hypnotizing her for the purpose of bringing forth a hyperesthesia to sensitize the inner cheek to the physiological cues of discomfort or pain.

PHENOMENA AS SYMBOLS

A fourth principle for deciding which phenomenon to choose is selecting one that can be used as a therapeutic symbol. In one of the training films issued by The Milton H. Erickson Foundation, Inc., entitled, "Symbolic Hypnotherapy" (Zeig, 1978), Erickson uses an arm levitation, elicited by him during the course of the session, to symbolize resistance. The hand of the subject, Leigh, is held upright between the two of them, almost as a vertical barrier or shield between them. Erickson then puts Leigh's arm down himself, indirectly suggesting to her that she remove the resistance. He does another, subsequent arm levitation, and this time has *her* drop the arm levitation, implying that she can remove the resistance herself. Later in the day, and in the follow-up session the next day, Leigh manifests another arm levitation, but this time one that is much more receptive and open: her arm is horizontal now, her palm up, her hand open. There is a gentle and clear sense of cooperativeness and receptivity. For Erickson, it is a symbol of her readiness to receive therapy and of her readiness to change.

These are the major guidelines to use in selecting the hypnotic phenomena for hypnotherapy that will be therapeutically most effective. The chapters that follow will mainly be devoted to a discussion of clinical indications and uses, and of ways to elicit individual hypnotic phenomena.

PART II

Hypnotic Phenomena for Intervention

Section A

Memory Functions

Chapter 4

AMNESIA

ABOUT THE PHENOMENON

In traditional thinking, amnesia is a hypnotic phenomenon that is usually associated with psychopathology (Zeig, 1985a). Generally considered a psychological equivalent to repression, amnesia is blamed for the generation and/or maintenance of unconscious conflicts, dissociated affects, and forgotten memories. However, in his seminal article on the therapeutic use of amnesia, Zeig (1985a) remarks that "if amnesia can be negative, it can also be positive" (p. 318). This chapter discusses a variety of ways in which amnesia can be a positive, constructive part of therapy.

EXPERIMENTAL STUDIES

In 1974, Nace, Orne and Hammer published a key article in *Archives of General Psychiatry*, suggesting that amnesia experienced posthypnotically was different from everyday forgetting or loss of memory. They did this with a very interesting research methodology utilizing a cue for the reversal of psychogenic amnesia. They then contrasted the amount of material remembered unprompted in subjects with the amount that they could later recall after the amnesia had been cancelled on cue.

This research has helped to spark an entire debate about the *hypnotic* genuineness of amnesia, that is, whether or not hypnotically induced amnesia is due to a state called hypnosis per se or is just a by-product of social-psychological variables. Research in subsequent years was directed toward trying to separate the nature of amnesia from other factors, such as demand characteristics, subject expectations, compliance, and role playing (Cooper, 1979). Another debate centers on the *definition* of amnesia, with experimentalists viewing reversibility of a subject's amnesia posthypnotically as a critical part of the process (Kihlstrom, 1985).

Clinicians, on the other hand, at least those of an Ericksonian tradition, emphasize the power of amnesia to create an *interactional* responsiveness outside conscious awareness (Zeig, 1985). Zeig describes the process as one where "a subject responds without full awareness of the response or of the stimulus that effected it" (p. 320). Reversibility is seen as unimportant, and even detrimental, to the therapy. In fact, Erickson would often use amnesia to promote the "settling in" of therapeutic material into the unconscious without conscious disruption by way of overanalysis, resistance, or defense (Zeig, 1985).

Fortunately, debates over which view of hypnosis is correct have actually provided insights into the essential nature of amnesia as a phenomenon and into its clinical applications. For example, Ashford and Hammer (1978) discovered that there was no significant relationship between a person's expectation of being amnesic and the actual occurrence of posthypnotic amnesia, although small positive correlations were evidenced between amnesia and overall hypnotic suggestibility, and between the expectation of becoming hypnotized to begin with and one's overall hypnotic performance. Since there was no support for the idea that posthypnotic amnesia was related to the prehypnotic expectation that it would occur, the finding appears to mitigate against the social-psychological explanation that preexperience expectation sets the stage for the actual experience itself.

In another interesting study, McConkey, Sheehan, and Cross (1980) demonstrated how robust posthypnotic amnesia can be by showing subjects videotapes of their hypnotic session from just moments before. This was partially in response to the social-psychological theorists' challenge that amnesia was not real and could easily be undone by some prodding. There aren't many things that will jog memories more powerfully than a videotape of oneself. Nonetheless, the amnesic subjects in general were unable to recall the events being viewed! For example, one commented, "I don't remember any of this, I don't remember it at all, so I can't make any comments." Whereas amnesic subjects reported difficulty in recalling the events during the videotape viewing, nonamnesic subjects used in the study generally reported no such difficulties. After viewing the videotape, recall of critical items was greater for both groups of subjects, but amnesic subjects only evidenced a substantial recall of 50% of the material; not one amnesic subject had total recall. Even when amnesic subjects were able to have *some* recollections of what went on, most often the memories seemed to be of the behaviors they had performed and not of their internal experiences. Whatever experiences were mentioned seemed to be inferred from viewing their behaviors as subjects.

At least for the high hypnotizables who evidence an excellent capacity for amnesia, this study appears to demonstrate that the experience is a robust one. With regard to clinical practice, it also suggests that it may be necessary for low and moderately hypnotizable clients to be taught to avoid situations that would risk jogging their memories. Because the amnesic subjects who did have recall remembered behaviors more than internal experiences, the results of this study suggest that when we help our clients work through previously repressed experiences, they might have trouble fully connecting to them. Therapists experienced in using hypnosis with clients who have remembered traumatic experiences from the past are aware that they will sometimes remember certain behaviors or sequences of actions but cannot recover the internal, and affective, aspects of the experience. This research suggests that this may be a normal and expected part of the process of remembering.

In their classic article, Kihlstrom and coauthors (Kihlstrom, Evans, Orne, & Orne, 1980) perhaps do the most to dispute social-psychological explanations of posthypnotic amnesia. The authors set up a number of experimental conditions that directly tested social-psychological explanations of why amnesia "appears" to take place in hypnosis. Social-psychological theorists often suggest that subjects *choose* not to use temporal or time-.sequencing cues to remember material, or that they don't try hard enough to remember out of some supposed compliance to what they believe the experimenter wishes.

Using 488 subjects, Kihlstrom and coworkers set up three experimental conditions where these social-psychological explanations were tested. In one condition, subjects were encouraged to try very hard to use the exact sequencing that they experienced in order to remember. In a second condition, subjects were exhorted to continue to exert more and more effort to remember. In the final condition, it was stressed to subjects that this was a scientific experiment and honesty was *extremely* important. These three conditions were seen as being rather extreme and ultimate ways to test whether social-psychological variables were producing the amnesias. The study demonstrated convincingly that for low hypnotizables, or for subjects who are moderately hypnotizable but not very good at amnesia, these conditions were successful at lifting any amnesia. However, for moderately hypnotizable subjects who were good at amnesia, and for high hypnotizables, the special instructions produced no greater effects on memory recall.

For clinical practice, and even for experimental considerations, this raises the very interesting question of whether these results can be generalized to other types of hypnotic phenomena. Perhaps it is that for some moderate and most high hypnotizables, a hypnotic phenomenon is experienced as a profound response emanating from a full dissociation. For low hypnotizables and some moderate hypnotizables not good at the particular hypnotic phenomenon in question, however, success is perhaps achieved with some buttressing from cognitive and mental strategies that are at least in part transmitted through environmental, contextual, and experimenter/clinician expectations and communications. This notion is discussed at some length by the author and the reader is referred to this article in particular as a way of familiarizing oneself with research issues in the study of amnesia.

It is important to note, though, that Kihlstrom and his coauthors' study, and many of the others reviewed both in this section and in other chapters of the book, illuminate aspects of a given hypnotic phenomenon that may hold true under some circumstances only. More tailored and client-sensitive clinical approaches may enable a hypnotic phenomenon to be experienced not only by more people (low and medium hypnotizables included here especially!), but also in a more robust manner. In the article just reviewed, the authors mention something on this order in the slightest of ways. They say that "the amnesia manifested by these experimental subjects is only a shadow of the profound disruption of memory observed in experienced subjects who are highly hypnotizable" (p. 614).

These experiments use many parameters that are not only unneeded but *unwanted* in clinical practice, especially by those working from an Ericksonian orientation. For example, hypnotic inductions in the Kihlstrom study were standardized, that is, the same for each subject with no attention given to customizing the induction to the client. Furthermore, hypnotic inductions and suggestions were all direct and authoritarian. They were also given to entire groups of clients at once and were very brief in duration (only minutes long in some cases).

The journal literature on hypnosis and amnesia also includes some articles that expand the domain of hypnotic amnesia. Evans (1979) discusses one form of hypnotic amnesia called "source amnesia." This phenomenon seems to be different from regular amnesia where a person cannot recall the facts of the situation. With source amnesia, subjects can recall the facts of the situation but cannot recall *how* they learned the information. This phenomenon occurs spontaneously in many of the subjects in Evan's study, apart from any suggestions offered. The design of the study involved hypnotized subjects being given the answers to difficult questions; when they were out of hypnosis later on, they were asked the questions. Although they found they knew the answers, they had no clue about how or why they knew.

In sum, Evans's study supports the idea that source amnesia is different from recall amnesia and not a matter of recall amnesia beginning to break down. Also, it does not seem to be a matter of some social-psychological artifact, inasmuch as simulators trying to fake hypnosis and amnesia never evidenced source amnesia in the absence of recall amnesia. That is, unlike the truly hypnotized subjects, they never recalled the facts without knowing how they learned the facts. They always claimed that they "couldn't remember anything."

Edmonston (1986) likewise expands our conceptualization of hypnotic amnesia by reminding us of some things from the past. He reminds us that prior to this century the two phenomena that were considered absolutely characteristic of hypnosis were non-voluntariness and spontaneous amnesia. He also reminds us that James Braid originally discussed two different types of spontaneous amnesias that arose in true hypnosis. One of these was an irreversible amnesia; it could not be undone with further hypnosis. Edmonston points out that we may be greatly limiting the study of hypnotic amnesia by looking only at suggested amnesias (which he thinks may be *more* influenced by social psychological variables) and ignoring the spontaneous amnesias that were once thought to be so central. He feels similarly about the lack of study of "involuntariness." He points out further that the suggestibility scales used to select high hypnotizables do not measure, or greatly undermeasure, the presence of either of the above experiences and thus may not be measuring what has classically (pre-1900) been considered really to be hypnosis. Interesting point.

AMNESIA AS A SUPPORTIVE INTERVENTION TO THE PRIMARY ONE

Amnesia can be used in therapy as a main intervention, or as a support for the primary intervention. This latter use is described below.

Amnesia was a critical part of Erickson's work and a central component to his indirect technique. One way in which he used this phenomenon was in preventing patients from bridging associations between trance and the waking state, thus sealing off the hypnotic suggestions from conscious awareness (Zeig, 1985a). Because with indirect approaches the mutative intervention is not apparent, clients can experience change as having been spontaneous. Seemingly spontaneous, self-directed change is useful for those needing to feel autonomous in their change patterns (Edgette & Edgette, 1992). Because amnesia can be used to encourage conscious forgetting of suggestions, directives, and other interventions, it can be a big boon in these latter cases. For the same reason, amnesia to buttress primary interventions is often critically helpful in working with highly resistant individuals, or with individuals calcified in maladaptive patterns of reacting; in such cases, the conscious mind (and character structure) would have difficulty resisting interventions/suggestions that had been forgotten. The secondary use of amnesia was also an important part of the hypnotherapy I (JSE) did with two individuals whose presenting problems were resolved at a wholly unconscious level in separate single-session therapies (see J. S. Edgette, 1993).

Gilligan (1987) also discusses the use of amnesia to protect unconscious change processes from conscious intervention. He notes that clinical progress can be hampered if a client becomes aware of hypnotic learnings or instructions before being able to integrate them comfortably into a conscious level of psychological functioning. Although some clinicians consider working at a level not consciously acknowledged by the patient to be an ethical bugaboo, the exclusion of deep, unconscious level work will undoubtedly limit the scope of a practitioner's hypnotherapy (see J. S. Edgette, 1989, for a discussion of ethics and Ericksonian psychotherapy).

Other instances where it could be important to prevent premature conscious awareness of learnings or interventions are with individuals who are traumatized and highly distressed, those who question the validity of trance learnings or posthypnotic instructions, and those whose conscious efforts to help themselves only make matters worse (Gilligan, 1987).

AMNESIA AS THE PRIMARY INTERVENTION

Rather than being used to seal off hypnotic suggestions, learnings, or ideas, amnesia can be used as the primary solution to a presenting problem. For instance, someone who is inherently good at the phenomenon of amnesia (i.e., a "good forgetter") can be taught to direct it toward the memory of his or her chronic pain. Since remembering—and thus anticipating—pain is a large part of a person's counterproductive management of chronic pain, using amnesia here can be a way of circumventing it. Another client who has a naturally good ability to forget things (an "absent-minded professor," for example), and who struggles with feelings of low self-worth, could use amnesia to extinguish internal, ruminative memories of inadequacy and failure. A gymnast can use amnesia to remove memories of a fall from the balance beam—a fall that has compromised her confidence level. A person quitting smoking can use amnesia to forget the compelling taste of that first drag off a cigarette. Zeig (1985a) described using amnesia to demonstrate to subjects that they have, in fact, been hypnotized. Other clinical uses cited by Zeig for amnesia include diagnostic assessment in terms of determining "memory style" and allowing clients to have "aha" experiences. These experiences happen when the amnesia has allowed the client to forget the *specific* therapeutic suggestions proffered and experience any changes as having come primarily from his or her own personal reassociations that took place as a result of those suggestions. Amnesia for the therapeutic injunctions thus offers a sense of ownership over the changes that take place.

INDICATIONS FOR USE

The principal of utilization dictates that amnesia should be considered whenever your client demonstrates a predisposition toward using it in his or her everyday life. How will you recognize these people? You can recognize them by picking up on the minimal (or not so minimal) cues they give that demonstrate a tendency to forget. For example, some people might call you two times before a session to confirm the appointment time; another might have forgotten the appointment and want a reminder. Clients may leave their keys or glasses on the couch after a session and you wind up walking down the hallway to give the items back. Another example of a minimal cue, suggesting that the therapist use amnesia, became apparent while supervising one of our trainees: The trainee had said to her client, "You can close your eyes now, just like the last time." The client looked at her and said uncertainly, "I did close my eyes the last time, didn't I?"

Apart from recognizing such cues, there are other ways of finding out if amnesia is one of the hypnotic phenomena that the person characteristically does. You can always test for amnesic ability in session by giving some amnesia suggestions during an exploratory or neutral trance and seeing if there is a response. Also, amnesia often occurs quite naturally at the end of the hypnotic session as the person leaves the altered state of consciousness characteristic of trance. Clients will vary in the extent to which they develop a spontaneous amnesia after the session is over. But those who do it naturally and broadly would more likely benefit from amnesia applied toward their problems than would those for whom the entirety of the hypnotic experience is vividly remembered after they have reoriented to the waking state.

Another possible indication for using amnesia is when a person uses it in everyday life but in a counterproductive fashion, unwittingly creating the problem. Excessive repression is an extreme maladaptive use of amnesia. People who use too much repression and shut themselves off from true thoughts and feelings often develop problems in their lives and in interpersonal relationships as a result. In these instances the treatment goal can sometimes become one of teaching the person to redirect the amnestic tendency toward an arena where it can function more adaptively.

Certain individuals with post-traumatic stress disorder can benefit from befriending the amnestic response that has caused repression of traumatic memories. Very often such people feel estranged from themselves, experience severe and/or prolonged dissociative episodes, and present and relate in a disintegrated fashion, largely because of their attempts to forget their memories of abuse and/or trauma and the associated affects. Anyone who spends a lot of mental energy trying to banish a part of one's self diminishes the self accordingly. Hypnotic efforts allowing people to wed their mental hypnotic phenomena to pursuits of emotional health can serve to counteract that kind of disintegration of the self.

First of all, it is often important to educate these individuals about the adaptive value of their forgetting—that their amnestic response was a ticket to psychological survival, enabling them not to be overwhelmed by the negative experiences. They then can be educated about how now, in adulthood, they are in a different position, a position of power that affords them opportunities to begin remembering at a pace that is right for them. And amnesia can be used as an aid in doing just that. For example, a person can be encouraged to remember *during* a therapy session, while also being instructed to develop immediate amnesia in the event of a disruptive flashback outside of the session.

Another situation in which one can redirect tendencies to forget toward less problematic arenas could be with certain passive-aggressive individuals. Characterologically predisposed to "forget," such individuals often can wreak havoc in their relationships by aggressing in that manner. Using hypnosis, direct and/or indirect suggestions can be made for the person to alter the location, time, or object of their amnesia/forgetting. Thus, instead of a man's "forgetting" his wife's birthday or their anniversary, he can "forget" the time two years ago when she called him lazy, which he uses to justify his petulant withdrawal. Or maybe he could forget whether it was four times or three times that she asked him to help with dinner that past week, which he's been using to fuel his perception of her as a nag. Now, even if the intervention for displacing the symptom is successful, the therapist would still have the passive-aggressive character to contend with—and the marital tension as well as the characterological and/or behavioral contributions of the wife. Those could be addressed with additional hypnotic work, through strategic interventions, or through some good marital therapy. However, the value in using amnesia as an intervention is in its splitting off the defense of forgetting from a characterological style of relating. This serves as a type of pattern interruption, an intervention useful in making inroads where a problematic constellation of behaviors offers seemingly little entry for therapy.

Another time to consider using amnesia as therapy is when a client uses the complement of amnesia—hypermnesia—to create the problem. For example, a woman I (JHE) worked with had, as one of her problems, extreme difficulty forgetting about an ex-boyfriend who had broken up with her months ago. Her *hypermnesic* ability was allowing her to remember in vivid detail every aspect of their good times together. Many people who do not get over an old relationship use hypermnesia to compound their problem. One antidote to this was to use amnesia—the hypnotic complement to hypermnesia. Of course, following the earlier line of thinking, a therapist could look for a way to redirect the hypermnesia more constructively, perhaps getting into the imaginary details of a positive relationship with a boyfriend-to-be. The point here is that there are any number of ways to work and it is up to the therapist's diagnostic acumen, creativity, and judgment to come up with the most appropriate course for each situation.

Similarly, obsessives frequently use hypermnesia when "doing" their symptom. They review or worry in evermore exacting detail, thereby making the symptom or problem loom larger than life itself. Often, with obsessives, if they will *allow* amnesia to take place, they can let go of their stranglehold on the worrisome idea.

As discussed earlier, amnesia can be useful in sustaining a partial or full forgetting that for the time being is psychologically adaptive. We've already mentioned both how Erickson used amnesia to "seal" in the hypnotic suggestion and Gilligan's and our thoughts on protecting unconscious change processes from conscious interference. Other instances in which to use amnesia would be, of course, when working with clients who could be vulnerable to premature resurgences of overwhelming affects and/or memories. In such cases amnesia is often used to titrate the experience.

Other examples of situations where the use of amnesia can be valuable are the following: a woman approaching the birth of her second child with trepidation because of her memories of labor pain can use amnesia to forget those earlier pains; a horseback rider whose memories of a bad fall compromise her current competitive riding can use amnesia to forget that fall; a man for whom being pointed a finger at, even in casual conversation, evokes an angered (and inappropriate) transference reaction can use amnesia to forget the meaning of this visual cue (this would be source amnesia).

CONTRAINDICATIONS

One generally avoids using amnesia when the person's conscious mind is in line with the goal to be achieved and with the method or process of achieving the results. That is, if resistance is low, the person's conscious mind can serve as an ally and further the healing in ways that are complementary to the ways of the unconscious mind; simpler is always better. Another general contraindication to the use of amnesia is with clients who lean toward paranoia. The hypervigilance of such individuals usually precludes the effective use of amnesia because they have made a characterological livelihood out of avoiding things being outside of their conscious awareness. Even if you are successful in enabling them to become amnestic for some part of the hypnosis, they are likely to be disturbed at this occurrence and rapport can be jeopardized. Why force someone's hand? In our work we are more inclined to help suspicious or paranoid people remember *all* of the suggestions and become aware of the multilevel communications that we use. Usually in that way they can relax. The meager trust of the paranoid will be most in evidence if you play to it, and if you do, such a person will be more likely to adopt the proffered suggestion.

Gilligan (1987) cautions therapists against using amnesia in order to have clients permanently forget some memory or part of themselves. This orchestrated repression would have the untherapeutic effect of leaving someone unconsciously dominated by the very memories or thoughts of which you are trying to rid him or her. Rather, he suggests, one should use amnesia to permit the uninhibited development of new learnings. We think this is an important caveat for the therapist using hypnosis in practice, and the use of amnesia to erase memory should indeed be used most judiciously. However, there are certain clinical situations where using amnesia to lock out memories can be therapeutic, such as in the sport-related and habit-control cases noted above.

ELICITING THE PHENOMENON OF AMNESIA

Direct and Indirect Suggestions

Direct, permissive suggestions for amnesia include such statements as "*You can allow yourself to forget*," and "*You can allow this information to go to the back of your mind and reside there only*," and "*You can let this information slip from your mind and have it operative at an unconscious level only.*" Direct suggestion is simple and can be used with people with whom there is negligible conscious interference. If the person is not only cooperative and receptive but also especially responsive to authority, suggestions could be somewhat authoritative as well. Here you would use nonpermissive language as in, "*You will forget this information.*" Diplomacy is noble but a therapist does well to do what works within the parameters of respect and benevolence: if a client responds best to being told what to do, why not tell him what to do?

Double binds, such as the phrase often used by Erickson that "you can forget to remember or you can remember to forget," are also effective. This is a particularly useful linguistic strategy for a client who prefers control and choice in their change processes. The cognitive confusion inherent in the statement also promotes amnesia as well, inasmuch as we tend to remember things through thought ordering and patterning. Here, the listening client is likely to become so disoriented by the linguistic confusion that he or she forgets the content of the statement and responds more directly to the injunction to become amnestic.

Zeig (1985a) stresses the superiority of indirect suggestion for eliciting amnesia compared to more direct means. He says that the latter is effective in eliciting those phenomena that deal with the *creation* of experience (i.e., positive hallucination, age regression, automatic drawing) but not good for generating phenomena that *delete* experiences from awareness (i.e., amnesia, negative hallucination, anesthesia). The reason is that in processing the direct suggestion to *not think* of a concept, *not hear* a sound, or *not feel* a sensation, a person first must recognize the reality of that experience which, of course, makes it all the more difficult to subsequently forget it. After all, people never oblige the request to forget gossip blurted out to them once—and *especially* after—the discloser says, "Forget I ever told you that!"

Indirect methods of suggestion as described by Zeig could include inviting the client to concentrate on a particular subject (e.g., the therapist), which implies that everything in the background can be ignored. Another method is to direct the client's attention to one category of experience (e.g., kinesthetic—"the feeling of the chair") to the exclusion of others (auditory, visual, ideational). In these examples, the indirection of the suggestion comes from one message being communicated on a social level (*"pay attention to me, pay attention to the feeling of the chair against your legs and back"*) while another message—the injunctive, therapeutic one—is **implied** (not spoken) at a psychological change level (*and you can forget the window, the lamp, that desk, the telephone ringing, the floor underneath your feet, and you can forget about your internal experience of distress or your [other kinesthetic] experience of back pain*).

Other indirect linguistic methods include ***presupposing*** that forgetting will occur (*"and **when certain ideas begin to slip away from your conscious mind**, you can..."*), and **interspersal** of the directive to forget (*"you can **forget** about how your breathing has slowed down or **forget** about how quickly your pulse rate slowed or **forget** about just how relaxed your jaw muscles have become..."*). Note that in this last interspersal example the word "forget" is purposefully used three times in the one sentence in order to shift psychological processes in that desired direction of amnesia. Other key phrases that can be interspersed to induce amnesia include "lose sight of" and "out of mind" (Zeig, 1985a).

Seeding is therapeutic foreshadowing, priming a subject to respond to the main intervention later (Zeig, 1990c). When you seed amnesia, as with any hypnotic phenomenon, it paves the way for a fuller and better response later on. Seeding this particular phenomenon involves making direct or obtuse references to forgetting prior to the working phases of trance. This can be done through interspersal, metaphor, double binds—anything that directs attention to the process of forgetting during or even before induction. To a person who comes into session thirsty but chooses not to get a soda, you can say during the induction as part of the seeding, *"A few minutes ago you had mentioned about being thirsty, but I bet you've forgotten about that thirst by now."*

Conscious/unconscious dissociative statements can also be used to suggest amnesia. An example is *"Your conscious mind can let go of certain fragments of thoughts while your unconscious mind lets go of entire texts of ideas."* Lankton & Lankton (1983) also talk about double-dissociative conscious/unconscious binds, which add the influence of confusion. Using this, one says to a client, *"Your conscious mind can know all about forgetting about extraneous and irrelevant ideas while your unconscious mind can really understand how to let go of the things I say, or instead, you can simply allow your unconscious mind to forget about the unimportant things* (implying that it will remember the important things), *and have your conscious mind be the one to really **let go of the things I say***" (said slowly and with emphasis).

Naturalistic Examples of Amnesia or Diminution of Conscious Awareness

Another useful means to elicit amnesia involves discovering and communicating to your client naturalistic examples of the development of amnesia from everyday life. One such story might be of a person driving to a familiar place and finding that he or she arrives there having not remembered anything about the trip: "*The driver knows that he must have stopped at stop signs and stoplights, he knows that he must have made right turns and left turns, but his conscious mind was thinking about something else while his unconscious mind was on a type of cruise control.*"

You can also talk to a client about how the unconscious alone can perform certain functions outside of the awareness of the conscious mind and that the process can be like going for a walk: "*You don't need to be aware or even think about moving one foot in front of the other, you don't need to think about alternating bending your knees, you don't need to know about or think about extensor and flexor muscles and working them in a type of synchrony. You can just allow yourself to let your unconscious mind do what it knows how to do. It has a wisdom of its own that you can trust....*" An anecdotal naturalistic approach to eliciting amnesia is limited only by one's repertoire of examples of forgetting in everyday life.

Structural Ways to Induce Amnesia

Structured methods of inducing amnesia are indirect means and are quite powerful. They involve creating amnesia by using a pattern or *structure* of communication that encourages the psychological process of amnesia without ever having to use words like "forget" or "let go of."

One basic structural method involves putting the suggestion to forget in the deep middle of the trance work. This takes advantage of the recency and primary effects of memory functioning, wherein what is said or learned last and first in a series of communications are recalled most and next most frequently. What is said in the middle of any series of statements or chain of numbers is most likely to be forgotten (Squire, 1987). Hence, in hypnotic work, you can embed into the middle of the induction whatever it is you desire the subject to forget consciously.

An especially well-developed version of the above is what is called a *structured* amnesia (Erickson & Rossi, 1974/1980; Lankton & Lankton, 1983; Zeig, 1985a). This is a technique through which some idea, suggestion, directive, or even dialogue between therapist and client can recede in the client's awareness or be forgotten about altogether. It can be used with or without trance. Essentially, one idea or discussion is encapsulated within an overarching one; for instance, discussion A is suddenly interrupted by discussion B, which a while later is abruptly interrupted by a resumption of discussion A at just the point it was broken off, as if nothing had intervened. The abrupt abandonment of the interjected comment or discussion, plus the renewal of the overarching one, helps to induce amnesia for the former. The confusion generated by such a sudden change also helps the encapsulated communication drop out of conscious awareness.

An example of structuring an amnesia for the suggestion of pain control follows below. This strategy was chosen for this particular client of mine (JHE) because the more he focused on suggestions for anesthesia, analgesia, dissociation, and other phenomena useful in alleviating physical pain, the more the awareness of the pain grew, and the more effortful and counterproductive the process became. The presenting problem was of knee pain.

> *So we were sitting there watching this movie in the theater and we were getting more and more absorbed in the characters and plot, so much so that we had forgotten about how we had felt it was chilly; we forgot about the annoying sticky stuff under our shoes, and I forgot about the lump in the seat cushion. The protagonist was falling in love with*————. *Suddenly I decided I had to have popcorn! You know, sometimes you just have an urgent need to* **change your internal state right away, Joe***. I rushed out to the stand where I got lost in the smell of the fresh popped popcorn and the decision over just how big a tub I would get! And to my* **inner delight** *this classy theater had real butter to put on the popcorn—not just "topping!" I paid and abruptly rushed back inside to ask Janet what had happened and she said the movie continued with him saying "When I'm with you, it's as if I'm transported to another world and nothing else matters or exists" and then....*

This is an example of a structured amnesia where the story of the movie (replete with suggestions for pain control through absorption in the external world) is abruptly interrupted, providing for the start of the amnesia. The embedded material concerning the popcorn purchase provides indirect suggestions for pain control through absorption in sensory stimuli that would compete with the pain, plus suggestions for inner change and comfort. When the structured amnesia is completed through the sudden return to the movie, indirect suggestions for pain control via dissociation ("another world") are offered as well.

The Lanktons (Lankton & Lankton, 1983) advanced the use of structured amnesia considerably with their development of the multiple embedded metaphor. These conversationally based structured amnesias are very similar to Zeig's "as if" technique (1985a) of inducing amnesia, wherein the therapist interacts with the client as if the hypnotic work for which amnesia is desired never took place.

Another method of effecting structured amnesias involves interrupting a social ritual. Erickson frequently did this with his "handshake induction" (Erickson, Rossi, & Rossi, 1979). Erickson would shake someone's hand, only to stop and hold the hand cataleptic in the air. He would then slowly withdraw his hand, leaving the person with an arm levitation. Erickson then distracted the person by delivering suggestions, new ideas, or other types of interventions. At the end of his commentary, he would take the person's hand again and finish the handshake.

The abrupt shifting of contexts is what induces the amnesia. Because a handshake is such an overlearned response, and because we all tend to think of it as always lasting a certain, preordained length of time, it is easy to have an amnesia develop in the middle of it being carried out by doing hypnosis in this manner. Erickson was brilliant when it came to finding ways for people to develop hypnotic phenomena easily and naturally. That is why he did not become concerned about how hypnotizable a subject was; he made it incumbent upon himself to be increasingly perceptive and responsive so that even a "poor subject" could respond well.

Utilizing Physiological Realities for Amnesia

Habituation is a physiological reality that can be manipulated in hypnosis to effect an amnesia. The physiological principle of habituation states that our bodies are programmed to no longer respond to a stimulus that is constant or repetitively patterned (Squire, 1987). In trance, we can create a habituation to verbiage and thereby create amnesia. A method of habituation that Erickson often used was to deliver suggestions with a monotone voice. Although some of his demonstrations are exciting and flashy, many of his audiotaped inductions and many of his recorded lectures use this monotonous and even droning voice tone. It has the effect of getting the person to dissociate, day-dream, not attend consciously, and thus forget the material spoken. Many students have listened to Erickson's lectures only to come away feeling that they don't remember a thing. Weeks later they discover that they have used—verbatim—some of his wording in their own trance inductions!

Another principle of physiological functioning is that when a shock to the nervous system takes place, retrograde amnesia often develops. This shock can either be a physical shock (as in the case of the amnesia that develops after a car accident) or it can be a psychological shock (such as a knock on the office door and someone opening it unan-nounced). Most of us have had the experience of getting a sudden phone call with some news and then forgetting entirely about what we were doing beforehand.

The same method can be employed in hypnosis by providing some (benign) "psychological shock" at the end of trance. In such instances we are simply disrupting the process of mental rehearsal that takes place at the end of trace. Since short-term memory is thought to be-come long-term memory through the process of rehearsal (Squire, 1987), disrupting that process interferes with the formation of an engram. In hypnotic sessions, this can be done by ending trance abruptly. It can also be done by changing the topic rapidly. It can occur also if you allow so much time in session to lapse that the trance ends at the very end of the therapy hour and you need to make an appointment quickly before ushering the person out.

The above suggests that, in general, no matter what technique of amnesia you use, you want to avoid reviewing the trance experience afterwards with the client. It may be characteristic for you to ask cli-ents after trance, "How was that experience for you?" or "What did you find useful in what we did?" but these phrases are not used when am-nesia is the goal since they would immediately result in an internal search and subsequent thwarting of the development of the amnesia.

Developing Amnesia at the End of Trance: Posthypnotic Suggestion and Follow Through

Apart from the abrupt interruptions and the disruptions of rehearsal described above, the end of the session can also be used to foster amne-sia in other ways. Posthypnotic suggestion is one example. These are suggestions that on a certain cue a person can do something else. Al-though posthypnotic suggestions for amnesia to develop later should be given throughout the trance state, they are often most effective when given at the end of a trance experience. It is a matter of creating an association of "if–then" in the unconscious mind. Here, for purposes of developing amnesia, some direct posthypnotic suggestions might go as follows: *"When you come out of trance, you can allow yourself to forget what we spoke about,"* or *"When you get into your car to go home, you can easily, quickly develop amnesia for the trance experience,"* or *"As soon as you arrive home, you can find the details of our conversations in trance slipping away, gradually receding...."* The cues for the amnesia would be *coming out of trance, getting into the car, arriving home*. Cues used in posthypnotic suggestions are best when they are inevitable, observable, and objective.

Another posthypnotic suggestion is *"As time elapses, more and more forgetting of what took place in trance can happen."* Note that this posthypnotic suggestion capitalizes on a common way in which people forget—gradually, over time. As is the case with hypnosis in general, amnesia is often best created when the suggestions are in line with how the particular event takes place in everyday life. Again, this is reflective of the naturalistic approach to hypnosis that underpins an Ericksonian therapeutic orientation.

With posthypnotic suggestion it is important that the person is cued as to *when* to forget (i.e., *as time lapses*) and not *what* it is he or she is supposed to forget. When you specify the material you want the person to forget, you enliven that very material (the "don't think of a white elephant" phenomenon). Therefore, be careful to phrase your suggestions along the lines of *"you can forget the things we spoke of"* or *"you can forget the suggestion"* rather than *"you can forget your pain"* or *"you can forget all about your work stress when you lay down to sleep."* Regarding word choice, be mindful to speak in terms of *forgetting* or *developing amnesia* and **not** in terms of *not remembering*. Since we respond to injunctions with little regard to the negatives in the phrase, what is left reverberating in the person's mind in this last example is the very word, *remember*.

SELECTED TRANSCRIPT MATERIAL

Cessation of Smoking

...that you can choose to remember to forget or forget to remember anything and everything about the suggestions that I give you, but in a similar way, you can remember to forget or forget to remember about that old habit. It can fade off into the past like a fading stimuli...it can fade off like a boat at night at the shore pulling out to sea, getting dimmer and dimmer... old habits can be broken and new habits can be established. Now, your conscious mind can cooperate with the suggestion by distracting yourself anytime you think about having a cigarette. Your subconscious mind, on the other hand, can develop an immediate amnesia, like when somebody interrupts you midsentence and you can't remember what the heck you were talking about. Or when something really surprising happens and you forget about what you were doing...and things can happen outside of awareness...I already know that you can be quite adept at doing one thing while focusing on something else. Well, your subconscious mind can have a thought about having a cigarette, but because it remains subconscious, your conscious mind can be unaware of it....

Amnesia for an Equestrian Traumatized by Falling Off a Horse

...I also know from what you've told me, Ann, that you're the type of person who really does like to do something and that's terrific...because there are really all kinds of things you can do now, different things you can do later...now, I know that you already know something about the phenomenon of forgetting...and that there are all kinds of things that you've allowed yourself to forget over time...there are many things that I'm sure you're just as happy to have let go to oblivion...and I want you to know that you really can add to that collection of things forgotten and you can include in that collection current thoughts, recent fantasies about what could happen or what might happen or what has happened in the past...there might be some reason why your conscious mind thought it was important for you to think about things that could have happened if you just had done this or just had done that...but those things too can become a little bit blurred at the edges as memory so that it really becomes a little gray....

Chapter 5

HYPERMNESIA

ABOUT THE PHENOMENON

Hypermnesia is the hypnotic phenomenon that involves vivid, near-photographic remembering. It is the complement of amnesia. Hypermnesia is sometimes confused with age regression, or the terms are used synonymously. But age regression refers to the reexperiencing of oneself in the past (which can mean the day before or decades before), and hypermnesia refers only to vivid remembering. Hypermnesia is often *part of* the age-regression experience, but you can be age-regressed and not be remembering much of anything at all or simply be remembering earlier experiences without feeling as if you are younger/back in time/dissociated from the present. With hypermnesia, the experiences of familiarity and nostalgia are what really stand out in particular.

EXPERIMENTAL STUDIES

Research findings on hypermnesia were summarized in a thorough review of the literature conducted by Relinger (1984). Though he points out that there is little consensus regarding the actual mechanism through which hypermnesia is possible, his vast review supports the existence of the phenomenon and the idea that it can be elicited on a consistent basis given certain parameters. It was found to be superior to waking-state remembering as long as the material to be remembered is mean-ingful (as opposed to nonsense syllables and the like). There was also some indication that if the initial material learned was learned under stressful or emotionally arousing conditions, then the magnitude of the hypermnesic effect increases.

We speculate that this may occur because of the secondary relax-ation effects of hypnosis. Perhaps the stress contributed to a blocking or inhibition of recall that is undone to some degree by the impact of the trance state (apart from the phenomenon of hypermnesia) on cogni-tive functions. That is, the relaxation and the ability to focus inherent in hypnosis may be the reasons for a stronger hypermnesic effect when stress was originally in the picture because remembering would be that much more difficult, as opposed to an experimental situation where there is no stress during the original learning period. In this latter case, hypnotic hypermnesia is being compared to waking-state remember-ing without the added barrier of stress. Comparatively, the effects would be easier to see when there is a barrier of stress or some emotional arousal.

Relevant to the current controversy about false-memory syndrome are the summaries of experimental findings on hypnotically retrieved memory in Kihlstrom's (1985) article. Specifically, any increase in valid memory obtained through hypnosis *may be accompanied by correspond-ing increases in inaccuracy of recollection or confabulation.* The likeli-hood of distortion increases if leading questions are asked while the subject is hypnotized, compared to biased interrogation in nonhypnotized states (Putnam, 1979; Sanders & Simmons, 1983; Sheehan and Tilden, 1983; Zelig & Beidelman, 1981). Dywan and Bow-ers (1983), Sanders and Simmons (1983), and Sheehan and Tilden (1983) also found no positive relationship between accuracy of, and subject confidence in, hypnotically elicited memories. Furthermore, it was dis-covered that confabulated memories produced via hypnosis can be found to be unshakable under cross-examination (Laurence & Perry, 1983).

Although the data may be discrepant with claims from many in the field, they warrant clinicians' full attention. Any therapist using hypermnesia as a means to "recover" memories in situations where the ramifications may be significant (i.e., forensics, trauma, abuse) needs to be well-versed in this literature and have a good grasp of the param-eters of its use. This issue is more extensively covered in Chapter 8 on age regression and interested readers are referred there for more de-tailed material.

Hypnotic phenomena are rarely discussed in terms of self-hypnosis. In broaching this topic, Fromm and colleagues (Fromm, Brown, & Hurt, et al., 1981), in comparing self-hypnosis to heterohypnosis, found that although personal memories and bodily sensations occurred spontaneously during self-hypnosis, they were seen as being distracting from tasks of self-exploration and imagery that the clients seemed to be invested in. Thus, something akin to hypermnesia and/or age regression, as well as tactile/kinesthetic positive hallucinations, appeared possible in self-hypnosis but were seen as being off-task events that were irrelevant and to be eliminated, rather than followed. On the other hand, subjects in heterohypnosis were much better able to use the therapist to guide them in their hypermnesia and age regression and they reported a heightened awareness and enjoyment of personal memories. In heterohypnosis, subjects could also experience positive and negative hallucinations successfully, whereas subjects in self-hypnosis were less able to do so even when they wanted to.

INDICATIONS FOR USE

One of the primary indications for the use of hypermnesia in psychotherapy is to undo the counterproductive use of amnesia in a client. Many clients have lost touch with certain aspects of themselves, certain experiences they've had, or memories and the like, and therefore they cannot resurrect them in the present as supports, motivators, or reminders of things once accomplished. They forget that they were once bold and assertive, or once happy and light-hearted, or that they once had a sense of humor, or sense of hope about the future, or goals, or even passions. Unable to remember, they sometimes remain mired in a depression, in a bout of passivity, in a loss of self-assurance, or in other similar unpleasant experiences. Hypermnesia for the lost self, or a lost and vital part of the self, can be exceptionally therapeutic.

Allow the person to spend some time over the course of a leisurely hypnotic session, or over the course of a few hypnosis sessions, reestablishing psychological contact with that lost, forgotten part—that resource—remembering what it was like to move about the world in that way. Invite your client to remember what things she or he would say at that time, how others reacted, how she or he coped, what things provided pleasure, how she or he felt about the self. Did the person dress differently, eat differently, read different things, go out to different sorts of events or places?

Really remembering something in this fashion works to enliven it again, and make it part of something in the present—even if just momentarily, in trance. From there the client can work to make it a larger and larger part of his or her current reality. One equestrian I (JSE) worked with had lost confidence in herself as a rider; under hypnosis she had a hypermnesic experience, remembering what it had felt like to gallop across fields without a second thought. Her remark upon exiting trance was an exhilarated and astonished cry of "Oh my God, I had forgotten what it was like to feel so confident riding! That was wonderful!"

Hypermnesia can also be used as part of a solution when it has been the mechanism of the problem. An example here is the person with low self-esteem who repeatedly remembers the minute details of every failing in life. In such a situation, the intervention could be organized around some task of remembering in equally vivid detail aspects of life's successes. This creates a situation in which the therapist is work-ing in a curiously similar way to how many cognitive therapists work. Augmented through the use of hypnosis, however, cognitive therapy can be more incisive, direct, and powerful.

Keep in mind that, for some people, changes for the better are psy-chologically frightening and can result in anxiety or the unwitting, unconscious erection of obstacles to progress. Immersing a client in a memory of "when it was good" may only be one (small, even) part of a therapy that speaks also to that individual's ambivalence about or felt inability to turn his or her life around. Hypnotic phenomena in therapy should never be applied in isolation from the personality dynamics of the client.

Apart from cognitive styles that indicate the need for using hypermnesia, there are particular symptoms and situations that like-wise indicate its use. We mentioned above the judicious use of hypermnesia in cases of trauma where amnesia predominates. Note that by its very definition, hypermnesia takes effect *after* people have already become aware of a memory. A person cannot be hypermnesic without already having access to some memory. Hypermnesia would refer here to the person's controlled and *therapeutic* absorption in a memory such that certain lost visual, auditory, tactile, emotional, ol-factory or other details become accessible again.

As mentioned earlier, hypermnesia is often used in combination with age regression when that which needs to be remembered has happened in the distant past; the two phenomena are very complementary. For example, if I wanted you to remember something in detail from your school at around the age of 8 or 9, I would not only need to instruct you to go back in time to that classroom, but I would also need to ask you to remember in evermore bright detail the color of the chalkboard, the smell of purple ink from the mimeograph machine, the feel of the eraser going across the blackboard, the sound of the bell indicating the end of a period, or the sight of the school buses lined up. When the relevant memories to be retrieved are not recent, age regression needs to be employed hand-in-hand with hypermnesia. Refer to Chapter 8 on age regression for an extensive review of the current research on, and ethical and legal issues involved in, memory retrieval work using hypnosis.

Another setting for the use of hypermnesia is when a person has difficulty remembering studied material during test-taking situations. Many requests for hypnosis to aid test-taking recall come from people when they are taking an especially important test—a licensing exam, orals, or boards. Hypnosis and suggestions for hypermnesia can facilitate the recall of information in clutch situations; however, it is important to note that for this kind of referral, it is also useful to work hypnotically on the *emotional blocks to remembering* that have been erected for that individual in test-taking situations. For example, it is common for people who don't remember during tests to become very anxious, which tends to block the process of remembering, or to begin thinking about success and failure issues, becoming so absorbed in trying to do well that they end up not focusing on the specific questions. It is indeed difficult to remember anything of importance while being absorbed in the issue of whether or not they were going to get an A or a B or thinking about what it would mean to one's academic career to get a D or an F. Another beautiful application of the phenomenon of hypermnesia is to use it to help musicians remember music, especially for solos and auditions when nerves can interfere with reading or when they are required to work without scores in front of them.

CONTRAINDICATIONS FOR USE

Specific contraindications for using hypermnesia have less to do with particular clinical conditions or diagnoses than they do with the way in which the client construes and uses the process of remembering. Be very careful with those clients who come specifically and only for "memory retrieval to see if there was some (physical/sexual) abuse." We feel that hypnosis and hypermnesia should generally not be used in this way (see Chapter 8); they can, however, easily be part of a therapy in which the goals include enhancing the client's *overall* sense of personal history. This may be relevant when a client feels disconnected from or amnestic for him- or herself as a child, teenager, or young adult. General memories and feelings (good, bad, and neutral) are retrieved as the person hypnotically courses through those time periods.

With clients for whom sudden recall might be overwhelming, this is a better course of action anyway, at least until you each have a sense of what defenses the person has available to ward off any affect or ide-

ation that is too much or too intrusive. One also needs to assess the
degree of adaptability of such defenses. If they are limited to disabling
degrees of dissociation, or self-destructive acting out (e.g., cutting, running away), or avoidance (e.g., suicidal ideation, abrupt termination of
therapy), then more resource building in the therapy and in the hypnosis will be necessary before proceeding with the uncovering work proper.
Those clients with severe characterological disorders or with propensi-
ties to disorganize under conditions of undue stress should necessarily
be treated by a more experienced clinician if hypnosis and hypermnesia
are part of the treatment.

Yapko (1990) speaks of the dangers of hypnosis being misused in the
attempt to have it wrongly applied as a lie detector. Pseudomemories,
created either by a condensation of a person's fears, distorted memories, and media influence or cocreated by the unwarranted suggestions
of abuse on the part of misguided, too-eager therapists, pose a threat to
the receptivity to and acceptance of those who really did suffer through
an abusive past. This does not demean the others' pain, but the clinical
community does, as Yapko rightly stresses, need to find ways to
differentiate between a true memory and a false memory when dire-
consequence material is recalled with the help of trancework.

ELICITING THE PHENOMENON OF HYPERMNESIA

Bear in mind that suggestions for hypermnesia should be given in a
very permissive way—more than for most other hypnotic phenomena.
This is because the "gun-to-the-head approach" is terribly counterproductive for remembering; although some everyday remembering can be
done by one forcing oneself, once a person gets to the point where he or
she is in need of hypnosis, it is an altogether different story. For the
unconscious mind to cooperate, it needs to be seduced, not muscled.

Seeding hypermnesia can be done easily during induction by inviting a hypnotic subject to go into trance either by *remembering* his or
her last trance experience or by constructing a new type of experience.
Similarly, a therapist could say, *"Allow your body to **remember** what it
is like to settle way down, slow down your pulse rate, and really relax in
the muscles, joints—how quickly can your body remember these things
from the last time? It can **remember so many things**, new and old…and
older…remember the feeling of trance and explore it even further this
time if you like…."*

Having a client go into trance by thinking about a favorite memento
is another way to seed. A client can be invited to think about a favorite
old toy, article of clothing, souvenir, or photograph. With a classical

musician, we might invite the person to go into trance by remembering a favorite symphony.

Words that are **evocative** of the phenomenon of hypermnesia include *refresh, unfold, unravel, recollect, commemorate, reminisce, nostalgia, wistful, relic,* and *keepsake.* Others await in the thesaurus on your bookshelves.

Use **presupposition** to predict, in a linguistically indirect fashion, the future occurrence of hypermnesia in the client. With a golfer who needs to learn how to quickly recapture the memory of good playing as a reference experience when his game goes off, we may say something like, *"After you remember, in all its glorious kinesthetic detail, the sensation of harmonic movement between your hands and eyes at that last tournament, you can start to discover ways to make that memory a keepsake, an inner experience that you can get to quickly, anytime, on any green, and be able to saturate yourself with that memory of effortlessness, rhythm, flow, harmony, and recreate it again, for real, right there in your body again...."*

Presupposition with a couple who can benefit from hypermnesia to regain some of the lost affection in the relationship might take the following form: *"While your conscious minds soon recall the different things you did that week of your honeymoon, your unconscious minds can begin to recognize inside yourselves the feelings you had then, of affection, or of seduction, or of whimsy, perhaps a special feeling of intimacy...."*

Double binds, too, can be used to elicit hypermnesia. Examples include: *"You can remember gradually, or the whole thing can come back to you in a flash,"* and *"You can be drawn most to the sounds associated with your memories, or you can be absorbed more fully by the tastes and smells."*

Conscious and unconscious dissociative statements that can be used for hypermnesia include the following: *"Your conscious mind can be involved in revealing what you already remember, while your unconscious mind can automatically begin to contribute new memories at a rate that's comfortable for you,"* and *"Your conscious mind can become aware of feeling wistful as your unconscious mind tenderly reveals an old thought or two that has some bearing on the things we spoke about today,"* and *"Your unconscious mind can already be thinking of an important keepsake for the memory that your conscious mind is beginning to crystallize for you."*

Although mention is made here of quickly remembering, in general, hypermnesia should be suggested as a gradual and evolving process. This is because most often a person remembers as a *process*: there is a blossoming of memory and associated affect. Suggesting that the evocation of vivid memory happens gradually conforms to the actual way in which people tend to remember. Another good reason for suggesting it as a gradual experience is that too often people don't remember simply because they conceptualize remembering as being an all-or-nothing event rather than a process that involves a continuum of remembrances.

Therefore, making remembering into a yes/no, black/white kind of experience is more counterproductive than productive and can actually create a pressure-cooker situation in which amnesia is elicited instead. Furthermore, gradual remembering is clinically more prudent, particularly in situations where trauma has taken place. This allows the person to integrate forgotten aspects of the trauma into the self at an adaptive and manageable pace. Abrupt and grand catharsis, although it is dramatic and makes for interesting movies, is seldom useful in clinical practice. As a matter of fact, this kind of abrupt lifting of amnesia can retraumatize the patient.

Metaphor

There are numerous metaphors that can be used in trance to engender hypermnesia. One is an account of a series of knots in a string being untied one at a time, gradually. You might say, for example, *"You pull a bit, you push a bit, letting it unravel, bit by bit, watching it unfurl, working it out, loosening the knot, getting the kinks out. Maybe you want to start with a small one and work from there, or maybe you prefer to start with a larger one, and as it unravels, you really recognize the textures, the feel of it as it unravels....Is the color of the fabric inside the knot lighter underneath than you remembered? You know the way something hidden from exposure is a little different...."*

Another useful metaphor is of a filing cabinet. Suggest to your client that he or she go into an *inner filing* cabinet, and one by one review the files lined up and the headings on each file. *"Do you see one of interest? Pull it out, open it up, see the notes inside..."* and so on. Alternately, the file can contain pictures of experiences to be remembered. A similar idea is having subjects experience, in trance, a visit to their unconscious, after having likened it to a storehouse of earlier feelings, ideas, pictures, and memories. Thus, you can lead a person through a visit to this storehouse, or an upstairs attic if you prefer, having them *"gaze at the innumerable boxes, some tied loosely, with easy access, others tied more tightly, a few with knots...."* Have the person *touch* the cardboard with his or her hand, or *smell* the mustiness, or the fresh spring air of a spring cleaning. The following is a paraphrased excerpt from work I (JSE) did with a woman in her mid-40s, seeking in therapy to recover a sense of herself as a child growing up. She spoke of having too few memories of any kind of herself as a child. She was using hypnosis as a vehicle to build a photo album of herself so to speak and was enjoying the experience as it took place each week:

> ....*Wow, look around now, that was a climb up those attic stairs but you've arrived...what's it like up there, Leslie? Can you tell me something about it?*....(Leslie responds with a description of an attic, with rays of sunlight streaming in through a window. She sees dozens of cardboard boxes stacked all around.) *Take your time, if you want, in deciding which cartons to look through first, or go right to what interests you, go ahead, and select, maybe an easy box for starters, where you can go through things, each item carrying with it memories of another time—dolls, pens from long-forgotten places, a letter from a childhood friend, from camp maybe, or from a sleepover...Have you found those clothes from when you were 11, yet? What's it smell like up there anyway?...That's right, fill in the blanks as you move along...ready for another box? Or are you enjoying the unfurling of memories just the way you are right now...?*

Another metaphor that we have used successfully is of a jigsaw puzzle. The puzzle becomes a living symbol for the fragmentation of memories that a person may have:

> ....*There are so many ways to put together a jigsaw puzzle. You can start by collecting the four corners and work from there, or you can start by collecting all the pieces with a straight edge and matching them together, getting an overall border and frame first. Alternately, you can collect all the different colors and begin assembling them. Some people zoom right in for the oddest shapes and connect those. In any event, you can afford to put a few of the pieces of the puzzle together comfortably, as no one can really tell what part of the puzzle is being assembled from only a few pieces. Piece after piece can be connected and it's only later—and this can be when the time is right—that the puzzle assembler says, "oh, that's the upper right-hand corner," or "oh, that's a picture of the farmhouse that I've been assembling." And you can bear in mind that some people like to look at the cover of the box of the puzzle first and use it as a model so they know the direction that they're going in. Other people purposefully like not to look at that end picture so that they can make the process even more chal-*

lenging or discover for themselves what the end picture is going to look like. Some people even go so far as to turn all the puzzle pieces upside down so that they're only working with certain shapes fitting together and no other visual cues.

Using a camera as a metaphoric backdrop for recovering and revivifying memory also works well. Talk about how a zoom lens *brings* images closer. Mention how the lens can then be focused so that the image gets *sharper and sharper*. Suggest that with each click of the camera something is *recorded* for permanent storage. We like this metaphor because apart from other aspects of it, it symbolizes the idea of "photographic memory."

Talk about TVs. One can say the following to a client:

You look at the TV and the TV is off and then you decide to turn it on and the picture comes in with only static. Then you discover that you're not on a real channel. You switch to the next channel and the picture's much clearer, but not quite clear enough. So, you adjust the antenna and the picture quality becomes sharper. Then, you begin to turn up the volume and you hear more and more clearly what's being said. Later in the day you call the cable company, have the cable company come over and install the cable and now the picture is vivid, sharp, and bright.

With the addition of a VCR, people could see themselves popping in a video of what is to be remembered and then controlling the unfolding of the memory by using their remote—fast forwarding through a prematurely revealed memory, pausing at select times, and rewinding or stopping it when desired. Of course, the person can also take the video back to the video store.

A final metaphor that we'll mention is that of morning fog beginning to lift. Fog is a natural for this kind of work; many people describe losing memories as "being in a fog" or "it's as if it's all foggy up there." During hypnotic trance, a therapist can trace the process of fog gradually lifting and clearing. One could also do posthypnotic suggestion for hypermnesia by talking in detail about how *"the fog can lift progressively each day as the sun rises."* Here, the emphasis on the sun rising suggests to a bereaved person that it is *through a mourning (morning) period that remembering can take place.* Apart from fog lifting through atmospheric changes, therapists can talk about someone putting on yellow-tinted glasses to cut through fog, or having yellow driving lights on the bottom of a car bumper, or having radar on the front of the car to scan for accidents ahead or animals in the road. Indeed, this is a dense metaphor.

Again, keep in mind that it's best to be permissive and not to implore a recovery process to take place. Also, we think that it's often best to have the person *practice* the process of hypermnesia by remembering innocuous or positive memories first. This establishes a feeling of competency and control over the flow of memory processes and over the management of associated feelings and reactions. Another principle that we'd like to mention is the characteristic Ericksonian idea of *working from the outside in.* You don't want just to suggest to people that they remember the most dramatic or the most important aspect of an event, situation, or experience. Start small, letting a person discover— through whichever senses he or she recollects with best—a tidbit here, a sliver of an image there, building up the process so that there is a rich crescendo of memory, unless of course full immersion would be overwhelming (even with positive memories sometimes). In these latter cases, the therapist and client should titrate the manifesting hypermnesia or in some way structure the hypnotic experience to more effectively support the client.

Using a Client's History of Success

Another way to elicit hypermnesia is by getting detailed descriptions of how the person has successfully remembered in the past. Ask your clients to tell you how this has occurred, describing it through all his or her senses, almost as if he or she were writing a play and a director in a far-off city needed to have explicit instructions in the script in order to direct the play. With this kind of intense detail, a person can tap into the process by which he or she previously best remembered something. The client and therapist can then piggyback on that history of success by directing it, focusing it, and pointing it at the situation currently in need of recall.

Naturalistic Examples of Remembering

Another means to elicit hypermnesia involves telling stories from everyday life regarding the common ways in which remembering takes place. For example, therapists could talk about the tip-of-the-tongue phenomenon:

And, just about everyone's had the experience of wanting to think about a word and not having it right in the conscious mind, but almost on the verge of being in the conscious mind. At those times, the more you try and remember it, often the harder it is. So, you can just distract yourself for a moment or two while giving yourself permission when the time is right to remember and—lo and behold—a few minutes later, the word pops into your mind automatically, having been allowed to pop into your mind through holding the conscious mind at bay with some distraction or absorption in an alternate activity.

Another example from everyday life involves discussing how someone recalls something that they had forgotten:

Most people have had the experience of trying to remember what took place in a particular situation and having difficulty doing so. What many people do is go back to the start. They experience themselves again walking into the building or into the school where something of interest or meaning took place and they trace their steps in a linear and sequential way until they get to the point where the event they are going to remember takes place. That makes it easier. Most people intuitively know that memories take place in a certain context and if you run through the context in the actual sequence it took place, the missing piece will fall into place like a domino placed between others.

This common, everyday method of remembering can be useful to people who are taking tests; in trance they can be encouraged to see the pages of the textbook one after another in a certain order. That's why educators teaching study skills know that the memorization of decontextualized fact after fact after fact isn't as useful for studying and retention as organizing the information in a particular sequence, demarcated by major headings. The major headings then almost become like tabs on the top of a file, which are not only easily spotted, but also trigger a train of associations. The same phenomenon can take place mentally.

Symbols

There are certain sensory events that constitute *skeleton keys* that are able to open up major doors of remembering. For example, in the visual sphere, a person could be encouraged to remember *looking* way up at her mother or could be encouraged to *look* down and see her father's big shoes. This would be a visual skeleton key. A person can be given suggestions for the sensory sphere that they tend to utilize most in experiencing the world. To try and hone in on an auditory master key, a person could be encouraged to *hear* again a particular song from the year in which they're trying to remember an experience.

In our experience, olfactory cues often seem to be the most effective master keys. For example, a person could be encouraged to remember the sight of his or her school gymnasium, but remembering the *smell* of the gymnasium—if he or she can do it—is even more powerful. Likewise, having a person remember the smell of his or her grandmother, her soap, her perfume, her clothing, can result in a wealth of memories "chockablock" with affect. In a similar vein, remembering the sight of one's childhood garage is less likely to evoke a memory than remembering the *sound* that the garage door made upon opening, or even better yet, *the smell of new grass clippings* in that garage or the *smell of gasoline* in the lawnmower. Since good hypermnesias entail rich sensory recall, including words evocative of the different senses facilitates their development.

SELECTED TRANSCRIPT MATERIAL

Hypermnesia for Doctoral Candidate in Psychology Preparing for Orals

So, it can be as if there's a tiny, little 007 spy camera inside each of your eyes...and your eye can dilate or contract ...depending on the light, just like the lens of a camera...and it can be used as a little spy 007 camera inside your head, every time you come to something important in your notes, you can photograph an entire page, you can photograph a chart, you can photograph an outline...you can organize the photographs...and when you're asked the question, it can be as if you open a well-organized file cabinet with folders each labeled and you pull the folders out and the photographs are right there, crisp, clean, smelling like photographs, as only photographs can smell...and they can be in black and white or vivid color—it's your choice....Now, alternately, it can be as if you're going through microfiche in the library...scanning...like the *New York Times* reel of microfilm...and you move the level from page to page—you slow it down, you skim, you scan—all the while, DiDi, going deeper and deeper into trance...your hand moving around and around, sometimes quick, like with the sports page, the automotive page and then you spot an article, you slow down...no, that's not all...and go further, faster, faster further...develop a rapid scanning technique for all that information that is in your subconscious mind, everything that you've learned in graduate school is encoded, everything that's been rehearsed sufficiently is in long-term memory...and all relevant information, all relevant memories can be refreshed, DiDi, it can be as if the information are like pillows upon a bed being fluffed up...a comforter being fluffed up...the memories can be fluffed up and freshened up....It can be like opening up windows in a house in spring and getting rid of stale air, your relevant memories can be fluffed up and freshened up, ready to be used...so, you can remember, DiDi, everything that you need to remember about what's been said...and with that in mind, permanently fixed, permanently fixed...you can bring yourself up and out of trance at a pace that's right for you....

Hypermnesia
for Recall of
Learned
Material
for the
Psychology
Licensing
Exam

...so deep, the suggestions that I give you will be able to be remembered vividly by your subconscious mind and implemented just when you need them....Your cue will be any beginnings of anxiety, your cue will be any doubt about knowing an answer and then at those times, these suggestions will come rushing out of your subconscious mind like a personal cavalry and it can be as if there are numerous filing cabinets containing the information that you've learned in graduate school and a special drawer for any information that you've learned and you can certainly do this as you review in the coming week...the information that you've learned can be organized in files, topics, headings, and in the test and in life you can have access to it...and you can go down into trance and that can be your way of opening the file cabinets ...you can go a little bit deeper into trance and that can be your way of opening up a file folder and you can see the answer to the questions right there in front of you...right there in front of you...trance can be your way of opening up the file cabinet and like using your thumb on that little piece of metal that unlocks the latch that holds the file cabinet closed...and you pull it open, you feel the metal on your hand...you feel the cabinet, the file on the runner, it opens up...don't open two at once, they might tip over...drawers, one at a time...and you can see a file with the relevant headings and you can pull it....

Hypermnesia for a Man Who is Anxious About an Important Decision He Made Regarding His Future

....Maybe now, maybe in a little while, you can have come to mind those times from the past where you *made good judgments...made sound decisions*...about what you were doing...a good decision you have made about the future....What is it you need to remember about how you learned to make distinctions between what would be right for you and what wouldn't? Remember that time you spoke about, just the other day, when you realized, several years ago, that you had good instincts about such things, that you finally felt that you could trust your inner amalgam of experiences and learnings, your ability to anticipate, your capacities for forethought...your ability to make sound decisions....

Hypermnesia for a Recently Divorced Man Who Feels Hopeless About Finding Another Woman to Love

....I suppose I could suggest bringing forward a memory from your college years, or from your high school years, to help you remember what it feels like to be hopeful, to be thinking about what's coming next in your life, but I prefer to let you select the most useful time period, something in your own history to help you rekindle that state of expectation, anticipation about the future, that there can be one, *another one* (an indirect reference to another wife), that's really right for you...and when you've come upon a memory of that feeling, go ahead and really experience it...now...so that you know...what it can feel like to look forward to what will happen new in your life...to know that this time it can be right....

Chapter 6

POSTHYPNOTIC SUGGESTION

ABOUT THE PHENOMENON

Posthypnotic suggestion refers to the subject's ability to respond at a later time to a suggestion given during trance. Such suggestions can involve the rapid reinduction of aspects or certain characteristics of the trance state, although this is not a necessary feature. Posthypnotic suggestions can be directed toward behaviors, attitudes, or feelings and used in any of the following typical situations: a woman giving birth, an anxious client about to undergo a medical procedure, an athlete needing to relax just prior to a competitive event, a speaker nervous for a speaking engagement, or a phobic about to approach the anxiety-provoking stimulus (e.g., airplane, bridge, elevator).

The posthypnotically suggested state can be one of relaxation, confidence, having a sense of control, being free of worry, or can involve any one of the hypnotic phenomena such as anesthesia, hallucination, time distortion, tunnel vision, and so on. For example, the person suffering from migraines can experience sensations of coolness *at the onset* of a migraine in response to a posthypnotic suggestion delivered by her therapist in session or in response to one delivered by her own self during self-hypnosis trances. *"As soon as you feel that first inkling of pressure, you can let loose inside, that rush of coolness, and let it go to your head."* This, incidentally, is an interesting suggestion for a client with narcissistic traits—for whom the suggestion will have added "characterological" appeal (let it go to your head)—*or* one who needs a boost in esteem.

Posthypnotic suggestion is based on the principle of association:

- "When you feel your first labor contractions, you can also feel a sense of power and control come over you...."
- "When you get the first hint of a migraine, you can quickly discover a coolness developing inside, first in your right temple and then in your left...."
- "As soon as you've checked your baggage, you can be surprised at how calm and composed you are...."
- "The moment the elevator doors close, you can take a deep breath and experience the ride as only a moment in duration...."
- "You can recognize the anesthesia that has already developed the moment you sit in your dentist's chair...."

Authentic posthypnotic suggestions manifest automatically, without conscious awareness. In fact, Erickson, in an article cowritten with his wife, Elizabeth M. Erickson, (1941/1980a) once specifically characterized the posthypnotic act as being executed without "any demonstrable conscious awareness in the subject of the underlying cause and motive for his act" (p. 388). He further wrote that a special, *albeit brief*, state typically develops spontaneously with the initiation of the posthypnotic act: It is somewhat of a dissociated act, one that interrupts and breaks through the stream of consciously directed activity.

However, in this same article ("Concerning the Nature and Character of Posthypnotic Behavior"), Erickson outlined several exceptions to the development of a *spontaneous* posthypnotic trance. One is the failure to have developed amnesia for the posthypnotic suggestion given during the hypnosis, so that the act is voluntary and consciously directed. It is posthypnotic, then, only in reference to the *temporal* relationship of suggestion and act. In these cases the person has remembered the posthypnotic suggestion but still retains the compulsive desire to complete it anyway. A second exception was with people who did not like the automatically responsive character of the posthypnotic act and would perform it only in a deliberate fashion. And yet another was where there was inadequate amnesia for the trance experience and the posthypnotic suggestion is identified by the subject.

Erickson also felt that keeping the posthypnotic suggestion unconscious made it more difficult for the subject to resist it. However, it is also important to know and to communicate to clients, where necessary or relevant, that people will never respond to a posthypnotic suggestion felt by them to be inappropriate or immoral. Storylines involving characters who respond to inappropriate posthypnotic suggestions make great movies (such as *The Manchurian Candidate*) but are wholly unfounded in "real life," inasmuch as suggestions given to a person in trance do not override that person's own ethical sensibilities and personal judgment.

Weitzenhoffer (1989a) has a different opinion about some of what Erickson says. He writes that the degree of conscious awareness of the intent or content of the posthypnotic suggestion has little effect on how the subject responds. This, too, is said to reflect that compulsive aspect of hypnotic behavior described earlier in this chapter; people do it no matter what. And even though the posthypnotic suggestion often implicitly instructs the subject to behave as if *not* hypnotized, the posthypnotic act, does, according to Weitzenhoffer and in agreement with Erickson, entail a brief reinstatement of the hypnotic state.

This is what often worries some clients. They anticipate that the posthypnotic suggestion will have them vulnerable to intermittent and unwitting walking trances. However, to the degree that any such reinstatement occurs, it can be expected to manifest real differently out of the office than in. It has not been our experience that clients move into an *externally recognizable* state of trance upon any posthypnotic cue; rather, they experience some *facet* of previous trance states—the composure, the hallucination, or the anesthesia, without the dissociation or physiological relaxation characteristic of trance. It is as if they have *extracted* the most relevant essence of trance for themselves. People continue to function within their environmental or social contexts and do not suddenly have their eyes defocus or move about as if walking or talking in a hypnotized state. They simply respond to the earlier suggestion to do, remember, or experience something that will be therapeutic.

Because the response to the posthypnotic suggestion occurs at a later time, this phenomenon takes it place alongside age progression as a phenomenon that allows the therapy to extend most naturally out into the future. Orienting toward the future in psychotherapy is a distinctive aspect of Erickson's pioneering work. Of course, giving therapeutic task assignments too could be considered a third way of promoting therapeutic progress at a time later than in the therapy session itself. Task assignments, however, do not involve hypnosis, are voluntary actions of which the subject is consciously aware, and are often considerably more elaborate and detailed in their delivery. The reader interested in the use of task assignments, homework, and prescribed rituals in therapy is referred to the works of Boscolo, Cecchin, Hoffman, & Penn

(1987), Haley (1963,1976), Madanes (1981), Selvini-Palazzoli, Boscolo, Cecchin, & Prata (1978), Weeks and L'Abate (1982), and other such pioneers of these strategic therapeutic interventions. The use of ambiguous task assignments in therapy is written about by Lankton and Lankton (1986).

HISTORY AND EXPERIMENTAL STUDIES

The duration of the effectiveness of the posthypnotic suggestion has been a subject of study. There appears to be quite a bit of variability, with reports ranging from a few months to several years (Weitzenhoffer, 1989a). There is one confirmed report of a posthypnotic suggestion having lasted 16 years (Weitzenhoffer, 1989)! Weitzenhoffer distinguishes posthypnotic suggestion from one-trial learning; he points out experimental studies that indicated that the posthypnotic response does suffer some degradation over time when not reinforced by renewed suggestions at periodic intervals.

In a fine research project, Berrigan, Kurtz, Stabile, and Strube (1991) performed a precise experiment measuring the durability of posthypnotic suggestions as a function of the type of suggestion given and the depth of trance achieved by the subject. Although most prior studies had demonstrated moderate initial drop-offs (during the first three weeks) in the effectiveness of posthypnotic suggestion followed by a plateau effect, Berrigan and coauthors observed that the research results were flawed by methodological deficiencies of various kinds. In addition, prior studies had not measured the drop-off in durability based on the type of suggestion given and trance depth. The Berrigan findings indicate that high hypnotizable subjects are able to respond posthypnotically for a period of at least eight weeks.

Further, true to the study's initial hypothesis, the type of posthypnotic suggestion *did* influence the amount of the drop-off. Simpler suggestions, such as the one that an arm would automatically lower given a special cue, evidenced little decline in posthypnotic response over time, whereas the suggestion that the person would be unable to remember the name of his or her hometown when asked was considered a far more difficult item; over time, this more difficult posthypnotic suggestion demonstrated a significantly lower degree of effectiveness.

In clinical circles the notion has long been propagated that greater trance depth would result in increased effectiveness of posthypnotic suggestion (Weitzenhoffer, 1950). This assumption, however, was only partially supported in Berrigan and colleagues' research. They discovered that subjects who were able to move to a greater trance depth during the *assessment* phase of hypnotizability were later able to respond posthypnotically at a higher rate. However, trance depth was not related to posthypnotic effectiveness when measured at the time the posthypnotic suggestion was given.

An interesting aspect of this research protocol is that *amnesia for the posthypnotic suggestion was not given*. Further, experimenters suggested that *prior to performing the posthypnotic suggestion subjects would go into trance* and then comply with the posthypnotic suggestion. A third interesting aspect of the methodology was allowing the subjects to *practice the posthypnotic suggestion once*, prior to having to perform it later; this had been shown in prior research to enhance results. Hence, the findings reported above may be due in part to the latter two methodological inclusions, and so clinicians may want to experiment with introducing these parameters when giving posthypnotic suggestions. Amnesia may or may not be correct to include, depending on your particular client. Remember too that results are more favorable when the work is individualized to clients and when the posthypnotic suggestion is given repeatedly at different levels of trance.

Readers may be interested in specific data from Berrigan's studies. For the posthypnotic suggestion to not remember one's hometown, responses dropped from a high of 12 respondents who were able to inhibit verbalization immediately after the posthypnotic suggestion, to 3 subjects who were able to inhibit verbalization at the end of eight weeks. For the posthypnotic suggestion to lower one's arm automatically, there was no significant drop-off: 10 subjects responded effectively immediately after administration of the suggestion and 9 responded effectively eight weeks later.

Evans and Staats (1989) performed an interesting experiment that measured posthypnotic responsivity to amnesia suggestions in four different diagnostic categories of hospitalized psychiatric patients. This interesting study confirmed the frequently found result that psychiatric inpatients perform similarly on suggestibility tests compared to normal control groups. The four subgroups, which were comprised of schizophrenics, eating-disordered patients, alcoholics, and patients suffering from major depression, likewise performed similarly to the control group with regard to the effectiveness of posthypnotic amnesia. There are only slight differences in the effectiveness of the posthypnotic suggestion between the different groups of psychiatric inpatients, with schizophrenics evidencing slightly more posthypnotic amnesia (perhaps due to the cognitive deficits that are part and parcel of the schizophrenia) and the eating-disordered patients, who experienced somewhat less posthypnotic amnesia (perhaps due to control issues).

However, besides demonstrating that psychiatric inpatients respond similarly to the control groups on suggestibility tests, the research showed that the inpatients evidence both responsivity to posthypnotic suggestion and responsivity to amnesia suggestions. High hypnotizables across all groups of inpatients performed in a superior fashion to low hypnotizables, and patient success at achieving posthypnotic amnesia seems to be related not to forgetting per se (inasmuch as material is eventually recalled when a reversibility cue is given), but to a *disruption in the retrieval process*, which is, most likely, an outgrowth of the confusion over the temporal sequencing of information that is to be forgotten. That is, subjects who are good at posthypnotic amnesia tend to achieve it by virtue of an inability to retrieve, perhaps due to an uncertainty about the ordering of information over time.

Another interesting study in posthypnotic suggestion was performed by Wojcikiewicz and Orlick (1987). This is one study that used actual athletic competition in the experimentation. The authors compared a posthypnotic suggestion for relaxation with a control group and found that the treatment was effective in reducing perceived anxiety prior to a fencing competition. In line with numerous other prior studies reviewed, researchers also found that hypnosis did *not* improve actual performance. (This research showed that hypnosis was most likely to improve performance when it removed some interference or psychological barrier rather then when it was used to affect physical/muscular performance per se.)

When the athletes of this study were interviewed, they were in complete agreement that for the hypnotic strategy to be even more effective, it needed to be practiced more frequently and also be highly individualized to meet the particular athlete's needs. Unbeknownst to themselves these athletes voiced a valid criticism of traditional experimentation and of the traditional application of hypnosis. Ericksonian approaches to hypnosis view intervention as an ongoing process rather than as a unidimensional/unidirectional firing away of a therapeutic or experimental salvo. Furthermore, good clinical sense mandates that intervention be "custom-fitted" to the client sitting in front of you.

In addition to the experimental studies cited above, a number of interesting case studies were reported. One study by Matheson (1979) demonstrated the use of posthypnotic suggestion with depressives by first age-regressing the depressed patient back to a time when he or she felt positive emotions. Then the context within which these positive emotions appeared was faded out, while the patient was encouraged to keep the positive feelings. Posthypnotic suggestion was then used to help the person retrieve the positive emotions while engaged in nondepressing activities (also for which there were posthypnotic suggestions). This strategy proved highly effective, with the author proposing that it enables depressives to engage in both the cognitive and action-oriented responses that are important to recovery.

Lewis (1979) also wrote about the use of posthypnotic suggestions in psychotherapy. He treated a patient with schizoid personality and, in attempting to insure behavior change at home, made posthypnotic suggestions central in his treatment plan. We think that whenever a well-spring of emotional problems, emotional deficits, or some kind of resistance mitigates against a person making real changes outside the treatment setting, posthypnotic suggestion can be very helpful. This had been the case in Lewis's study. Follow-up showed that significant behavior changes were recorded during the therapy and maintained at five months and at one-year and two-year follow up interviews.

In the above case studies, posthypnotic suggestion was used to help clients change specific ways of acting and feeling so that the changes invariably led to other changes, including changes in interpersonal and behavioral processes that would become new habits, snow-balling them for therapeutic effect. Making suggestions that the symptom will disappear, then, is not such a good idea. Such was the experience of Singh (1989) in taking a two-pronged approach to the treatment of refractory headaches in three patients. He combined using a posthypnotic suggestion for the absence of the headache with a posthypnotic suggestion for using a coping mechanism for the headache. The latter strategy was found more effective.

Sometimes posthypnotic suggestion can be used to counter behavior over which the person has no voluntary control. Koe (1989) gave a client suffering from night terrors the posthypnotic suggestion that the sounds that precipitated the night terrors (nocturnal noises that awakened him) would go unheard by him and he could continue sleeping. This suggestion, which is tantamount to a posthypnotic suggestion for negative auditory hallucination, successfully eliminated his night terrors. The author summarizes that inasmuch as his experience shows night terrors to be an arousal phenomenon, the posthypnotic suggestion to the client to not hear what is arousing him or her can be effective in ameliorating this disorder.

INDICATIONS FOR USE

One clinical indication for the use of posthypnotic suggestion is when a client is highly suggestible. Clients who present or describe themselves as very self-suggestible can be called upon to use that part of themselves to solve the problematic situation. Suppose, for example, that a person desiring pain control through hypnosis responds to the question of how he managed, as a child, to control the discomfort after scraping a knee by saying, "I would just keep telling myself that it's going to go away, it's going to go away." A prudent therapist uses this client's already successful methods of self-generated posthypnotic suggestion in this current situation of pain control.

Another time to consider using this phenomenon is when (self) posthypnotic suggestion has become part of the problem. Remember, too, that if posthypnotic suggestion is the mechanism of the problem, it can sometimes become the mechanism of the solution. How many times, for example, have we worked with people who foul up their lives by repeatedly badgering themselves with negative suggestions, that is, suggestions of what *not to do* in a given circumstance. They tell themselves to "not yell back at the kids," "not walk this hitter," "not slip on the ice." This is very counterproductive. When a person negatively programs himself or herself by thinking of what not to do, what has been accomplished is *repeated reminding* about the unfortunate occurrence.

There's another drawback, too. The unconscious mind does not process negatives in the same fashion as conscious-level linguistic functioning and therefore is left with an image or concept of the very activity referred to; there is no "picture" for **no**, which is a conceptual term. Therefore, what resonates in the person's mind is *yelling* at the kids, *walking* the hitter, *slipping* on the ice. This is especially counterproductive in situations involving physical action. The body tends to automatically organize itself in the direction of the idea in mind (ideomotor responding), so don't be surprised to find yourself slipping on ice if you have been entertaining images of losing balance and falling. Help clients to countermand these habits by using positive statements: *"Calm is Mom," "Straight over the plate,"* or *"Balanced real nice right over this ice."*

These sorts of statements are really a variation on the theme of posthypnotic suggestion. They are consciously effected and typically not associated with trance. We include them here because people manage to "hypnotize" themselves without hypnosis as we think of it—they train themselves to respond to ideas automatically *as if* they were posthypnotic suggestions. Since this happens often in the negative ways described above, why not extract what we can from the phenomena of posthypnotic suggestion and ideomotor responding to make self-suggestion more profitable?

A third opportunity for using posthypnotic suggestion is when the desired change is to take place outside of the session. There are a number of specific indications by problem area for posthypnotic suggestion. Migraines, chronic pain, anticipatory childbirth anxiety, labor pain, performance anxiety, competition nerves, and many of the phobias are all good examples. This is because a change in perception or in habit pattern or in phenomenological experience can be orchestrated to take place at a certain time—and in the relevant context. The intervention of posthypnotic suggestion thus becomes like a long range, highly accurate missile—precise and parsimonious.

- The chronic pain patient uses posthypnotic suggestion to have the sensation of numbness (practiced in session) kick in *at precisely the moment when the pain reaches the threshold of discomfort.*
- The woman in labor begins to feel a dissociation of upper and lower parts of her body *as soon as she hears the door of the car shut on the way to the hospital.* Or she feels a reinforcing sense of control and calm *as she passes through the doorway into the delivery room.*
- A tunnel vision sets in for the batter *the moment he steps up to the plate.*
- The child giving her first piano recital is reminded of how well she does when there is an audience by *touching her hairband just prior to going on stage.*
- The college student with a speaking phobia finds himself feeling a rush of confidence and relaxation *the moment he steps onto campus the day of his oral report.*
- The businesswoman with a fear of flying goes into an exquisite, dissociative trance *once she feels the plane roll onto the runway for take off.*

In all these situations a posthypnotic suggestion has been used to trigger the desirable response by connecting it with something the therapist knows will happen just prior to the symptomatic response.

A fourth indication for its use is when there is sluggish transfer of positive gains made in sessions into the person's daily life. These are situations in which a client needs help mobilizing change outside of the therapy session. Consider clients who do not implement the work of therapy in their everyday lives or futures. They work brilliantly in the therapy hour, develop terrific understandings of themselves, are active in formulating strategies for overcoming problems, appear urgently to desire change, and so forth. But the work of the therapy just does not transfer over into everyday life. Stymied therapists often end up simply providing more and more of the same in the hope that a threshold is eventually reached, and that the "pot boils over" into daily living. Therapists using hypnosis, however, have used posthypnotic suggestion as a way of priming the pump so that the transfer is made more easily. Bridges are made during trancework between a person's resources and their application toward solutions; posthypnotic suggestions are then used to remind the client of this when behavior or attitude change is needed.

Let's say a woman with a panic disorder avoids employment because she fears becoming immobilized by anxiety on the job and therefore she thinks she will be unable to get herself home. Her problem is not about getting anxious per se—she feels able to tolerate that. What holds her back is the worry that she will not be able to get back to her house. The posthypnotic suggestion here could be as follows:

> *....Each time you even begin to think "what if" can be the cue for your conscious mind to remind you of all the ways in which you have been able always, always to take care of yourself and do what you needed to do when feeling more anxious than you cared to be at the time. Each 'what if' will bring another memory of getting home, safe and sound, passing through your mind like a video, assuring, reassuring, allowing you to continue to move, comfortably, toward change....*

In this way, posthypnotic suggestion is used to preempt the automatic but counterproductive response in favor of a more adaptive one.

Of course, the situation is not always as extreme as the one mentioned above. Other clients transfer some learnings, but when they get into a pressure or clutch situation, they regress, switch ego states, and do not do what they intended to do. For example, some couples demonstrate new, more constructive types of communication in most situations but lose that during heated arguments, going back to old unproductive and inciteful ways. This would be a perfect situation in which to use posthypnotic suggestions. The couple could be instructed, together in trance, to use any cursing as a cue to remember the circumstances surrounding the last time the couple had made love. Even if it does little to change the affective tenor of the argument, it certainly serves as a pattern interruption.

Another situation where posthypnotic suggestion can be used prophylactically to preempt automatic counterproductive responses is with people who are trying to stop habits like smoking or overeating. Here the posthypnotic suggestion might be something like the following: *"The moment you think you want a smoke will be your cue **to inhale deeply and really appreciate the air capacity of all those newly discovered alveoli**,"* or *"Whenever you begin to think of eating more than your body needs, you can vividly and sharply **remember the discomfort of a distended, overstuffed stomach**."*

PRINCIPLES FOR DELIVERING POSTHYPNOTIC SUGGESTION

1. Say it many times throughout the client's hypnotic experience.
2. Give the suggestion at many different levels of trance (unless amnesia is critical, in which case one should only offer the suggestion at deeper levels where conscious awareness has been suspended).
3. Say the posthypnotic suggestion in many different ways, using a variety of linguistic and anecdotal means to communicate it.
4. Base the posthypnotic suggestion on something that is noticeable or observable that you know for certain is going to happen. For example:
   when the sun rises
   when you put on your running sneakers
   when you feel the first hint of anxiety
   when you enter the room for your interview
   when you shake hands
   when you step inside your in-laws' front door
5. Find out how your client successfully reminds himself or herself in everyday life to do something (i.e., How do you get yourself to remember where your car is in those large parking lots? Is it with a spatial or visual orientation? Do you use the color or letter of the symbol to locate your car?). Try to use those same cues in your suggestions.
6. Remember to use your voice to emphasize the significance of the suggestion (even at unconscious levels of reception) in some way (i.e., pausing before and after the suggestion, voice softer, rhythm slower).

ELICITING THE PHENOMENON OF POSTHYPNOTIC SUGGESTION

Direct and Indirect Suggestion

To **seed** the idea of responding to posthypnotic suggestion, you need to think about what would reference the phenomenon in a subtle, undetectable way now and yet build toward an affective crescendo as you deliver the suggestion. If you are working with a couple in preparation for childbirth, you might have learned that the act of being seated in a wheelchair upon arriving at the hospital and being wheeled toward labor and delivery is what precipitates anxiety for the woman. The anxiety may be related to feelings of loss of control, associations to being ill or damaged, discomfort allowing herself to be taken care of, or any number of other issues. Given that the wheelchair has become conditioned as the anxiety-provoking stimulus, you might already be considering the use of a posthypnotic suggestion to help this woman have a different, or at least attenuated, reaction in response to the chair. You can seed your intervention in the early part of your induction with something like the following:

- *"...With your next deep breath you can sink down into that chair (office chair) a little more deeply and let that be your cue to really relax and look forward to what's coming...."*

or

- *"...Go ahead and rest your arms on the armrests and let that be your trigger for feeling centered, composed, and in control...."*

Once the client is in trance, or even before, you can also use **presuppositions** to orient the client toward responding to posthypnotic suggestion. Presupposition and seeding have in common the fact that they are preludes to the phenomenon that one is trying to elicit. However, presupposition is a little more verbally direct in its alluding as to what can take place in trance for the client. A couple of examples of presupposing the posthypnotic response are *"After you have reacted calmly upon first seeing the plane, you can rejoice in your change,"* or *"Soon after you feel the inner quiet at the start of the exam, you'll be pleasantly taken aback."* On the other hand, seeding these same ideas might take the following form during the early part of the induction phase of the hypnosis: *"And as you relax in your seat, you can discover a calm inside, allowing you to drop quite comfortably into trance,"* or *"I don't know, Steve, if you'll experience an inner quiet before or after a relevant image shortly comes to mind."*

Double binds, too, can be used to elicit a posthypnotic response. The therapist could say, for example, *"It may be that as soon as you arrive home from work you feel the urge to become physically active, or maybe it will be the moment you walk out the door at work that you feel this desire to exercise."* Remember that the desired response needs to be made contingent upon something that is concrete, observable, and bound to be experienced by the subject. In the above example, the cue upon which the new behavior (desire to exercise) was contingent was leaving the work site or arriving home—two safe bets. These may also be the two junctures in a day when someone who overeats could easily make a poor decision, either stopping for fast food, snacking, or simply "vegging out." In that case, use these very junctures as your trigger for better decision making. Connecting posthypnotic suggestions to expected behaviors or situations is what gives this intervention its pinpoint precision.

Conscious/unconscious dissociative statements can be helpful in creating compliance to a posthypnotic suggestion. One could say, *"Your conscious mind can think to itself, 'Pause,' and just take a deep breath if you feel the urge to smoke, while your unconscious mind can immediately give you the experience of a nicotine high."* These conscious and unconscious dissociative statements give two posthypnotic suggestions at once; if the person ties up some resistance in avoiding one, then the other one may slide through and become operative at an unconscious level.

The use of posthypnotic suggestion will usually require the concomitant use of amnesia for the suggestion. This is especially indicated in cases where the client is an overanalyzer of therapeutic interventions or is one who tries too hard; here, the *automaticity* of the suggestion gets lost under the client's conscious scrutiny. When amnesia for the posthypnotic suggestion is desired by the therapist, suggestions for it should be part of the trance as well. These suggestions can be direct:

- *"....You can forget now these ideas for comfort you just heard and allow them to resurface at the designated time and place...."*
- *"....Go ahead and dismiss from conscious memory these suggestions, knowing that your unconscious will hold onto them and effect them at the correct time and place...."*
- *"....It's really OK that these ideas for relaxation and composure recede from conscious awareness now, as they will return when the time is right...."*

Or the suggestion can be indirect:

....You know how easy it is to forget what kind of appetizer you had for dinner last night, or what dreams you had, or even what a person might have just said to you moments before . . . it's that easy to let there be changes even now in what one is aware of and what one is not....

The suggestions can even be part of inductions for confusion and distraction:

....People can sometimes forget things they hear even before they hear them, as they find something else in their own current experience of the world to better absorb their attention, such as a bright shock of color, or a moment of music in their heads, no less a funny word, or maybe a funny colorful song that fully absorbs your conscious attention for the next several moments in a way that allows your unconscious alone to register these next ideas....

Metaphor and Symbols

Metaphor and symbols can be incorporated into your hypnotic work for the express purpose of eliciting posthypnotic suggestion. In these instances, the therapist can draw upon all the technology through which something is programmed to happen at a later time. For example, one could discuss in hypnosis (or out) how she programmed her oven to go on at a certain time and cook the meal so it was ready when she got home. Other metaphors include VCRs that are programmed to tape a show even when someone is away on vacation; alarm clocks that are set to go off to remind someone to do something; pill cases that beep so people are reminded to take medications; watches that can be set to beep when something needs to be done; compartmentalized feeding units for cats that reveal each day's food supply at a certain time (an arrangement that allows owners to go away for days at a time); and the like. Of course you don't need technology to have a working metaphor for a posthypnotic suggestion: just talk about the old-fashioned method of tying a string around one's finger as a reminder of what needs to be done—a homespun, folksy way of concretizing the notion of a posthypnotic suggestion.

Naturalistic Examples

In providing naturalistic examples of posthypnotic suggestion, therapists need only to casually scan their historical and experiential backgrounds to think about when they and others may have employed it in everyday life. One can go on and on about all the different ways people cue themselves to remember where their cars are parked. Likewise, a therapist can go on and on about all the ways people remind themselves where they left their keys. We all have a long history of reminding ourselves to do something, whether it be remembering to pull down the blinds before the baby's nap so that the light doesn't interfere with his sleep or remembering to pick up some milk on the way home. All of these typical commonplace events become the fodder for naturalistic examples of posthypnotic suggestion. We believe that by providing a wealth of such examples, the client's very own capacity to find ways to cue him- or herself in relation to some problem where posthypnotic suggestion would be useful will be sparked.

SELECTED TRANSCRIPT MATERIAL

*Post-
hypnotic
Suggestion
for
Candidate
in Clinical
Psychology
Taking Oral
Exams*

So, your cue can be being asked a question about any aspect of clinical psychology...upon that cue, your mind can work in a clear, crisp, highly effective, cognitive, efficient manner and you can then engage in rapid scanning, like microfilm scanning in the library, finding just the information that's relevant to you...retrieval can be easy and smooth, Cindy...like a water pump primed, your mind can respond immediately. In the last session I gave you some suggestions and your mind responded very quickly, very fully...it can do that with these suggestions....I directly and indirectly asked you to remember about your own elementary school...that was a long time ago, your graduate school is more recent...you can remember that more easily....

*Post-
hypnotic
Suggestion
for Coping
with Shy
Bladder*

Now, anytime you step up to a urinal, you can automatically have this relaxation come over you...seeing the handle that you flush with—seeing it can be your cue...you see that—relaxation comes over you and you daydream...think about something else...all the while having the subtle intention, just a subtle intention, just a permission...to pee...and if these straightforward things don't work, you may need to smoke yourself out, and how might that happen? Well, I can give you the posthypnotic suggestion that if the straight forward things that I've mentioned don't pan out, you can smoke yourself out by going to the bathroom when you only have to go a little bit and not really a lot, just a little bit...this is Plan B...and purposefully stand there when you know that you don't have to pee and stopping yourself in fact purposely from peeing, trying to get yourself not to pee...and so, Plan B can involve you going to the urinal and trying to get yourself not to pee, going when you don't have to pee that much or going when you do have to pee a lot, but as an experiment, you're probably pretty good at holding your pee at this point, as an experiment you can go and see if you have the willpower, see if you can try so hard to control the peeing that you cannot go...and yeah, sure, maybe your penis will get so confused by all this that it just says, piss on you, and goes, lets it fly and then screws up the whole experiment, but maybe you can try and stop yourself from peeing...

Post-
hypnotic
Suggestion
for Coping
with
Migraines

....Certainly I have no objection to the first signals that a migraine may be developing as being your cue to go deeper into trance more quickly....

Post-
hypnotic
Suggestion
in Sport
Psychology
(Maintaining
Erect Upper
Body
Posture)

....As you look at your horse's ears...that really can be your cue to retrieve any or all aspects of this particular trance experience...in whatever manner you like...it's possible that by looking at the tips of your horse's ears, it can serve as your cue to once again bring your shoulders back...up and back and stay there...know that you really can nail that scene in your inner experience and transpose it into a reality....

Post-
hypnotic
Suggestions
for
Reinduction
of Trance
Using a
Physical Cue

....You can go into trance remembering the sound of my voice or remembering the soft cushion behind your head...or...you can squeeze yourself on the shoulder and have the experience of deep trance in a moment's notice...like a signal...you can pick your hand up now and do that...and when your hand reaches your shoulder and squeezes it, your subconscious mind can recognize that anytime you do this, you can go as deep, as quickly as you would like...you can have trance in a flash...it can come over you very quickly...you can move like a child after a developmental arrest is undone. They often, after a fixation is undone, they often move forward in time, go through the developmental stages that they've missed at a quicker pace, covering them in the same sequence—the sequence is inalterable—but people go at different paces. An older child released from an arrest will often move forward very, very quickly in time...through the stages of development...growing in leaps and bounds....Now, you can go down into trance through the sequences of trance depth...the sequence can remain inalterable...but you can do it faster and faster, deeper and deeper...let it go...and one way of doing self-hypnosis, other than touching yourself on the shoulder and having that be your cue...you know, when my mentor was working in trance on me, he would have a cue for me to go into trance on a moment's notice so that we could spend more time in the working place of trance...and he would give two knocks on an object (knock-knock) and immediately, like the flood of a chemical through my system, I would just—like taking a drink on an empty stomach—I would feel a familiar wooziness, the familiarity of the trance relaxation...isn't classical conditioning an amazing thing?...a baby can cry and breast milk can begin to flow...the mind can have a thought, the mind can experience a sensory experience and then something else can be associated with that, a physiological response that's at once healing....I can remember being in undergraduate school and having some air blown into my eye and I would blink and the student next to me would ring a little bell. And then, of course, after only a few trials, the student would ring the bell and I'd blink my eye. And you know, and I know, that classical conditioning is a reality and works at the subcortical level...well, anytime my mentor knocked on an object, it was so associated in my mind with trance, that I would go deep down right away...and you can once again reach up and squeeze your shoulder and as you do, your mind can associate this with deep trance...anytime you do that, you can go into trance quickly, easily, or abruptly and easily...deep down...it can be an inalterable association in your mind so long as you want it to happen...it can even happen when somebody else does it if you desire that effect. That can be your signal, your cue...to have a trance experience...there's nothing that you need to do to have it happen...you can just allow yourself to be conditioned and it will do it on its own...outside of your awareness, subcortically....

*Posthyp-
notic Sug-
gestion for
Ameliora-
tion of
Anxiety
Attacks*

....I can tell by the slackening in the muscles in your cheeks that you've moved very well down into hypnosis...and I don't know if you always consciously experience this change in your physiology inside yourself when you sit at home, but there certainly can be an increasing sense of familiarity so that you can now, Sherri, go home and retrieve this experience of comfort, this experience of whatever positive mindset you've developed...you can take that with you and you can know that in the morning, at your kitchen table, by looking down at your hand raising the coffee cup to your lips, these feelings really can all come back to you....

*Posthyp-
notic Sug-
gestion for
Maintaining
Muscle
Relaxation*

....It's the client I worked with who had a furrow—he often would develop a facial tension, a furrowed brow. When solving problems, he'd develop a lot of tension in his forehead and he wasn't even aware of it until he had hypnosis here and learned how to really let go of those forehead muscles, really let go of the muscles around the eyelids, around the eyebrows, muscles in the cheeks, letting go...the more you let go, it's as if the stress just dissipates, stress that's been accumulated...releasing...disappearing...and as he learned to do that, he gave himself that post hypnotic suggestion to...make this his reality—do it this way, muscles, anytime he began to get tensed up. But, there was a preliminary posthypnotic suggestion that he gave himself too. To notice the bad things beginning to happen so that he could nip it in the bud....

Section B

Toying with Time

Chapter 7

TIME DISTORTION: CONTRACTION AND EXPANSION

ABOUT THE PHENOMENON

Time distortion is a frequently experienced hypnotic phenomenon, which also has numerous clinical applications. It refers to an alteration in one's subjective experience of time, wherein it becomes dissociated from standard measures (Gilligan, 1987). Thus, time can be experienced as having lapsed more quickly or more slowly than real "clock" time. Time expansion refers to a feeling that the time elapsed is longer than clock time, and time contraction refers to a feeling that time is passed more quickly than clock time.

Many therapists using hypnosis are familiar with clients who report that a 20-minute trance experience felt more like a 35- or 40-minute session (time expansion) and with other reports of 15-minute trances feeling as if they were only 5 or 7 minutes in duration (time contraction). These are beautiful examples of unsolicited time distortion.

HISTORY AND EXPERIMENTAL STUDIES

As Ernest Rossi points out in his introduction to the section on time distortion in Volume II of *Erickson's Collected Papers* (see Rossi, 1980b), Cooper (1948/1980) was the first to discover the hypnotic phenomenon of time expansion in hypnosis. In fact, it is described as the first new hypnotic phenomenon to be discovered in over 100 years! Subjects in Cooper's studies were able to vividly experience "performing" such tasks as churning butter for 10 minutes or picking 800-plus cotton balls in an actual time of only 3 seconds! Amazingly, all subjects reported that they had felt able to take their time to accomplish the tasks. They not only had felt unhurried, but also were able to detail the exact nature of their personal experience to such an extent that it was clear that at a subjective level they had partaken in a rich and differentiated experience. For example, one of the subjects who picked cotton described how she knew which balls of cotton to pick and how she would pick up certain leaves of the plant to check for balls that had been missed. Interestingly, experimenters initially found that 10 seconds was more than enough time needed for a variety of lengthy functions, and 3 seconds seemed to be a type of minimum; if the subjects were brought out of trance after 2 seconds, they felt as if they had been interrupted during the performance of the experimentally required task.

In a second article on time distortion in the same volume, Cooper collaborated with Erickson (1950/1980) to produce a very scholarly report replete with rigorous and sound experimental research findings. They discovered that although subjects vary in how capable they are initially in producing time distortion, almost all were able to be trained within 3 hours to produce this hypnotic phenomenon. Some were able to produce it in as little as 20 minutes. Although 20 minutes sounds like a long time for a phenomenon that is often experienced by subjects within the first several minutes of trance, keep in mind that the time distortions referred to in this article are extremely deep ones accompanied by very intense experiences. This finding should be well heeded by readers who fall into the trap of expecting to produce some type of hypnotic phenomenon quickly during a first trance induction of maybe 15 minutes duration. Remember that although some subjects are able to respond that quickly, a good therapist is willing to be patient and wait for the development of the phenomenon, particularly for the fullest development if deep trancework and intense experiences are therapeutically desirable.

Cooper and Erickson (1950/1980) also found that to produce time distortion it was important for subjects to get far away from both everyday surroundings and the objective sense of time passage. In reading their descriptions of this, it appeared that what was also being manifested as part of this degree of time distortion was a solid experience of dissociation. Although many current experimentalists and traditional hypnotherapists tend to view hypnotizability as something fixed and innate, Erickson saw hypnotic skill as something that could be developed and honed over time. The time distortions studied involved richly lived experiences of altered time and were mainly evidenced in highly convincing accounts of imagined numerical counting that took place in a subjective time of many minutes and even hours, while objectively only 3 seconds had passed. Although the authors discovered that during any prescribed task to be performed in hypnosis, there is a strong tendency for time distortion to take place, they further concluded that "time sense can be deliberately altered to a predetermined degree by hypnotic suggestion, and subjects can have an amount of subjective experience under these conditions that is more nearly commensurate with the subjective time involved than with the world time" (p. 265). They also concluded that "the continuity of these subjective experiences during distorted time is good" and therefore noted that "hallucinated and time distorted experiences were different from dreams or accessing a memory" (p. 265).

The authors also tried to rule out the possibility of a retrospective falsification of memory entering into subjects' reports. This is one way in which subjects could provide detailed accounts while in fact not having had, in subjective reality, the experiences of time expansion during the allotted seconds. Today's social/psychological theorists regarding hypnosis and hypnotic phenomena would probably say that a retrospective falsification **had** occurred, probably in line with the subject's need to please the experimenter or to comply with the perceived task demand. Erickson and Cooper addressed this issue but came up against the wall of the fact that the subjective experience of time is nonetheless that—subjective—and they could think of no objective way to ascertain whether or not the seemingly sincere reports of their subjects were actually experienced.

However, they did offer this convincing information: each subject felt that the experience had been absolutely real, each experienced having had ample time to complete any task (even in that 3-second span!), and when subjects found out about the nature of the experiment, they were invariably astonished at what they had been able to achieve. Perhaps, however, the most convincing evidence that this is a real scientific event and not a matter of conscious or subconscious role playing and falsification has to do with the *flavor* of the subjective accounts. They not only have incredible richness but also contain spontaneous mishaps and events that would not be expected in role-playing accounts. Here are some examples of these accounts. In the first one the subject is counting bullets being made during a hunting club party:

> It was at a molding (of bullets) party at the club. There was quite a crowd there. I counted for maybe six minutes and ran out of bullets so I waited for more. I didn't count the full ten minutes. While I was counting them, this other boy walked up—he was talking and waving his arms. The pot of lead tipped over and burned his foot rather badly. I got up and sat down again and continued counting. The others were running all over the place. The remainder of the lead we put back on the stove. I counted 493. That's when I stopped and waited. Then later I got up to 546. (Cooper & Erickson, 1950/1980, p. 242)

Below is another account from a woman who was choosing to count cookies as she once had in a factory. Here is her version of what took place during the 10-second interval allowed:

> ....I was down in the basement. There were work tables. I was counting. I counted them as I put them in the smaller sacks. I counted 1,003. That was all I got. In the middle the telephone outside rang on and on. Just after that there was so much cookie dust all over that I started to sneeze. I sneezed ten or twelve times. I just couldn't stop. I dropped a package. I didn't answer the phone. (Cooper & Erickson, 1950/1980, p. 243)

Cooper and Erickson also offer a list of some of the events that were reported to have taken place during these brief durations, many of which again lead one to believe that for the subject an actual *experience* was taking place. Here is an abbreviated list:

- While rowing a boat, a subject lost an oar lock.
- While picking up shells, a subject stepped on a jellyfish.
- While changing a tire, one subject found only three lugs in place. Later he found the fourth one in the hubcap.
- While drilling, the man next to the subject passed out from heat prostration.
- Subject had trouble opening a barn door because it was sticking due to recent rains.
- While the subject was getting shaved, a barber spent so much time talking to the other barber that the lather began to set. (Cooper & Erickson, 1950/1980, p. 250)

In the third article in this series (Erickson, 1954c/1980), Cooper and Erickson take all of this one step further by applying time-distortion techniques to actual clinical cases. They describe a number of cases notable in their use of time distortion. One case involved a man who had intractable painter's block. Erickson's therapeutic use of time distortion with him resulted in the painter being able to paint a picture in a 6-hour time span (in reality), instead of his usual 70 hours. Further, the man had total amnesia for everything that had taken place; all he remembered was having begun to eat a sandwich and then, after a blacked-out span of time, going back to eat it and finding it dry and crusty. In fact this had been Erickson's specific posthypnotic suggestion to the artist.

Another case was of a woman who experienced massive amnesic fugues throughout her life periodically. Erickson felt that the amnesias were secondary to some severe traumas, yet every therapeutic strategy he tried over a period of 3 months, for 2 to 4 hours each day (!), was to no avail. He had the subject agree to do an experiment in time distortion. When the time came in session for him to assign her the experimental task, Erickson directed her as follows: "From childhood to now—remember!" In a 20-second time period, the subject was able to review in detail her entire life, which was believed by Erickson to be the factor in eliminating the fugues.

Another case was of a musician whose need for money forced him to take a job where he no longer had time to practice. However, he needed to practice in order to maintain his skills as a musician and eventually find employment in that field. Erickson suggested to him that during his regular work day he could take a few moments, go into trance, and practice entire pieces of music, and even his entire repertoire, within the span of moments. The subject was not only able to do this in a highly effective fashion, but, also via suggestions to himself, he was able to learn new selections; in addition, in his time-distorted hallucination, he was able to procure a tape recorder, tape himself playing, and then learn from his mistakes on playback! Again, this kind of creative contribution by clients during time-distortion work makes it hard for us to believe that the experience is merely role play. In this musician's case, there is also independent evidence of the effectiveness of his "time-distortion therapy," which is important to note: other musicians, and people who were employing him as a musician, saw great improvements in his playing.

In summary, we can say that this article spells out a variety of ways to incorporate time distortion into our clinical practices. However, only in the third case described above, where the musician uses a sort of time-condensed mental rehearsal, are we able to see precisely how the person was able to use the phenomenon of time distortion to therapeutic advantage. The way in which the woman with fugue states used her conscious review of life events to become asymptomatic is not apparent, nor does the article explain how the first subject's experiences, for which there was no conscious recollection, changed the presenting problem. In these latter cases, time distortion does not appear as the specific agent of therapeutic change but rather as part of what sets the stage for the change, a worthy contribution in its own right.

In the fourth and final article on time distortion in this series of studies in *The Collected Papers*, Erickson and Elizabeth Erickson (his wife) (1958/1980) discuss what had been a neglected aspect to their research on time distortion—time condensation. It was actually Mrs. Erickson who noticed this discrepancy and promoted the scientific inquiry into this phenomenon. As an aside, we note that Mrs. Erickson's contributions to hypnosis research and theory are both significant and scholarly, yet they are frequently overlooked. This article starts off by discussing the frequently observed phenomenon of time condensation in everyday life. The authors discuss how during moments of love or during vacation or other pleasurable experiences it is common that a person feels as if "time flies." The remainder of the article discusses a number of very interesting cases: In situations involving great boredom or great pain, patients and subjects were able either to reduce hours of torment down to a matter of subjective minutes or, as was the case a couple of times, actually to stop the clock so that there were huge gaps in the subjective experience of time, with the minute hand appearing to have leapt from, say, the half-hour mark to 10 minutes to the hour.

Perhaps the most interesting case cited is of a dental patient who was able to achieve, simultaneously, both time expansion and time condensation. This patient was having dental work done and during the work the suggestion was given to her that time could pass very rapidly. At a conscious level it did, because when she came out of trance, she felt as if only minutes had passed. However, in the trance she dissociated, regressed, and "became a little girl and played all afternoon on the lawn." She was amazed that at a second level of awareness she was able to have an extensive, afternoon-long experience of playing, while at a conscious level she had condensed a hour's worth of dental work down to a matter of mere minutes.

The next studies found in our literature search were considerably more recent. In summarizing for the *Annual Review of Psychology* findings on hypnotic time distortion in the 1970s and 1980s, Kihlstrom (1985) reports one study that found that memory for a word list was improved during hypnotic time distortion—a finding suggesting that effective study time had in fact been increased—but subsequent studies did not find such an effect. However, the majority of these latter studies did find that the subject's sense of time had been effectively altered, apart from any research results showing enhanced learning. Kihlstrom also reviews a handful of studies confirming Erickson's and Cooper's findings that there is a strong tendency inherent in neutral hypnosis that contributes to a personal sense of time elongation, apart from any suggestions offered by the therapist. In other words, there has been experimental validation of the tendency for hypnotized subjects to overestimate the time spent in hypnosis.

INDICATIONS FOR USE

Indications for the clinical use of time distortion are varied. Time expansion is helpful for the anxious test-taker who always feels as if time is speedily running out; once that individual is helped to experience time in a more leisurely way, an hour that feels like 20 minutes can instead become one that *feels* like 90. Along these same lines, we have used this phenomenon extensively in the area of sports performance. Uneståhl (1979) discusses the time distortions that are often a part of the elite athlete's experience. Athletes who rush through gymnastic, archery, or dressage performances, feeling as if they do not have ample time to make adjustments in their movements, often can benefit appreciably from learning to experience their actions in a relaxed, slow-motion tempo. This can also be applied to music soloists who rush through their performances.

There are a number of applications in the area of behavioral medicine. Chronic pain clients can learn to self-hypnotize so that pain-free periods are experienced in an expanded, near ever-lasting way. Time contractions can then be used by the same types of clients to shrink the perceived length of time that pain is experienced. Medical patients undergoing uncomfortable (e.g., dialysis, chemotherapy) or anxiety-provoking (e.g., MRI) types of treatments can use time contraction to make long blocks of time seem shorter.

Besides the applications to hysterical amnesia, painter's block, and dental anesthesia mentioned earlier, time distortion techniques have also been used in treating cancer patients (Rossi & Ryan, 1986), in counteracting a severe fainting reaction to the sight of blood (Erickson, 1954c/1980), and in lessening the discomfort associated with childbirth. I (JHE) used time distortion with a 25-year-old man with Hodgkins disease who relapsed after a first outpatient treatment of chemotherapy and needed to go into the hospital for more intensive chemotherapy, the duration of which would be one month. He was terrified of hospitals and the long duration of his stay, alarmed by the conditions of it (to have his bone marrow removed meant that his environment needed temporarily to be utterly sterile), and revolted by the likelihood that he would suffer severe side effects from the chemotherapy. All of these combined factors made him consider foregoing the treatment and facing death.

In our work I convinced him to give the treatment a try and taught him how to go into a deep trance, contract time immensely, have profound amnesias, totally dissociate his mind from his body (and hence the hospital), and have vivid hypnotic dreams. At the end of his stay he said that he had felt he was only there for a couple of hours at most, that he could only remember a few pleasant conversations (he was shocked to hear that he had vomited violently through most of his stay), and that he had been lost in a never-ending series of dreams. The medical treatment was a success, by the way, and he remains symptom-free five years afterward.

Other applications of time distortion include those miscellaneous situations where temporal factors are directly related with the presenting problem. These include both retarded and premature ejaculation, chronic tardiness, and procrastination. Time distortion can also be used as a trance indicator (Rossi & Ryan, 1985) for purposes of ratification. Feeling certain that only 10 minutes passed when it was actually 45 minutes is a great experience to convince one that time distortion can be induced in hypnosis. The use of time distortion in therapy would be contraindicated only for those clients who do not have enough plasticity in their experience of time to evoke a significant enough degree of the phenomenon to use it in practice.

One case in which I (JSE) did *not* use time distortion when the presenting problem was chronic tardiness and procrastination was the following. We include it here because it is illustrative of the need to factor in dynamic understandings of the client's interpersonal world in treatment planning; otherwise a therapist runs the risk of having brilliant interventions that don't work. A 30-year-old woman in the human resources field entered therapy requesting hypnosis for her problem of always being late. She's late to work in the morning, she's late to meetings, she's late handing in reports. It became very clear very quickly that this individual struggled enormously in her dealings with people in positions of perceived authority and control. Responding in a timely fashion to hypnotic intervention would have been construed by Maria as one more submission, and had I handled it without regard for such factors, the therapy would have been destined to falter. Since there was too little plasticity in Maria's personality at that time to embrace hypnosis as *her* process, *her* tool, rather than that of yet one more "authority figure," I opted to deal with her problems more forthrightly. Maria was one of those individuals who moves more quickly with direct feedback about herself. This better prompts her to change because of needs for control over how she is perceived.

ELICITING THE PHENOMENON OF TIME DISTORTION

Direct and Indirect Suggestion

Seeding time distortion is easy because there are so many ways to make references to time in the induction phase of the hypnosis. You can talk about going into trance in a *timely* fashion, or comment during the induction about how *once you decide to allow the body to really settle down, it can happen in a split second* (for a time contraction). Or, you can comment on how *"there is, especially today, the pleasure of having plenty of time to allow the body..."* (for a time expansion). The therapist can pace and lead the client's hypnotic response as either *"slow and gradual, taking one's time,"* or look for signs that the client is experiencing a *"rapid descent, moving briskly into trance, more quickly than one might ever have imagined!"* Seeding and **presupposition** can take place in one statement as in the following example: *"You can become even more curious about, and open to, new experiences **as soon as you begin to notice those changes in the timing** of your breath rate."*

Other presuppositions that facilitate your clients' perception of change in their experience of time are apparent in statements like, **"When you begin to feel things really slow down..."** (here, "things" can refer directly to physiology and only *indirectly* to time), and *"**Once your unconscious mind realizes how easy it will be to adjust its experience of time**, your conscious mind will find itself rushing to do the same...."*

Double binds that encourage time distortions include telling clients that they can *"go into trance with a delightful sense of timelessness, or instead with a sense of time suspended"* (both for time expansion). Other double binds can offer clients the option of *"experiencing time in your own subjective way or, if preferred, in a way of your own creation"* (time expansion or contraction).

Conscious/unconscious dissociative statements are especially helpful with time distortion because dissociation from standard measures of orientation is the foundation upon which this hypnotic phenomenon rests. You can talk during your induction about the *"conscious mind experiencing clock time while the unconscious instead experiences trance time"* or about the *"conscious mind being concerned with* *how much time there will be left, as the unconscious proceeds in an unhurried fashion."* You can also speak about how the *"conscious mind can remain oriented to time yet the unconscious mind be oriented instead to the experience at hand."* This latter suggestion would be particularly useful for clients who have trouble "shaking" their experience of real time; instead of watching and waiting for a conscious experience of time distortion, they can simply turn their attention to how they can dissociate conscious and unconscious levels of awareness and feel time altered on a different phenomenological plane.

These suggestions for dissociation and time distortion are made with reference to either or both the client's experience in session and the real-life application. Bridges are made between in-session experiences of time distortion and outside session experiences by remarking, during trance work, on how these distortions can happen *here and there*, and *now and then*. You can also facilitate the client's reexperiencing time distortion in the relevant real-life setting by giving frank, direct suggestions that are disguised with interspersal techniques or story telling. An example of the use of interspersal for eliciting time contraction is the following:

> *When was the last time you cooked an egg? Tried to make it scrambled but it cooked up so **fast** you had to **run** over to the pan and stir it up in a **hurry** because it had already partly become an omelet. **All of a sudden** the liquid turned solid—**how does anything transform that fast?***

Don't forget about using undisguised direct suggestion, too—nothing fancy here, just straightforward, permissive suggestions for the perception of distorted time. For instance,

> *When it's time, you really can go ahead and speed up your experience of time. It might be as soon as the technician comes to set you up for your dialysis, or waiting until the I.V. heparin lock is reopened.*
>
> *Feel free whenever you need to shorten those uncomfortable periods while you're waiting for the medicine to kick in, so that they zip by and before you know it your medication has taken effect. Ask your unconscious mind to really help you—it contracts muscle fibers all the time and it can do this job, too.*
>
> *As soon as you take your seat in the examination, you can become aware of an altered sense of time, a slower sense of time, giving you all the time you need to answer each question thoughtfully and correctly.*

Note that this last example of direct suggestion incorporates post-hypnotic suggestion as well (see Chapter 6 on posthypnotic suggestion). This is an excellent intervention for helping clients make their in-session experiences with time distortion (or other hypnotic phenomena) cross over productively into their lives.

Metaphor and Symbols

Watches with worn-out batteries, cuckoo clocks with worn-out mechanisms, and windup clocks in need of winding can all serve as symbols for time expansion. Daylight savings time is another useful concept. Old movies in which clocks are shown with the hands zipping around illustrate the concept of time contraction. Slow-motion videos and recollections of trying to run through water generate the opposite feeling. A baseball pitcher who rushes through his wind-up can be instructed to wear a watch with a dying battery to remind him to *slow down*. (Hall of Fame hitter Ted Williams would experience beautiful time distortions, reporting that in his best moments the baseball was seen so well that sometimes it seemed to almost stand still for him. [Gallway, 1981]).

Naturalistic Examples

Examples of naturalistic time distortion abound. Think of a one-hour car trip between the same two cites that sometimes breezes by and at other times seems to take hours. Compare the temporal experiences of a teenager in summer school and one in summer camp. The two hours of a gripping movie evoke a very different experience of time than the two hours spent waiting in the airport for a delayed plane. Lankton and Lankton (1983) remind us of other colloquial experiences of time distortion such as waiting for a kettle to boil, watching the second hand on a clock, and waiting for a line of people to move. Also remember to store in your mind examples your client gives you (inadvertently or not) of his or her own experiences of time distortion, for example, with regard to prior trances or session lengths. This also includes the times the client may have used daydreaming to make it through a boring dinner engagement (naturalistic time contraction) or taken off a watch so that a vacation week would pass more slowly (naturalistic time expansion).

SUGGESTED TRANSCRIPT MATERIAL

Time Distortion (Contraction & Elongation for Pain Control)

...time, as a psychologist you know and I know, that time is a matter of perception...perception of time can vary, can change in drugged conditions, can change in sleep situations....How many times has someone, yourself perhaps, fallen asleep and awakened and just not really known how much time has passed—sometimes a short amount of time can be experienced like a long amount of time; pleasurable time can be that way for you—it can expand, it can contract, too...people have had the experience of falling, deep and soundly asleep, feeling as if one moment has passed, when in actuality it's been hours and hours...any experience of pain can be like that for you....Steve Gilligan says to his headache patients that "you can have your whole headache in one minute of clock time. It can be painful, but one minute of clock time...all the time your subconscious mind needs to be headachy...one minute of clock time...deeper and deeper down...when a person's deeply and soundly asleep and slips off the bed...they perhaps have a beautifully vivid dream of parachuting...the dream seems to take hours and hours, minutes and minutes to complete, but it's completed in its entirety by the time you hit the floor and it seems like it took forever to do that...the perception of time can change for you...when you play tennis, you can slow time and allow yourself a much longer time to react...practice seeing the ball come to you in slow motion....Learn, pretend at first...fake it 'til you make it...pretend at first and then learn to see the fuzz of the ball coming toward you...the lines, the fuzz, the smell of the tennis ball...you might imagine the smell of the tennis ball and it can take you deep, down in trance, ever more deeply...perception of time changes when a person's taking drugs...and just about everybody's had the experience of being on vacation and taking off your watch and not really thinking about what to do when— doing what you want to do, when you want to do it. Really allow yourself to give into some of those personal pleasures and incorporate it into your day and on vacation. Vacation can be a symbol of a time when you meet your needs and do as you please...deeper and deeper...deciding on vacation and *it doesn't matter what time it is....*

<table>
<tr>
<td>

Time Distortion

</td>
<td>

....I know, for instance, that people often will experience changes in their experience of time...while in trance and other times as well...so, I don't know if this particular experience has seemed longer than it actually is, or shorter than it actually is, but couldn't it just be possible that your experience of how long you've been in trance is just the slightest bit different from actual clock time...and couldn't that actually be a very fun and whimsical concept to think about on a Monday morning...how time can be subjectively altered....I don't know the last time, Bette, that you were sitting at dinner with company...whose conversation was tedious or boring and time seemed so slow that it appeared as if it would never really move...and that can be so easily contrasted with the time experience of another occasion where the company and the company's conversation was brisk and witty....

</td>
</tr>
<tr>
<td>

Time Contraction

</td>
<td>

....Now, time is a very intriguing phenomenon...and time can be both objective and subjective...and there are ways to experience time to be just so malleable that you can do really all sorts of things with it...it's interesting to think how 3 minutes can sometimes seem like 3 minutes and sometimes seem like a little bit more than 3 minutes and sometimes it seems like a little bit less than 3 minutes....Now with your conscious mind you may be really curious about what this notion of time distortion has to do with anything that we've been talking about...and what it has to do with the goals that you want to attain...and I would encourage your conscious mind to be that curious and even be more curious and more curious as time goes on...so that it can feel increasingly prepared...for the unconscious mind to grasp in a moment the significance and the relevance of this notion of time subjectivity to the things that you'd like to have changed in your own subjective sense of the things that you do in your life....I don't know if you can tell the difference between 2 seconds and 3 seconds and

</td>
</tr>
</table>

it's entirely possible that you might, but I'm not as sure that you can tell the difference between 2 3/4 and 2 1/2 seconds...and I am even less certain that you would be able to detect the difference between 2 1/2 seconds and 2 3/8 seconds....Now it may be that your conscious mind might say it knows the difference between 2 3/8 seconds and 2 1/2 seconds...but I think your unconscious mind knows that even if it could tell the difference, it may not wish to even bother, instead settling for the smaller amount of 2 3/8 seconds...and if instead your unconscious mind decides that it does in fact know the difference, perhaps it could be just your conscious mind that decides that the difference is so slight it will just go with the 2 3/8 seconds...it's possible that both consciously and unconsciously you decide to abandon the seeking of differentials and simply decide that 2 3/8 seconds is enough of an accurate interval of time to work with, and decide to simply go with that and that would be perfectly all right to do....

Time Expansion for a Golfer Who Rushes Through Her Swing

....You can find yourself delightfully experiencing an altered sense of time...and perhaps even now with your own visual inclinations you can see yourself, although there's no need to do so immediately, or experience yourself playing golf...but with a slow motion...notice changes when you swing in your experience of time, in your experience of movement...so that you can understand that you have all the time you need to think about what it is you'd like to do and what it is you need to do...and once you recognize that you really can work time in your best interests, you can understand that you can choose to maintain whatever degree of cool you think would be useful for you at that time....You can also be the one to choose just how long that experience of change in your experience and perception of time will last...so that if there's any reason whatsoever, if there's any need whatever for you to reconnect with reality time in order to do something that needs doing, you can always know that you can do so immediately ...in a way that keeps you on top of everything as you wish to be...so that all alterations in time are adaptive ones and are ones that bring you closer and closer to your goal of maintaining your mind set that allows you to do whatever you need to do while you're playing....Now, it can be now or it can be later that your unconscious mind allows you to experience a new-found sense of confidence, a different experience of yourself as a professional golfer when on the green....

Chapter 8

AGE REGRESSION

ABOUT THE PHENOMENON

Hypnotic age regression entails a therapist using hypnosis to facilitate a client's going back, experientially, to an earlier time in life. This can happen with varying degrees of intensity for the client, depending upon the client's "talent" for age regressions, the quality of the induction and trancework, and the degree and steadfastness of any counterforces, or resistances (conscious or unconscious), to the client's regressing. Whereas hypermnesia refers to intense *remembering*, age regression refers to *reexperiencing*.

Erickson (1980c) loosely defined age regression as a tendency on the part of the personality to revert to some method or form of expression that belonged to an earlier phase of development. True age regression was described as being not just an experience of memory, but rather a total reorientation in attitude, affect, and/or behavior. Whether or not age-regressed individuals actually revert to earlier modes of cognitive and affective functioning has been the subject of considerable study (see section on Experimental Studies), with the majority of experimenters concluding that they do not. Weitzenhoffer (1989b), though, describes age regressions where subjects mentally return to the patterns of behavior, emotion, and thought with a "partial ablation of later influences" (p. 136). These regressions, characterized by age-appropriate childlike perceptions and judgments, are however referred to as "revivifications." They are differentiated from other age regressions that are more like

104

hypermnesias, where the subject responds to the experience with attitudes and judgments of present-day ego and chronological age. To Weitzenhoffer, these latter responses are seen as adult conceptualizations of childhood; he calls them "pseudo age regressions." Some subjects manifest what Weitzenhoffer refers to as a duality phenomenon. In these situations, the past is vividly experienced from the dual, simultaneous perspectives of both child and adult. Weitzenhoffer criticizes these experiences as being "incomplete regressions."

Weitzenhoffer's incomplete regression is actually the one that we believe is most adaptive, at least as far as psychotherapy is concerned. After all, it is rarely the reexperiencing of past events in trance alone that is therapeutic; it may even be retraumatizing. Instead, it is the preservation of some observing ego during the regression that makes new meaning or gets a new perspective on events, abilities, or attitudes from an earlier time in one's life. There is a myth among some therapists who use hypnotic age regression with post-trauma clients that a massive and hysterical catharsis is desirable in its own right. To just reexperience a negative event from the past does little to help a person.

The observing, working ego is manifested *precisely* in the simultaneous appearance of current and prior perspectives. Because the individual brings to the age-regression experience greater wisdom or psychological maturity, he or she can use it to much better advantage. Clients can gain new insights, review different facets of memories, rediscover in past experiences dormant abilities, or uncover repressed memories in a more secure emotional context (Yapko, 1986, 1990). Cognitive restructuring (amplified through the effects of the hypnosis) (Beck, 1983; Beck, Rush, Shaw, & Emery, 1979) and the modification of old learnings are other ways to use age regressions therapeutically, both of which require at least some involvement of the adult ego faculties of cognition, synthesis, integration, reality testing, and judgment during the working phases of hypnotherapy. For instance, clients can mitigate overpersonalizations ("I must have really been a bad kid for Dad to have been so sad/drunk/tired/broke/angry all the time"); magical thinking ("My baby brother got sick and died because of that time when he was crying all night and I wished him dead"); self-blaming ("If I'd acted more caring, my niece would never have started using drugs"); and the like.

However, there are situations where, either by accident or design, clients regress so thoroughly that the therapist cannot find any remaining adult or observing ego. Clients may reexperience events as if they were happening again and lose an awareness of the present. Sometimes this can be OK, especially if the client is immersed in a *positive* experience or emotion from the past, or if the client reorganizes well after a painful regression and is able to get some therapeutic mileage out of it. Severely traumatized clients with fractured egos or disturbed clients with impaired egos may be more vulnerable to this kind of all-encompassing regression, albeit without concomitant abilities to integrate the experience constructively.

Sometimes, though, all-encompassing regressions where a person loses awareness are not OK, and the person feels overwhelmed, disoriented, frightened, and retraumatized. This person cannot deal with the experience productively, may not be able to recover by the end of the session, or may have negative sequelae lingering for days after. It is always the context that determines whether or not a therapeutic strategy—hypnotic or otherwise—is indicated and not the presenting problem or diagnosis. Personality, resiliency, working alliance, the presence or absence of support systems, and so on are only some of the variables to factor in when deciding whether or not age regression is the intervention of choice. Therapists will need to set different parameters in these instances where there is greater risk of a disorganizing regression; these parameters would include shorter periods of trance, more structured trance experiences, more dialoguing during trance, more resource building prior to trance so that a client can restabilize quickly or exit the experience, and other like strategies.

Another way to ensure a client's safety and comfort in trance involves having the person first go back in time to a place where he or she felt safe, invulnerable, and protected. By remembering such a place and "housing" it inside, the client learns to have a symbolic location to which he or she can go in a moment's notice to regain feelings of security. Being able to exit an overwhelmingly uncomfortable mental experience quickly is critical. To this end, Weitzenhoffer (1989a) recommends setting up, prior to trancework with a client, a nonverbal signal that will serve to reorient the person to his or her current age and time in case rapport is lost during trance or if the client feels that he or she has lost control over the situation. He offers the idea of the therapist squeezing the client's right shoulder as one example of such a signal. Dolan (1991) also discusses the importance of setting up associational cues for clients for purposes of comfort and security should they spontaneously regress to the trauma as well as the importance of setting up symbols for safety in the present.

Age regression is not just for returning to negative experiences, though! Retrieving dormant or forgotten attitudes, perspectives, emotions, and thoughts can be therapeutic, as can be a revisit to a time/place/person that offered solace, support, joy, or other pleasurable experiences.

EXPERIMENTAL STUDIES

Over the years there has been a wealth of research performed on age regression and many case studies reported. However, in this area of the literature particularly, the case studies seem either biased toward the point of view of the examiner or self-satisfied with the impressive results of the clients. Therefore, we will refrain from any in-depth reporting of case material in this section, at least the case material that appears in journals.

One whole area of debate in the experimental literature concerns the question of the actual extent to which a person is, in fact, physiologically, cognitively, and emotionally transported back in time during hypnotic age-regression work. Although there have been a smattering of widely publicized studies claiming an actual return to the past (see, for example, Reiff & Scheerer, 1959), by and large other researchers have come to the opposite conclusion—that during age regression, clients experience something that is emotionally important (and therapeutic), but it involves *a subjective reliving of the past* from the perspective of the present and *not* an actual return to past levels of functioning.

Perhaps the most comprehensive review of this debate is contained in the work of Nash (1987), who reviewed 100 studies that had been conducted over a 60-year time period. This culminated in a report on memory during hypnotic age-regression from the Council on Scientific Affairs (1985) that found that hypnotic age regression is a subjective reliving of earlier experiences as though they were real. It is important for the reader to understand that none of the above findings diminishes at all the potential therapeutic impact of age-regression work in hypnosis. All it points out is that clinical hypnotherapists should not automatically assume that a client has actually returned to an earlier mode of mental or physiological functioning.

Another debate concerns the degree to which memories retrieved during hypnosis are accurate. This issue becomes especially important when retrieved memories are relevant either to forensic crimes committed or to abuse (physical, sexual, or emotional) that is thought to have taken place. The stakes involved are high; based on memories recovered during hypnosis, families are torn apart, legal charges are pressed, and identities are shaken. It has been popular for a number of years for therapists to use hypnosis as a means of enabling a person to recollect events that may have been repressed. It is beyond the scope of this book to cover this debate in-depth, but it is nonetheless important, with our clinical emphasis, to summarize findings that bear on practice issues.

Loftus and Yapko (1995) note that at present, no studies demonstrate the validity of repressed memories of childhood abuse that resurface in adulthood. Further, we have found in our review of the literature little or no evidence to support the notion that lost memories can be reliably and accurately recovered during hypnosis. In general, we think that readers should avoid organizing a whole therapy principally around the active pursuit of repressed memories and instead view the appearance of these memories as an outgrowth of other work and as part of a larger context of therapy. Exceptions to this may be where catharsis is sought specifically, as in the treatment of certain post-traumatic stress disorders and where the veracity of the memory is not a critical consideration (e.g., war- or crime-related traumas without forensic involvement, natural tragedies, and the like).

A second finding in this review of the literature is that clients can construct an inaccurate memory during hypnosis and then believe it with utter conviction. Thus, the magnitude of a client's belief or insistence about a memory does not correlate positively with validity. Yet another consideration is the evidence that therapists sometimes inadvertently ask leading questions during hypnosis in a way that promotes the development of false memories. This is not just a matter of asking an obviously leading question like, "Did he touch your vagina?" but it involves seemingly neutral lines of questioning that may be misconstrued by a client as an indirect suggestion that something *did* happen. Asking "Did he touch you?" is a seemingly more innocuous question, but it too is far from neutral: There is presumption of touch and presumption of male gender. "What happened?" implies that something *did* happen and is a poorer choice of question than is "Tell me what you are experiencing in trance now?" The upshot is that therapists should avoid using hypnosis to engage in "fact finding" or when information gathered needs to be absolutely accurate. (See Yapko [1994], Loftus [1993], and Loftus & Yapko [1995] for more extensive review and coverage in this area.)

Corydon Hammond (1993), however, takes a more moderate position and argues articulately in favor of continuing to consider the validity of many recovered memories, including some of those recovered under hypnosis. Hammond cites numerous criticisms of research that show that recovered memories are inaccurate and that people often cannot distinguish between accurate and inaccurate recollection. He finds much of this research seriously flawed and therefore sees this entire issue of false memory syndrome as being far from an open and shut situation.

For example, Hammond points out that much of the research has been conducted on normal populations and not on individuals with traumatic memory. Furthermore, he comments that most of the flaws noted have been in the recollection of *details* more than in the recall of entire events. He also suggests that traumatic memory may be encoded in an entirely different manner than regular memory and that this has not been addressed in the prevailing experimental research. He cites a number of other criticisms as well, suggesting in sum that the recovery of repressed memories can be accurate and is still a viable endeavor.

However, Hammond offers some cautions to therapists using hypnosis for memory retrieval, and these should be well heeded. He suggests that therapists be very well trained in the recovery of repressed memories and be especially sure not to ask leading questions of clients. Since an exhaustive review of the experimental memory literature and of the criticisms of Hammond is beyond the scope of this book, we underscore Hammond's caveat about doing work in this area in a judicious and informed manner.

Even under the very best of conditions and therapeutic management it is obvious that a false memory can arise and be believed by the client. The relevant clinical issues to be acted upon involve the ways through which the therapist can help a client make inroads toward differentiating what was real and what was not, or how can the therapist and client make constructive use of the memory in a manner that does not depend on its verity? We have not yet seen these issues addressed in the literature.

A final caveat is to avoid hypnotizing potential or prospective witnesses in legal situations to "refresh memory" or regarding anything that concerns a committed crime. Orne (1979) points out that when it comes to details of a crime, hypnotized subjects can recall false information with a concomitant conviction of its truthfulness. Well-meaning but mistaken witnesses could inadvertently mislead judges and juries because of their sincerity. In general, forensic hypnosis should be respected as a very specialized area requiring specialized training and knowledge. In addition, laws vary by state; some laws even vary regarding whether hypnosis is permitted in forensic situations.

In Pennsylvania it is not permitted, but we have heard anecdotally from another therapist that in the western part of the state, some defense attorneys are encouraging their clients to get themselves hypnotized (from uninformed therapists) so that the fact that they were hypnotized about their cases would later be revealed in court. Since the client would then be unable to testify on his or her own behalf, the entire case would be thrown out!

However, Orne (1979) notes some legitimate applications of forensic hypnosis, if the therapist is adequately trained and the procedure is videotaped in order to ascertain that leading questions were not asked.

Also, in situations where there are no witnesses to a crime and police are desperate for any possible clue, hypnosis for memory retrieval might be worthwhile even if what is remembered is inaccurate, inasmuch as *some* piece of information may be recovered and be enough to crack the case. In any event, the cautions noted above constitute contraindications for the use of age regression unless you are expert enough to know exactly where you stand legally. In addition, it is inadvisable to use age regression if the client has an ego weakness such that the lack of grounding and structure inherent in age-regression work could contribute to poor reality testing.

The fact that false memories can be created during hypnosis, and that clients can come to believe them with conviction, is an important discovery for therapists for more than the obvious reason. It also speaks to the plasticity of human memory and experience and hints at the possibilities for its utilization. It provides a lot of support for what Erickson did in his February Man case (Erickson & Rossi, 1979). In this case, hypnosis was used to help a woman feel as if she had been loved and prized as a child through the benign *implanting* of a kind and supportive figure into her past. This revision of personal history was done using age regression over the course of several sessions. The woman discussed, while age-regressed, the small and everyday experiences she was having as a child. Erickson listened, and he listened in what seems to us today to be a very "client-centered" fashion, with the result that she internalized his caring. When he gave her amnesia for the hypnotic work, she wound up feeling good about herself—loved and loveable. This enabled her to alter her adult sense of self by retrospectively *weaving in* an experience that fostered self-esteem.

An elaboration of age-regression techniques that capitalize in other ways on a client's ability to evoke a loving or otherwise supportive figure is the reexperiencing of a traumatic event in trance with that figure remaining at the (age-regressed) client's side. Intermittently, the trauma can be stopped, just by the subject's intention, and the whole situation discussed with the hypnotically evoked person. It is often helpful if this caring person maintains some "physical" contact with the client in trance, such as placing a hand on the client's shoulder, or even by holding the client's hand. It is also helpful if the caring person communicates important messages in the dialogue with the client about the experience that is unfolding. One message might be that the client isn't at fault for what is happening (i.e., isn't causing the physical or sexual abuse, for example) but that the person or persons doing it have a type of sickness or emotional handicap. Imparting this message helps to relieve guilt, shame, and the all-too-common belief of children that somehow they were wrong and caused the abuse, and the perpetrators were right.

A second important message for the loving figure to communicate can be the normalization of the child's (or adult's, if it's a later trauma that the client is reexperiencing) anger, rage, and even homicidal feelings that arise from his or her abusive circumstances. The therapist can then suggest that, of course, actions can be different from what is felt and thought, enabling the person to comfortably allow the angry feelings to be a part of his or her personal experience. Just knowing that these are normal reactions to a trauma will allow the person not to fragment and disdain him- or herself for a reaction that he or she had (and may still be having) to the experience. Having such feelings usually adds a secondary overlay of pathology for people since they have not only experienced a horrible situation, but also they end up hating and disowning themselves for their response to it. In communicating these emotionally supportive messages, the loving person is undoing, at the time of the trauma, some of the cognitive and emotional sequelae.

Importantly, simply being listened to by the loving person can help to reduce the aftereffects of trauma. Studies (Dolan, 1991) of people who experienced similar traumas to each other but who adjusted differently demonstrate that the ones who coped well were able to talk with somebody (preferably family) at the time of the trauma and were believed and supported. It is part of the utility of hypnosis that one can create this same effect retroactively; in therapeutic situations the results are often immediate and impressive.

By utilizing this plasticity in human cognitive functioning, we therapists using hypnosis can, like Erickson, think about how to purposefully and therapeutically augment our clients' personal histories with figures and experiences that enhance present day functioning—but only in conjunction and in alliance with our clients—and with their consent. The idea here is not to dismiss a client's real history or feelings but to find a way to assuage mental pain through the hypnotic development and subsequent activation of "transplanted" memories that heal. Not everyone is going to be a good candidate for this use of age regression, particularly those who need to come to terms with their past more directly and put closure on events by working through events consciously. Other clients may not have the ability to "hold" the emotional influence of an imagined figure or occasion. Further, if there is ongoing abuse deal first with that, ensuring its end. This still leaves plenty of clinical situations where the innovative use of a hypnotic phenomenon such as age regression can be enormously helpful.

INDICATIONS FOR USE

The clinical uses for age regression are numerous and varied. They include resource retrieval; investigation of one's past (Lankton & Lankton, 1983); an induction strategy via temporal disorientation (Gilligan, 1987); exploring the origins of symptoms; opening channels for forgotten memories and experiences; therapeutic abreaction (Brenman & Gill, 1947; Weitzenhoffer, 1989b); treatment of amenorrhea; treatment of stuttering; rehabilitation of polio victims and stroke patients (Kroger, 1963); and resolution and integration of trauma into the personality (Dolan, 1991). Fromm (1970) notes the fascinating return of a forgotten childhood language via age regression. There are numerous other applications; the above is just a sampling of what is in the literature.

As is alluded to above, a frequent use of age regression occurs in the context of helping clients deal with traumatic or negative experiences in the past that are compromising their emotional or social functioning in the present. A second major indication for its use is when there is a lost *positive* past experience that would be useful to recover. Here you use hypnosis and age regression to revivify a reference experience of health or to recover a resource from the past that can be utilized again in the present.

One premise of Ericksonian therapy is the belief in the value of reconnecting clients to resources that have been used in the past, or that exist in latent form, or that have not yet been applied to the present problem. An example of this is the hypnosis that could be helpful for a couple that have worked through conflictual issues in their relationship but have not yet regained the warm emotional tenor of earlier times. I (JHE) worked with such a couple. They complained that although they had worked through their issues, they could not get back the feeling of love that they once had. They were so used to fighting with each other and resenting one another that a self-consciousness developed around the expression of loving feelings. I used age regression to bring them back to their first date, then to when they each knew that they were in love, to their wedding day, their honeymoon, and other instances of special joy in their relationship. At the end of a series of age regressions, conducted over a number of sessions, they each felt as if the lost feeling of love had been rekindled. The self-consciousness about expressing or accepting affectionate overtures attenuated over the course of reexperiencing the affection together in trance.

Another example of using age regression to reconnect with a resource is with the athlete who has lost a sense of confidence in his or her performance. This is not an uncommon experience when an athlete goes through a streak of bad luck or poor performances. Athletes commonly complain that they can't get back the same mental set that existed when they were winning. Age regression used in this context can revivify the winning feeling so that the person can carry it again into current performances.

Therapeutic age regression is also indicated when it is something that the person does well naturally. Take a depressed individual, for instance, who is able to vividly recall aspects of her past but who has never used this "ability" in a constructive, self-therapeutic vein. Such a person could age regress in session with the goal of returning to an earlier time in which she was happier in her life, felt more in charge, and felt more hopeful. The experience of the regression would then be constructively used even further by having the client describe, either during the trancework or afterwards (out of trance) the conditions—internal and external—that contribute to those more positive feelings and experiences. Clinicians must be careful not to be seduced into thinking that terrific, therapeutic things are taking or will take place simply because a client reexperiences a poignant moment in trance; the object is to help clients find ways of *using* these positive experiences and feelings toward therapeutic gain. Helping clients to identify "good" time and "bad" time variables and helping them to make bridges between the earlier nondepressed mindset and the present time via direct suggestion and/or posthypnotic suggestion are ways to reach this goal.

Along similar lines, age regression can be used with easily regressed smokers to bring them back to the time before they smoked. Once there, clients can be directed to reexperience what it was like to be able to breathe deeply and easily, to run up the stairs comfortably, and to walk into a closet full of fresh-smelling clothes.

There are also ways to use age regression therapeutically when it has been the mechanism of the problem. Let's say you are working with a person who suffers intermittent, painful flashbacks to a traumatic event. The person can be taught age regression as a mental technique over which he or she learns to have control rather than feeling controlled by it. Practicing age regressions to innocuous events, where the client learns to stop, start, or escape the experience, can attenuate the feeling of being at the mercy of spontaneous, affectively overwhelming regressions. Clients can also learn to use age regressions to have "flashbacks" to pleasant experiences in the past.

Age regression for therapeutic gain can be part of the treatment plan for someone who is too future-oriented. Phobics, for example, often imagine in lurid detail the "bad experience" they fear will happen in the future. Age regression can be used to have them remember in equally vivid detail all the plane flights they have flown comfortably and easily, or all the times they have walked far from home in a relaxed fashion, or times when they went up into a tall building and felt at ease. I (JSE) have often used age regression with people who complain they have no memories of childhood in order to help them build up a sense of personal history. In such instances hunting for a specific memory is supplanted by offering clients a context where they can fill up a "mental photo album" with snatches of memories—positive, negative, benign—and thereby feel less dissociated from their pasts.

ELICITING THE PHENOMENON OF AGE REGRESSION

Direct and Indirect Suggestion

Erickson's initial efforts at eliciting age regression were based primarily on direct suggestion, which yielded inconsistent results (Erickson, 1980c). Erickson viewed 20 minutes as the minimum amount of time necessary for the development of such a mentally complex hypnotic phenomenon. He states that these are "not matters of simple prompt obedience to emphatic hypnotic commands" but "the results of a profound psychophysiological process requiring time for the organization and development of patterns of response and behavior" (p. 106). In contrast to this, Weitzenhoffer (1989a) contends that he has seen spectacular regressions take place—with highly suggestible subjects—by using no more than a signal.

With regard to eliciting age regression, Erickson further advised that initial suggestions for the regression should be vague and confusing—precipitating in the subject a gradually increasing sense of uncertainty for the phenomenological situation, and leading toward a disorientation, followed by amnesia for the present. This is then followed by indirect suggestions for the regression itself. The mental transition is from feeling, to believing, to "knowing" the regressive experience.

There are many ways to **seed** the phenomenon of age regression. A therapist could say, "*Cindy, as you go back...down into trance.*" Here the therapist has, through pauses, seeded the idea of "going back." Words and phrases like *returning, back in time, retrieve, daydream about a* *time back when,* and *remember* can also be used to seed. Zeig (1990c) reported on Erickson's prehypnosis inquiry about a subject's familiarity with a *nursery rhyme* as his way of seeding age regression during one of his teaching seminars. Playing with a toy prior to induction also hints at what is to come and does nicely as a seeding technique when the regression desired is to childhood.

Therapists can **presuppose** that the age regression will take place with comments like, "***When you're back in time*** *as a 7-year-old, you'll be interested to see the things that you can remember about your classroom, who's sitting off to your right, whether the desks have metal legs fixed to the ground or not.*" Other remarks that indirectly suggest age regression by presupposing its appearance are "***As soon as you become aware of the sensation of drifting back,*** *you can focus your attention on whatever seems most interesting, or relevant...*" and "*While your unconscious mind begins to select the best moment for your conscious mind **to become aware of the changes in time,** you can simply become absorbed in the sensation of movement of breath through your body...*"

Double binds can be useful here, too. Therapists can suggest that clients go back in time to when they were "*7 or 8 years of age, or perhaps 11 or 12 might be a more enlightening time.*" Another double bind suggestion is "*You can remember a certain feeling from when you were a little boy, but maybe things will come to you instead through an image.*" Yet another is, "*You can allow yourself to remember things in a piecemeal fashion, like a patchwork quilt being made one section at a time, or maybe you'll find yourself suddenly, curiously immersed in an experience of long ago, one that brings with it further recollections, new learnings...*"

It is desirable to switch the tense of verbs as the individual is becoming immersed in a regression (i.e., go from, "*remember how that backyard looked,*" to "*look around at the backyard now; remember the smell of your mom's kitchen,*" to "*go ahead, breath in and smell your mom's kitchen again*"). Note that comments and suggestions shouldn't be randomly chosen but selected to mesh with the client's actual experience in trance. Find out what that experience is by asking the client about it during the hypnosis or by setting up yes/no/I don't know finger signaling (see Dolan, 1991).

Other comments that can help the client feel more involved in the regression are "*...and as this experience becomes more and more vivid,*" and "*...you can go ahead and even begin to mix the distinction between what was then and what is now,*" and "*...that air of confidence you had then you can have now, right here, for as briefly or as long as you feel comfortable with it.*" To elicit age regressions, Yapko (1990) mentions making affective and somatic bridges from the present to the past through such comments as "...the first time you had that feeling/ sense/experience..." (p. 262). Temporal disorientations are mentioned as another strategy for facilitating regression, as are age progressions leading subsequently to a regression; Yapko feels that these strategies enable a client to get more emotional distance from a negative experience in the past, which allows the person to access memories and experiences more easily and use them more constructively in therapy.

Because the use of dissociative statements often encourages a hypnotic subject to experience two different things at once, the therapist is offered the unique opportunity to use conscious/unconscious dissociative statements that will help the subject to age regress and also take back with him or her valuable resources from the present that can allow experiences to be reworked. For example, you can suggest to someone that *"Your unconscious mind can go back to that uncomfortable painful childhood memory that we spoke about, while your conscious mind brings back in time with it your intellect, and you can use your intellect in a way that wasn't available then, to really help you master now that earlier experience so it can settle, and be understood in a more useful way, a less personal way perhaps, a way that allows you to finally be able to say that this is resolved..."* Another illustration of this is *"As your unconscious mind begins the process of orienting to that experience, your conscious mind can go back also with all the understandings that you've acquired in your years of training as a therapist"* (this client who was herself a therapist). Another example is *"Your conscious mind can orient immediately toward that exquisite experience of feeling competent, while your conscious mind invokes the memory of how you managed to effect that."* In essence, the format of conscious/ unconscious dissociative statements offers an immediate opportunity for the therapist to encourage the combined use of present-day and past-day resources in a way to promote psychological change.

Metaphor and Naturalistic Examples

We have found the method of using an "evolving metaphor" to be very helpful with age regression. This refers to beginning a certain story line in conjunction with what the person is remembering and using the introduced metaphor to help modify the client's regressive experience so that it is maximally therapeutic. One example would be a metaphor that proffers safety. For instance, a client who is reexperiencing a painful or distressing aspect of a past event can be invited to imagine that he is watching the event as if it were being played on a TV through a VCR. This is our adaptation of a common clinical intervention where the traumatized client sees a trauma being played out on a movie screen. We like this adaptation better because it provides the client with more personal control via the display panel of the VCR or via a remote control. At any time the video can be put on stop, fast forward, rewind, or pause. In fact, we've even suggested to some clients that they take their video back to the store and "rent" it some other time when they feel more equipped to deal with it.

Individuals can build up entire libraries of videos inside their heads using this evolving metaphor, with sections for "self-help," or "comedy" films perhaps, or maybe with rooms for "editing," or one for "screening." All of these words can be interspersed in subsequent hypnosis sessions to organize clients' attention toward their own abilities to edit, screen, help oneself, or add comic relief to disturbing memories and experiences. Another way to produce some safety and distance is to have the person view the experience as if looking through glass, with an intercom at his or her disposal.

It is essential that the client feels able to modulate the age-regressed experience prior to doing that kind of hypnotic work. Feeling in control of and modulating a painful experience allows for a safe context in which the reworking and healing can take place. Often people unconsciously do not want to remember past negative experiences because the pain is expected to be so severe. By demonstrating to clients that they can control their discomfort, the unconscious resistances to undoing the repression can begin to attenuate. We sometimes start our trauma work off with a *mildly* painful memory (such as a bad birthday) so that the person can take "batting practice" with these strategies for feeling in control of inner experiences before moving up to more emotionally challenging situations.

Naturalistic examples of age regression appear whenever people daydream, become absorbed in a memory, stare at a picture, or reminisce. You can give examples of people loosening up and getting playful or silly during moments of whimsy or while playing with children.

Drawing people back into their own histories by describing (near) universal experiences is another way to use storytelling in the context of psychotherapy. Erickson used to elicit age regressions through his early learning set induction, also known as the "ABC" induction (Erickson, Rossi, & Rossi, 1979). This famous induction orients subjects back to their first year or so of grade school, when they are learning to write the letters of the alphabet. It subtly traces one's development of a sense of competency, starting with the initial experience of doubting one's ability to ever learn to get all the letters right and ending with the mastery of the skill. What really makes these kinds of stories magical is their accent on sensory revivification. To help clients regress in our adaptation of the early learning set, we refer them to the smell of the purple mimeograph ink that came off those old machines, to the feel of fat brown pencils in their hands, to the sounds of children saying the Pledge of Allegiance. Later on in developing the regression, we might bring up other familiar experiences—the colored lines along the gym floor, the squeaking of sneakers, the cold metal feel of the monkeybars. Hearing about the sensory aspects of past experiences creates an irresistible urge on the part of the client to go back and participate in the sensory memory, thereby eliciting the age regression.

Another story we use to help clients retrieve memories of mastery and accomplishment is of learning to ride a two-wheel bicycle. We'll start this one by talking about seeing the bike in the garage, or noticing the tiny rust marks on the handlebars, *"the plastic handlebar ends— maybe with plastic flyers—the sound of the bell on the handlebars, flags on the bars maybe, too...."* If any of these details resonate with the person's background, he or she will likely be transported right back.

Erickson was masterful at evoking regressions with examples from everyday life that would be common to most people and yet unique to a certain time period in life. An example of working this way is encouraging a client in trance to look down at his father's shoes and notice how very large they look and how small the client feels by comparison. Instead of directly suggesting that the person go back to the fifth year of life, the suggestion is indirect and *inserts* the person into a particular experience. Once someone starts to participate, he or she inevitably regresses to the age desired: if you look at your father's shoes and they look huge to you, you therefore must be a young child. This methodology may seem roundabout to the conscious mind, but it is effective in speaking the language of the unconscious.

Symbols

Symbols of age regression that can be used to elicit the phenomenon involve many of the same mechanisms that are spoken about in the next chapter on Future Progression. These include clock hands spinning backwards, old newspapers with headlines spinning into one's field of vision and then stopping so that the headline can be read, a digital clock moving rapidly backwards, a safe time machine through which one can go back to an earlier time, calendar pages being stuck back on a calendar. All of these symbols or props provide a mechanism through which a person can transition back in time.

Live symbols can also be used to elicit age regression. Give your hypnotized client a Lincoln log to hold. The feel, texture, and even smell of it is so unique that it serves as it own time machine right back to kindergarten age. How many parents spontaneously age regress at their first contact in many years with the smell of Play-Doh, the taste of a zwieback cookie, or the touch of finger paints as they parent their child? Why not utilize these natural tendencies in therapy?

Symbols can also be used to anchor a desirable age-regressed affective experience. For example, if in a childhood filled with mainly negative memories, one sole positive memory is of playing with marbles on the floor and shooting them into a shoe box, then a person who feels empty, or unloved, or unhappy can maintain a couple of special marbles in his or her pocket at all times to touch or to look at whenever there is an emotional need to balance out the experiential world.

In a similar vein, athletes can hold onto a special symbol of a moment of triumph and make contact with it to rekindle the feelings associated with triumph. For example, in *The Philadelphia Inquirer* (Sunday, March 7, 1993) Philadelphia Phillies right hander Curt Schilling discusses how at this point in spring training he had been a little nervous about recapturing his form from the end of last season. He then describes recapturing the feeling of confidence that he had last year by watching a number of his performances on videotape. This is a little more cumbersome a symbol than we'd been talking about but nevertheless illustrates the idea. Closer to the point are symbols that immediately transport people to an earlier and desired head set, perspective, or feeling, simply by mental association or touch.

SELECTED TRANSCRIPT MATERIAL

Age Regression for a Photographer Who Has a Learning Disability and Was Traumatized by an Aunt Who Ridiculed Him for Feeling Pressure

....So, what I'd like you to do is travel back in time—to do that you can imagine yourself looking at a clock, maybe a clock in the darkroom and watch the hands swirl backwards, taking you back backwards, taking you back in time...it would be good for you to go back in time, keeping your feeling of capability, your knowledge of how adept you are—go back in time until you see that little boy in fourth grade, talking to your aunt...and when you get back to that theme, you can watch it—it will come into focus very clearly...to begin...walk up to the side of that little boy...put your arm around his shoulder and raise your thumb up again to let me know that you're there...OK...and you can afford to allow yourself to hear your aunt saying again, "how can a fourth grader feel pressure?"....What I'd like you to do is squat down next to yourself as the little boy and whisper in your ear—go ahead, tell her...tell her that you do feel an awful lot of pressure...that it's hard for you to learn and then just keep your hand on his back, maybe wrap it around so you're holding his hip, rubbing his stomach a little bit...so that he knows you're right there with him as support...and you can listen to him talk to her and stand up for himself and trust his own reality....

She really doesn't understand and it doesn't even matter if she understands what he's saying, but it's really important for this little boy to say, to affirm what he knows to be true...and you can hold your hand up and make her stop while he continues to talk about the pressure of the demands and she's probably forgotten just how difficult it is to learn how to read and write...and how hard it is to cope...and whisper in his ear too "go ahead, you can tell her"...continue on...and as he talks, maybe she can have an impassive response. I don't know this woman—you do—maybe she can see the light and remember how difficult it is to remember whether a "b" is a backward "d" or an upside down "p" or maybe she can remember how hard it is to draw an "s," a snake—which way does the snake point...and doesn't "m" have two humps—or three?....And is a "z" a flattened-out snake "s" or is it something completely different? And does it point in the same way? LMNO, LMNO, LMNO...and is the number "6" an upside down "9"?...or is it something altogether different? She may have forgotten these things and how difficult they are for somebody with a learning disability, but maybe as you talk, she can understand—or not...that's OK too....The most important thing is that you encourage this little boy to continue to believe in the validity of what he's experiencing...and I'd like you to whisper something in his ear—I'd like you to tell him it's not his fault, even as he talks to his aunt, I'd like you to periodically whisper to him that it's not his fault, that he didn't do anything wrong, that he's trying the best he can and that's just fine—that's all that anyone can expect....You can tell him that he's a wonderful, wonderful little boy...you can tell him that if he has problems in school, it's not his fault...you can tell him that you know for sure that later on he'll find lots of things that come easy to him and that he does them very, very well...that he's going to be extremely successful and happy....You can tell him that you're a visitor from the future and you know this...with absolute certainty...after you tell him that, you can stand up and...while keeping your hand on his shoulder...you can look at your aunt and notice how you're her height, or taller, now...and you can say to her, you know, it's hard for him to learn—he probably has a learning disability—he feels a lot of pressure, but he's trying the best he can...he really wants to please very badly...and you can tell her too that you're a visitor from the future...and the fact of the matter is that once learning is no longer just a matter of what it is in the early grade school, particularly once it involves creativity, visual, motor ability, artistic ability—he's going to really flourish....

And you can tell her that it's all too possible for a fourth grader to feel tons of pressure and doubt...and then I'd like you to wish her well...and then I'd like you to bend down again and give the boy a hug...ask him if he has any questions for you before you take off— you can tell him that you'll be back to visit plenty of times...but ask him if he has any questions....If he does, you can answer them in a fatherly kind of way...you can brush his hair a little bit with your hand as you do...you can assure him that you'll be back to visit plenty of times...and answer his questions...and you can, when this process is complete, when you feel a sense of comfort in what you accomplished with this little boy, for now anyway, you can raise your thumb again and I'll help you to reorient to the present....

Age Regression for Shy Bladder

Everybody's had the experience...you know when you're a little boy and somebody says—what happens when somebody says, you know it's going to be a long time until we get to a bathroom?...do you hear that adult voice saying that to you? And what effect did that have on that 8-year-old right away? I can remember and you can go back in time and reexperience that....I can remember being in pain, well, I would have been just fine if my dad hadn't said to me, you know you won't be getting to another bathroom for another hour and you just have to hold that, hold your pee....I never had to go to the bathroom so badly in my whole life at just that exact moment...and it was so bad that, well, it was so bad that I needed to pretend to myself that I could go to the bathroom anytime I wanted...and then I didn't have to go...even though I really did...but I didn't know it....

Age Regression to Healthy Time in a Person with Chronic Fatigue

...so deep that your immune system gets stronger and stronger and you know what it's like to have a really strong immune system...and you can experience that again now...because for a while the mono at age 16 maybe derailed your physiology, we're going to give your physiology right now, Sarah...a way of reexperiencing what it feels like to be really healthy and robust, so I'd like you to allow yourself to go back in time...back in time...to a time before the age of 16, when you were healthy...really, really healthy and you can, you can understand that you are a very healthy, robust person...sure, you get sick from time to time, but basically, even then you are healthy waiting to happen....And so I'd like you to experience a day in the life of time when you are feeling particularly strong and healthy, when you have that image in your mind, you can raise your thumb up...OK...it would be good if you could open up all your senses to this experience, see everything there is to see around you, even smell what there is to smell, the particular smells...as vividly as possible...you can hear the sounds special to that place...hear the sounds special to that place...maybe run your fingers across some sort of texture that's right there...and you can really experience, Sarah, most fully this feeling inside of being an utterly healthy, vibrant, robust, strong physiological person...and this can be a reference experience for you....

Chapter 9

FUTURE PROGRESSION

ABOUT THE PHENOMENON

When I (JHE) was in elementary school, there was a teacher—a nun—who helped me a great deal. At the time I was struggling to learn, despite a mild visual-spatial-motor learning disability. Reading was difficult and laborious, and taking work off the board was incredibly slow and tedious. Arithmetic columns were skewed and I failed penmanship report card after report card. Now this was well before the time when learning disabilities were commonly acknowledged, diagnosed, and remedied. My struggle and my pain were compounded by the fact that the teachers did not understand what I was experiencing and would only implore me to "try harder," "go faster," and "do better."

My family was moving and I was about to switch schools. I can remember one particularly kind teacher taking me aside, bending over, looking me right in the eye and saying, "I know, I'm certain, that you're really going to amount to something someday, that you're really going to make something out of yourself. I don't know whether you're going to become a teacher or a doctor or a businessman, but I do know you will be successful, even though you're struggling now. I can see that you have a lot of potential."

I think that kind teacher knew a whole lot about how the mind worked. When she said what she did, she gave me hope. I felt she understood that I could and would do better at some point. She helped

123

me to be more optimistic by instilling the awareness in my mind that things would work out well one day. Although she did not use a formal age-progression technique, she certainly did have me wondering about and imagining which of those different professions I could choose when I got older. Today, although only remnants of the learning disability remain—my persistent difficulties with getting family genograms all on one page in some semblance of order and learning from which side one correctly saddles and bridles a horse—I do feel I have a lot to thank that teacher for. I think she provided me with a great deal of emotional damage control at a juncture when I could have begun to think of myself as a scholastic failure.

HISTORICAL PRECEDENTS

For ages the prospect of some future outcome—positive or negative—has been utilized to influence man's behavior in the present. For example, some religions have held out the prospect of heaven or hell to influence behavior. Likewise, in the eastern part of the world, the prospect of endless cycles of rebirths and the bliss of enlightenment have also been used to alter behavior. Whether or not you believe in heaven or hell or in reincarnation, one does have to admit that these ideas have profoundly influenced man's behavior.

Philosophy and religion have recognized the impact that the future has on the present. Aristotle (1943) for instance, with his concept of entelechy, conceives of man and the world in general as proceeding toward a certain state of pure forms, that is, pure or perfect examples or archetypes of each object, person, and thing. Unlike the above movements, however, Erickson did not count on either a prospective external future to influence the present nor an innate tendency to grow toward future perfection, but instead he used hypnosis to help people create internal "future experiences" that could alter current functioning. He did, nonetheless, have some predecessors in the field of psychology.

Alfred Adler (1927) was perhaps the most widely respected theorist who credited the future's influence on the present. In contrast to Freud's great stress upon experiences during early childhood as determinants of personality, Adler, in his theory of fictional finalism, proposed that man is more motivated by his expectation of the future than by experiences of the past. Again, unlike Aristotle and the religions noted above, these goals do not exist in the future as part of some teleological and preordained design. They exist subjectively and mentally in the here and now as strivings or ideals. As was the case with Erickson, Adler's theory has no place for predestination or fatality, but only for man's ability to envision himself at a future time. He said that "individual psychology insists absolutely on the indispensability of finalism for the undertaking of all psychological phenomena. Causes, powers, instinct, impulses and the like cannot serve as explanatory principles. The final goal alone can explain man's behavior" (p. 400).

AN ORIENTATION TOWARDS THE FUTURE

The hypnotherapeutic technique of future progression, that is, orienting clients toward the future and then helping them to *experience* themselves there, was a very important contribution of Milton Erickson to the field of psychotherapy. Several writers on Ericksonian technique speak of Erickson's future orientation in therapy, in general. Havens (1987), for instance, makes a strong case for considering most, if not all, of Erickson's interventions as being future-oriented; metaphor, task assignments, and describing consequences of actions are all viewed by Havens as techniques that position clients vis-à-vis the future. Likewise, Zeig (1987) sees as one of the central principles of Erickson's work a futuristic or teleological perspective. He discusses an intervention that Erickson made with his granddaughter, Laurel, that was not going to take effect until 16 years later, long after his death! De Shazer (1985), in a description of Erickson's "crystal ball technique," discusses Erickson's future orientation in general and his own model of Erickson's age-progression techniques in particular.

All in all, probably one of the most distinctive qualities of Erickson's approach was his use of the future in psychotherapy. While other approaches focus largely, if not exclusively, on the client's past, Erickson understood that making a concrete reality of the positive vision of the future could be more curative. By and large when Erickson did focus on the past, it was to garner diagnostic information for future-oriented work or to retrieve personal resources to be applied in the present or a future situation rather than because a focus on the past had any therapeutic value in itself.

There are many synonyms for Ericksonian age-progression work. In the literature, it is variously called future pacing, age progression, pseudo-orientation in time, and time projection.

MECHANISM OF ACTION

Erickson (1954b/1980) cited numerous cases in which tremendous psychotherapeutic gains were made in otherwise intractable conditions with the use of future-progression techniques. It is interesting to speculate about the means by which these techniques have their profound effect. It would appear that the importance of a future orientation rests in its ability to have a person experience a completely different biopsychosocial reality from the one regularly experienced. From a neuropsychological perspective, it is commonly understood that the development in humans of the prefrontal lobe makes goal setting, planning, and hypothesizing about a future reality an organic reality (Luria, 1973). Hence, projection into the future is a neurological reality. Eric Fromm (1955,1956) stated that this fact provides the foundation for man's existential condition: man is not just grounded in the here and now but simultaneously aware of his past and also aware of his future, including the inevitability of his own death. This awareness gives his life meaning and a certain existential intensity whereby, since he knows his days are numbered, he lives life with intent, seeking goals in the future. Erickson can be credited with not just observing this fact of the human condition but with manipulating it for therapeutic gain.

Erickson himself made a number of statements that concisely and cogently expressed what he thought was the mechanism of action for his age-progression technique. In his seminal article entitled "Pseudo-Orientation in Time as a Hypnotherapeutic Procedure" (1954b/1980), he speaks of the "general appreciation that practice leads to perfection, that action once initiated tends to continue, and that deeds are the offspring of hope and expectancy" (p. 397).

Erickson also seemed to have a sense that an experience lived in the mind's eye and then forgotten by way of amnesia could be experienced subsequently as a history, a personal historical fact that one could then base his or her actions upon, almost as if it had happened already. To quote Erickson again, "the patient could respond effectively psychologically to desired therapeutic goals as actualities already achieved" (Erickson, 1954b/1980, p. 397).

HISTORY AND EXPERIMENTAL STUDIES

In the last decade there have been relatively few reports in the literature on the use of age progression, and almost all are exclusively of the case study variety. Lehman (1978), for example, demonstrates the effectiveness of age progression with a patient suffering from neurodermatitis; this report had the advantage of a four-year follow-up at which point the patient was still asymptomatic. Tilton (1983) demonstrates the use of pseudo-orientation in time with an agoraphobic, while Orman (1991) uses age progression as part of an entire treatment package integrating a number of hypnotic and nonhypnotic approaches to help an alcoholic drug addict recover. In this latter report, age progression was used to enable the patient to see himself as being successful in abstaining from alcohol and cocaine at various future times. The patient was encouraged to visualize situations in which he would be tempted to go back to using alcohol or drugs and then to experience himself being able to resist temptation while using a number of techniques for mastering urges, techniques that were cultivated during the therapy proper. At six-months and one-year follow-up the patient was still not using any substances.

Havens (1986) describes using Erickson's age-progression technique with populations in addition to those that Erickson worked with. He cites improved performances for athletes and students as well as improved salesmanship and increased effectiveness of hypnotic weight loss and smoking cessation. Using Erickson's technique verbatim, Havens provides what is tantamount to a case study replication by demonstrating that Erickson's age progression approach works with a variety of other cases beyond the five that Erickson himself reported.

An article in the July 1979 edition of the *American Journal of Clinical Hypnosis* discusses an age-progression strategy that is really quite creative. Authors Sexton and Maddock worked with psychotic and depressed suicidal patients, all of whom revealed upon age regression that both their psychoses and/or depression and/or suicidality were related either to guilt or to reunion fantasies that developed subsequent to the death of a close family member. One case, for instance, involved a woman who prayed for the end of her husband's suffering during a difficult illness, and when he unexpectedly died a couple of hours later, she felt as if she had caused his death. The guilt was so severe that she not only wished to die, but also to be reunited with him in heaven. Another case involved a woman who promised a dying person that she would be with the person before very long. In her grief over the person's subsequent death, the woman felt a commitment to the promise; when this commitment mingled with her depression, a very grave suicidal situation was created.

With these cases, the authors reported that they first age regressed patients back to the point where the initial promise or death wish took place. Once the nature of the patient's self-perceived transgression or commitment was discovered, they were age progressed *into heaven*, where of their own accord they engaged in conversations with the lost loved ones or with Jesus Christ himself. In the patients' conversations with the loved ones, they worked through the promises that they had made and had the chance to see that the person was doing well. In their conversations with Jesus, they would hear that they were understood, forgiven, and that it was not their time to be in heaven. This was a strikingly imaginative technique, and one that the authors reported being so highly effective that the psychoses improved dramatically, the depressions lifted quickly, and ego functioning improved significantly.

We are impressed with the innovativeness of this technique but caution readers that this procedure is **not** for the beginning or even for the intermediate practitioner of hypnosis, inasmuch as a "botched" therapy session using "heaven" could result in *increased* wishes for the client to reunite with the loved one in the afterlife! This raises the question in our minds of how the therapist is to handle the situation if the dead loved one is less than forgiving or does not look so good in heaven or perhaps cannot be found in heaven and the subject feels the need to search hell; or perhaps the good Lord is not quite so reasonable in forgiving. Provisions need to be made for these situations, too, inasmuch as the subject's hypnotic experience rests largely on his or her projections, especially if he or she is unamenable to guidance and constructive leading on the part of the therapist.

However, these authors reported all positive outcomes and positive experiences in "heaven," without therapist mediation or coaching. This seems incredible for a psychotic and severely depressed population, but nonetheless this is what is reported. In any event, this is a creative strategy in a world filled with hypnotic ho-hum, and the authors' efforts are to be applauded.

Another addendum does seem to be in order, however: Sexton and Maddock insist that cooperation on the part of psychotic patients is essential. One of us has found that although consent to treatment is essential, cooperation need not be present. Psychotics in my (JHE) article on hypnotizing acutely psychotic and dangerous inpatients (1988) were able to be led into trance with excellent, therapeutic results despite their utter disengagement from the world, their rage, their hallucinations and even, in one case, a complete distrust of the staff.

A bit more experimental in nature is Deiker and Pollock's (1975) report of a patient with a chlorine bleach phobia who underwent a combination of hypnosis and systematic desensitization. This article is interesting for its discussion of ideas for integrating hypnosis and a behavioral orientation and, in particular, the authors' discovery that future progression might hasten a client's passage through the hierarchy of anxiety-provoking items that is part of systematic desensitization. In their treatment approach, the patient moved at a much faster pace through the second portion (after the age-progression intervention where they experienced themselves comfortable in the phobic situation, at a future time) of the hierarchy than the first and then also successfully completed an in vivo trial of close contact with the phobic object.

Another discussion on the integration of hypnosis and behavioral approaches is in an article by Bornstein, Pychtarik, McFall, Winegardner, Winnett & Paris (1980). These authors used age progression as one of many techniques in a hypnobehavioral treatment in a composite package applied to three highly hypnotizable nail biters. These subjects had their nail biting measured over a number of months and all three showed excellent clinical progress over time, including at three months posttreatment follow-up. In concluding, the authors felt these results to suggest that a combined hypnotic and behavioral package may yield results superior to a behavioral treatment approach alone.

INDICATIONS FOR USE

Future orientation as a psychological phenomenon can obviously be experienced either in or out of trance. What distinguishes it as one of the hypnotic phenomena, however, is that when experienced in trance, it becomes more than a superficial overlay of time orientation on one's reality; the client ideally attains a whole different phenomenological world of time, sensation, and experience of the self. Therein lies the ability of future progression to function as a therapeutic tool. And because an individual can, for the time being, move out of the present and what may be concomitant rigid conceptualizations of the self, of others, and the problem, this technique can often catalyze a process of change where there had been little movement.

Apart from its general usefulness, future progression is particularly indicated with depressed individuals to mitigate the often accompanying feelings of hopelessness. It is also especially useful with those who find themselves—for reasons of despair, passivity, or characterological cynicism—completely unable to imagine a positive event taking place at a future time. Others for whom this technique is useful include people who feel hopelessly mired in the muck of the past or whose (mis)understanding or belief that therapy needs to be oriented exclusively toward uncovering work cannot be dislodged. Sports performance and habit control are other excellent areas of application.

Yapko (1986) mentions the use of future progression with depressed persons in order to help them build positive expectations about the future. Building a vision of a future that they can visit and "try on for size" using hypnosis offers "experiential reference points" around which people can begin to focus their energies, hopes, and resources. Gilligan (1990) also describes the therapeutic advantage of orienting clients toward a future self around which the unconscious mind can begin to organize and to direct its energies. In his text *Trancework*, Yapko (1990) also mentions the use of future progression in orienting clients to the *negative* consequences of continuing current maladaptive patterns. He writes that facilitating in trance the actual, concrete experience of the negative consequences can serve to "kick-start" better patterns of behavior and thought, giving the healthier process more momentum.

Erickson's (1954b/1980) article on future progression shows how he successfully used future progression with some chronic, pervasive, and seemingly intractable problems. His emphasis was on change through a focus on the individual, and the therapeutic thrust was of an intrapsychic nature. We have had good results using future progression with couples and families as well. Some case examples of its use in these contexts, in addition to applications in the areas of sport performance and habit control, follow.

Karen and Sam came to marital therapy wanting to mend their relationship of over 20 years. They had had a good relationship until he failed to defend her to his parents when they criticized her for something she had done. This precipitated a huge blow-up between the two. Although they had processed and resolved the experience of the betrayal in marital therapy with me (JHE), they were both having difficulty truly forgiving each other for the pain they had inflicted on each other as the struggle had taken place. Moreover, they were also having difficulty recapturing the tenor of love for each other that they had previously felt.

When I used future progression with this couple to help them experience a time when they would have those elements present in their relationship again, neither of them could come up with an image or an experience. Sam fell asleep during the hypnosis and Karen drew a total blank! I initially thought this meant the prognosis was rather poor, but I persevered and attempted to reframe the situation by saying, "*Your unconscious mind probably recognizes that there are just too many experiences like this to choose from and that choosing only one would somehow do the future richness of your relationship an injustice.*" I went on to suggest that their unconscious minds could choose many such future experiences and present it to them as a gift; however, the experiential reviews could occur in, and remain in, the unconscious so that they may not ever be consciously aware of what these experiences might be before their actual happening!

In the weeks to come I saw Karen and Sam looking more fondly at each other, making more eye contact, touching each other more often, and talking about the things they were beginning to do again together. They were able to terminate therapy a few weeks later, saying that they had mended the hurt in their relationship and had recaptured the love that had been lost. Attributing these changes to the future-progression work is presumptuous, but the case does demonstrate how it is used as part of a therapy. It also demonstrates a process orientation of hypnotherapy, wherein applications of technique are not fixed and static but are modified to fit the situation as it unfolds.

Bill came for therapy reporting a great amount of difficulty in being able to get emotionally close to women. He had a long history of choosing women who were either distant geographically, distant emotionally, or distant sexually. He also wanted help with his chronic discontent. Future progression was used to help him find a time in the future when he would feel at peace with himself, comfortable and calm. When he was able to experience that vividly in trance, I (JHE) thought to capitalize on his success and help him make gains in his relationship difficulties as well. When I went to make the next suggestion, I looked at my notes and noticed that he always referred to females as "girls." I then made the error of using this same terminology in my suggestion. I said, *"Perhaps you can also experience yourself in this setting with a girl."*

Being the responsive subject he was, he promptly proceeded to report that in the park in which he was sitting, a girl that looked a lot like Goldilocks was coming down the path skipping. I then said, *"That's right, and that's just about all you'll get looking for a 'girl.' Now perhaps in this experience there can be a woman with whom you can feel close and intimate and experience a true and gratifying reciprocity of support and ideas."* He then experienced a woman coming up and sitting on the park bench with him. They discussed a number of subjects together and the atmosphere warmed appropriately. This appeared to be a healthier relationship than the one he was accustomed to. Subsequent to this session, Bill seemed to shift, attitudinally, toward a more mature conception of male/female relationships and began to speak with sincerity about wanting to date a different kind of woman, one with whom he could have a more intimate relationship.

Lisa was an 8-year-old, competitive horseback rider who was working in therapy with me (JSE) to rebuild her confidence for jumping fences. In the 2 years preceding the 10-session therapy, she had suffered two bad falls and numerous near misses, which had shaken her confidence considerably. Lisa's goal, at the therapy's inception, was to make it around a simple course of four small fences. This was what was required of her in the classes in which she competed at horse shows. Future-progression techniques were one of several interventions used to help Lisa catapult herself out of her mental set of lapsed confidence into an experience of herself as a competent and confident rider.

This little girl was an excellent hypnotic subject who was able to kinesthetically experience herself riding while in trance in the office. This was evidenced by her movement back and forth on the sofa during trance, as if in the saddle, and the unwitting positioning of her hands raised and in front of her, as if holding reins. Reviewing her hypnotic experiences together revealed that she had been able to feel herself comfortably jumping a course of fences and enjoying the experience immensely for the first time in years. I returned her to that experience in subsequent sessions, offering her posthypnotic suggestions about being able to recreate those feelings whenever she wished.

The sensations of confidence, competence, and pleasure were furthermore connected to actions or objects (touching her horsehead earrings, gazing at a part of her pony's bridle visible from when mounted on him) that Lisa could use to access those feelings whenever she wished (for instance, right before entering the show ring). The championship ribbons that Lisa began bringing to session, plus her exuberant accounts of riding and jumping, attested to her regained confidence.

I (JSE) also used future progression with a woman who recently had quit smoking. Jill was struggling fervently with urges to abandon her nonsmoking regimen and resume the habit. She was having trouble getting past the discomfort of the moment and had been unable to use the prospect of future health to reinforce her nonsmoking status. I progressed her in trance to a time several years later where she could look back upon the experience of being a nonsmoker for the intervening years. She was able to imagine the expanded breathing capacity of her future self, a richer voice (Jill was a singer), her enhanced olfactory sense, the clarity of air in her home, and so on.

After *immersion* in that trance experience, I asked Jill to have the "future Jill" talk with the "present Jill" and to tell her whatever she thought was needed to convince the present Jill to sustain her smoke-free status—to describe just how good it felt to have a nonsmoker's scope of breath and lung power, and how happy she was that the earlier Jill had quit, and how she didn't miss smoking at all anymore and hadn't for years and years. The client reported this to be a very powerful experience that effectively supported her decision not to become a smoker again.

ELICITING THE PHENOMENON OF FUTURE PROGRESSION

Direct and Indirect Suggestion

Seeding future progression can be as simple as inviting clients at the beginning of trance induction to "*wonder what this experience will bring* *in the future"* or *"wonder where the experience can take you, what kind of adventure will you have?"* You can tell clients to allow their conscious minds *"to pick the depth of trance, while the unconscious **picks the time*** (references to time especially foreshadow the concept of the altered time dimensions inherent in a future progression) *for the desired trance depth to be attained."* Telling clients to *"**go ahead** into trance"* or to *"move comfortably forward into trance"* are similarly effective in seeding a future orientation.

Presuppositions can take the shape of *"**When you find yourself in a different dimension of space and time,**"* or *"**As soon as you begin to become aware of feeling wiser, a little older,**"* or *"**Once you recognize your experience as one from next year,** you can start to remember the intervening months, and see what happened, what are the outcomes of your decisions, what might you be thinking of now that you forgot to consider before...?"*

Another way of using presupposition is to ask a future-oriented diagnostic question prior to trancework that contains a presupposition. An example of this is the question, "What will things be like **when the problem is over**?" This is a question that we have heard Jay Haley sometimes ask of the families with whom he works. The clinician should try and make sure that the answer given to this question is relatively realistic given the capacities of the patient. Note that the presupposition contained in the question is that the problem *will* be over at some future time.

Double binds can be used to allow subjects to select their own speeds or means by which they enter a future orientation. You can say, *"Feel free to go ahead in time gradually and at a leisurely pace, or you can go swiftly, eager to see what it feels like to feel lighter/happier/at peace...."*

Examples of **conscious/unconscious dissociative statements** that elicit future progressions are the following: *"Your conscious mind can take its time selecting the precise time in the future that will be most productive to visit, while your unconscious mind moves more quickly, trying on many possible times for size, discarding some, considering for approval others, picking, choosing efficiently and double checking before offering it up for final consideration,"* and *"Your conscious mind can imagine what it feels like to comfortably experience intimacy, while your unconscious mind thinks about the kinds of conversations you can have with your wife that will lead to that experience."*

Dissociation through **disorientation** is an excellent way of eliciting future progression, and one which Erickson frequently used. The disorientation can be to time itself or it can be to a place or even a person. For example, were one going to disorient a client to time in the future, the following statements and suggestions could be said:

"...sitting there, comfortably experiencing the level of trance that your unconscious mind has chosen for you today, your conscious mind might have begun to lose track of precisely how long you've been experiencing trance for....It could be that you've been in trance for 3 minutes or 6 minutes or maybe it has been 12 minutes...your conscious mind can experience time in that way, while your unconscious mind experiences time in an entirely different way....Experiencing tomorrow already now, and the day after that now, and it could be that a week has already passed, already passed, easily and comfortably, and now your unconscious knows that it's September already. Can you smell the changes in the air? Isn't it crisp? Everything has turned orange already! Do you notice in your hypnotic visions how the autumn lighting is different from late summer, and your unconscious mind can really appreciate that and share it with your conscious mind too if it wishes so that it can also share in this experience...."

As with age regression, it is very important when eliciting a future progression to help the client have as vivid an experience as he or she can. Therefore, you want to capitalize on whichever sensory faculties that particular client experiences most richly and incorporate those experiences into the trancework. Further enhancement of the disorientation could come with other comments and suggestions about olfactory, tactile, gustatory, auditory, and visual experiences of autumn to really stamp in the hypnotic experience of it being September or October rather than, say, August.

A disorientation to place (useful, for instance, if working with a graduate student anxiously preparing for the oral defense of a dissertation) can elicit a future orientation through something like the following (abbreviated) induction:

"....You may not have yet discovered the ways in which you can experience changes...in your surroundings...in your experience of yourself in your new surroundings...the specific feature of this chair and this room can begin to recede...in your conscious mind, or begin to meld with features of another chair in another place...you may have thought that you were sitting here, in this office, talking with this person...and your conscious mind can continue to wonder comfortably if that's true or not...while your unconscious mind can allow you to experience yourself in a different place, a different chair, with a different person. Have you begun to wonder who that person will be? I don't know yet if you've recognized that the new place that...you can be now...is a differ-

ent office, a professor's office maybe, or a conference room in the university library, or a classroom and here and there you are, sitting in that chair, feeling terrific because you have just successfully completed your dissertation defense...hats off to you...."

In addition, you would ideally want to seed the induction with earlier references (either in the trance or prior to the trance proper) of the concept of place disorientation as well as include in the session several stories, anecdotes, or naturalistic examples of when/where people get disoriented to time or place. Consider, for example, what it's like to wake up abruptly from an unexpected nap after the sun has gone down and the room has darkened or what it's like to drive with unwarranted assurance to a location before realizing that you had been thinking of the wrong place altogether.

Disorienting a client to his or her own person can also promote a future orientation by having the client suddenly recognize that the person that he or she has been seeing or talking with in trance is the self in the future—thinner (if presently overweight); older and wiser and more confident (if lacking in self-confidence); as a competent therapist or parent (if unsure about one's ability to master a new role); addiction-free (if struggling to give up cigarettes or alcohol) and so on. The essential point in eliciting disorientations to person is to make the recognition unanticipated and sudden for the subject; it is this element of surprise that causes the cognitive and experiential confusion, resulting in the client being able to break, at least momentarily, with the experience of the self in the present.

Metaphor

Metaphors that can serve as backdrops in your trancework for eliciting future progression include the obverse of some examples mentioned in the previous chapter on age regression. For instance you can have the person imagine clock hands spinning quickly forward or the red or green lights of a digital clock rapidly spinning as the numbers change kaleidoscopically toward later times. Similarly, clients can visualize calendar pages being torn off in rapid succession or imagine newspapers spinning around, like in old movies, in such a way that future headlines appear one after another. Other metaphors include the use of (safe) time machines or crystal balls. When using time machines, be sure to underscore the idea of safety, inasmuch as these machines are often associated in the movies with misguided adventures that frequently leave its occupants stuck in wrong or dangerous time periods!

The use of crystal balls as imagery also warrants a caveat for judicious use because of the way in which they smack of palm reading, fortune telling, and the like. Although Erickson himself was fond of using them in future progression work, we tend to think that in the spirit of his (and most hypnotherapists') wishes to dissociate hypnosis from hocus-pocus, they are best avoided.

All in all, many methods are available to help the client adopt a future orientation. The specific method chosen will depend both on the clinician's facility with certain methods and, most importantly, on the personality and preferred trance style of the client. An old movie aficionado may delight in visualizing spinning newspapers, whereas a compulsively time-managed executive will scoff at that idea but take readily to the digital clock image. An individual who orients more toward sound than vision may do better focusing in trance on the sound of time whirring past the windows of a time machine, while a science fiction fan would prefer to look out the machine's window and, as in the classic film *The Time Machine*, view the rapidly changing fashions in a clothing store window display.

Maintaining a Process Orientation

It is critical that therapists establish some means to be assured that clients in trance actually attain an experience of themselves in the future. Too often, therapists are content to concern themselves primarily with the execution of a technique and not with the degree of responsiveness elicited from the client. Therapeutic communication must always be evaluated in terms of response, not by structure (Zeig, 1990b), and this can never be emphasized enough. Therefore, through either ideomotor signaling (e.g., finger movements or hand gestures) or talking, therapist and client must establish a vehicle of communication so that the therapist maintains a pulse reading on the client's experience (or lack thereof) and calibrates the trancework accordingly. This is, incidentally, as relevant for age regression as it is for age progression.

If the client has not been able to attain a future-oriented experience of the self, you should coach and coax them toward one. By using the Ericksonian principle of breaking something difficult down into smaller steps, co-create their future scene in a piecemeal fashion and put it all together at the end. Make comments such as *"OK maybe you can't yet experience yourself far away from home without anxiety…but can you be two blocks away and calm for now?"* or *"If it's difficult right now to experience again a family life with warmth, comfort and happiness, can you close your eyes in the experience and know it's OK that you don't hear anything because that means there are no arguments taking place now....Can you instead just smell a nourishing delicious meal cooking...fresh bread baking, chicken broiling, perhaps...."*

Don't be concerned if it takes time to complete the work—even in a number of sessions. Future progression, like therapy in general, needs to be a process and not a procedure. Glitches become grist for the mill; if a client cannot experience this phenomenon, a clinician can then consider the problem an *inability to generate a future state* and not just the lack of the finished product.

Take, for instance, my (JSE) recent experience with a demonstration subject in a workshop I taught on Ericksonian hypnosis in Saratov, Russia. This gentleman had volunteered for the proposed demonstration of future progression, stating that he would like to learn how to create a vision of himself as a psychologist in a community and economic climate in which professional opportunities appeared bleak. It would have been a nice occasion for a positive result, but when I saw my subject smirk during the trancework and gleefully tell me that his unconscious mind wished for no such experience, I knew I had better switch gears fast. Therefore, utilizing Vladimir's rascality, I underscored to the audience the importance of communication during trance and of maintaining a process orientation. First, I reframed the absence of future progression as Vladimir's unconscious mind's demand for greater respect of the uncertainties that abounded and of his worries about his future as a psychologist in Russia. Second, I moved Vladimir toward age regression to complete the demonstration of eliciting hypnotic phenomena with one that I thought would appeal more to his somewhat passive-resistive (and thus somewhat regressive) interpersonal style.

Once the client has an experience of the self in the future, it can be suggested too that he or she clearly experience a future time when the problem is *gone*. In most cases, clients should be encouraged to utilize fully all senses and experience this scene as a first-person event. That is, rather than seeing themselves acting on a stage, so to speak, they should be encouraged to experience the events as if seeing them through their own eyes rather than watching themselves as spectators. Clients can be reminded of the wonderfully funny scene in the movie *Ghost*, where the character played by Patrick Swayze steps into Whoopi Goldberg's body to have some physical contact with Demi Moore. The resulting dance is one of the most tender scenes in the film. If you can recall the way in which Swayze went behind Whoopi and "stepped into" her, you can describe this scene to your client as an anecdotal example that can help the person "step into" his or her future self.

In other cases, however, it may be more therapeutic to have the future-progressed client *not* step immediately into the future self and instead remain an objective observer for a while. Erickson dialogues with Rossi about the advantages of allowing the subject to watch before experiencing the future self (being appropriately sexual in a new relationship, being a parent, being in a pain-free state), so that he or she can use the dissociation to "test the waters" at a comfortable pace or degree of involvement. This objective observer stance also allows the subject to become *curious* about the future experience rather than frightened by it or anxious about it (Erickson & Rossi, 1980b, pp. 393–396).

Once a person has and is comfortable with the experience of being in the future, it is time to explore the ways in which it can be therapeutically used. It might be enough for the client to have this experiential reference point in what had previously been a "futureless" perspective on life or to use it to reinforce current actions that are difficult or anxiety-provoking to sustain (e.g., not smoking, dieting, going to therapy). Others can use a future progression specifically as a means of inspiration, motivation, or hope.

Some clients find it useful to imagine what steps took place between the present and the future that were helpful in orchestrating a positive situation. Erickson frequently used future progression in this way (1954b/1980). In such cases, it is useful to provide some bridges between current and future experiences. For example, asking the question (in or out of trance), "What was needed to help you get from where you were before to where you are now (the future point?)," can really help to start the movement towards that end point. Note the use of the past tense in this last sentence: this helps create a stronger sense of the future positive experience being in the present. Again, it's important that the stepping stones be realistic. That is, hitting the lottery as one of the stepping stones to the future point is a nice idea but not something that is either likely to happen or under the person's own control. It's good if the client can see the events leading up to the desired end state as being made up of processes or of skills that can be developed or enhanced, rather than as events that must take place at the hands of someone else.

Other clients who don't like their future progression experience can consider what they need to do in their current lives to avoid that situation. Erickson often used amnesia in conjunction with future progression so that the person had no conscious memory of the future experience (see 1954b/1980, p. 397 for examples of this). The decision of whether or not to induce amnesia for the future progression depends upon whether or not the client's conscious awareness of the experience would help or hinder its being effected in reality. Awareness of the experience can catalyze and/or support the movement toward change in many instances. As Zeig (1988b) notes, a person's conscious mind can empower a suggestion. If, however, a therapist thinks that the reference point of a future experience needs to be a more subtle influence on a person's psychological functioning, then amnesia will be the prudent choice.

Ask your clients to talk about their experiences as they are taking place. That will help you therapeutically monitor and guide the events as they unfold. As scenes come to a satisfactory end, suggest that the individual "lock in" both the experience as well as the positive emotions associated with the experience. This tends to provide a much fuller and richer experience than if the client were to remember only an image. In situations where you are not using amnesia, you can also give the posthypnotic suggestion that the client practice remembering the future experience two or three times in the next week. This is a suggestion that we have heard Steve Lankton give to subjects on numerous occasions.

SELECTED TRANSCRIPT MATERIAL

Group Induction of Future Progression at a Workshop for Therapists Learning Hypnosis

So you can begin to make yourself comfortable in all theways that you already know how to and you can allow yourself to focus gently on the sound of my voice in your conscious mind while perhaps your unconscious mind focuses on the sound of your own inner voice. You can maintain that dual perspective as you allow yourself to head down slowly, or perhaps quickly, into a trance state that you can find pleasurable inside or outside. And as you head down into trance you might want to allow yourself to search back in time to the experience of a good trance you've had before…remember vividly and reexperience vividly just what that deep trance was like and how your body felt with that experience and just how good your mind felt with that deepest experience of trance. I don't know where you had that experience and I certainly don't know when you had that experience but I do think that you can allow yourself to reexperience that trance again here and now, now like then, now and then, again and again, over and over again. And you really can recognize, as you absorb yourself in that great experience, you can recognize that if I say anything that doesn't feel quite right, you can ignore it, and if there is something you'd like to hear that I don't say, you can say it to yourself, for yourself, and respond to that suggestion also.

And I don't know whether you'll be surprised, or whether you'll expect it, but the best experience of trance can get even better over time as the next moment becomes this moment becomes the last moment and is yesterday. And how tomorrow can be today and then can be last week. Next Sunday is this Sunday is last month's Sunday. And how you can experience time moving quicker and quicker, forward to a time when you're experiencing yourself over a certain problem or achieving a certain end. I certainly don't know exactly what that could be but I wonder how many of you would really like to experience yourself now as an accomplished virtuoso of Ericksonian hypnosis—even better than you were at the conference. Virtuosos with techniques that you have mastered with therapeutic skills of all sorts, appropriate and accurate empathy with your clients, technical mastery as well as close alliance and rapport. I'd like you to experience yourself in that place, experiencing it through your own eyes and looking at it through your own eyes. What is there to see? Does it have a smell—perhaps the wood in an office? The special smell that houses or offices have, maybe even smells like the smell of a special ink pen or fountain pen. What is there to touch? Is there a special and favorite therapy chair? Allow all your senses to experience this completely and fully.

You can remain absorbed in this experience, really having mastered the practice of hypnosis, being effective and appropriately caring—bringing yourself along at a pace that's just right for you, really developing as a therapist, really developing as a therapist, heart, soul, mind and body...developing into the therapist that you know you can be and feeling really comfortable in that fashion....

And perhaps in the one minute of clock time that you have to use this experience fully, it can feel like an hour or even two hours of experiencing...taking your time and absorbing yourself in it for as long as you need. Even if you come back before the experience is over, you can experience it again and again, now and then,

then as well as now. And you can allow yourself, too, to have a dream. I don't know whether the dream will be tonight, or whether you'll have the dream later on, but I do know that you can have a dream, a very vivid dream about the experience of yourself as a wonderful therapist, a very vivid dream, a dream that you can have easily and comfortably. And so you can reexperience it as often as you would find useful and you can experience it unconsciously even while your conscious mind does something else, if you wish. So the practice and the re-remembering can take place effortlessly even when you don't know that it's happening, even when it's outside of your awareness. These changes can be taking place and the memories can be accumulating, the memories of that experience and incredible competency and caring and full ethical responsibility. All the pieces can come in place.

And perhaps if you'd like, you can now absorb yourself in that experience for the one minute of clock time [time passes silently]. That's right. Now you can allow yourself to experience some of the experiences that led up to where you are now....

I wonder what those can be, perhaps you know what they are and perhaps your unconscious mind can give them to you now as experiences, as gifts of what led up to this moment, or perhaps you'll just need to be curious about how it all took place. Perhaps you won't even care because maybe the important thing to you is that it did happen and somehow intuitively you orchestrated it all, somehow you knew a whole heck of a lot more than you knew that you knew. And maybe the succession of experiences leading up is clear and maybe it's just a few or maybe there's just a wonderful innocent curiosity as to how to it all took place.

A minute or two of clock time is over now and you can allow those experiences to taper and come down to a satisfactory end point. And as that happens, you can recognize that last Sunday can become this Sunday and can once again be next Sunday. And that's OK because you can revisit all these places as often as you'd like. As you come back to the present time you can recognize that you can have a choice either to remember the experience fully and completely or you can forget as much of the experience as you would like. You can forget as much as would be useful to you, even the whole thing if you wish. Or, you may allow yourself to remember with your conscious mind half the experience and your unconscious mind the whole experience. You don't need to remember anything but you may want to. And so last month can become this month can become once again next month.

And you can find yourself reorienting, allowing yourself to come up and as you come up out of trance, I'd like you to give yourself a hand, coming up to face things with a new perspective. I'd like you to allow yourself to reorient to the external world and as you come up and out of trance I'd like you to recognize that you can, if you want, keep as much of the experiences that you've had...and you can keep it throughout the day, you can keep it throughout the conference for as long as you'd like.

Section C

Duality of Reality

Chapter 10

DISSOCIATION

ABOUT THE PHENOMENON

Dissociation refers to one part of a person's mental or physical experience functioning distinctly and independently from another part. This usually entails the person's mind dividing itself up in some way, such as visual images being distinct from emotions or, in its extreme, even two or more separate personalities sharing one mind. However, dissociation can also involve one part of the person's body experienced as being separate from another part. It can also involve a person feeling a sense of detachment from the immediate physical environment and the events taking place in it. An important aspect of dissociation is that the dissociated parts of the person are autonomous or semiautonomous in that they function with some degree of independence from one another.

Dissociations happen naturally with or without trance. Kroger (1963) likens the detachment of dissociation to reveries that people experience in the course of absorbed thought. Erickson believed that hypnotic trance did not necessarily or always entail dissociation and that dissociation was one characteristic of trance, but other theorists, namely Hilgard (1977), viewed dissociation as the fundamental phenomenon upon which the experience of hypnosis rests; in this latter view, all hypnosis entails dissociation.

It is important to understand that dissociation is a mental mechanism that can be used either productively or counterproductively. Most often, as therapists, we hear about dissociation in connection with its maladaptive uses. Dissociative disorders such as multiple personality states, fugue states, feelings of derealization, depersonalization, dissociated affects (no feelings connected to a memory or an immediate experience), or dissociation buttressing amnesia and repression that keep one from remembering anything about his or her past are some of the many manifestations of dissociation that come to our professional attention. But dissociation has its adaptive aspects, too.

We dissociate in normal, healthy ways daily as an essential part of navigating through life. For example, we all dissociate from preoccupying personal worries when we are in session with clients so that our work with them is not compromised. We dissociate from distracting auditory stimuli (e.g., a telephone ringing, someone whispering) to engage fully in a really good movie. In fact, we couldn't even walk down the street if we were fully associated! Imagine constantly thinking to yourself, "Move the right foot forward, look up, move the left foot forward, bend this ankle, look here, slide the right arm forward, now the left arm forward." When our automatic pilot takes over, we are using dissociation adaptively to live our lives. In his survey of the literature, Lars-Eric Uneståhl (1988) reports that studies repeatedly find that 90 to 95 percent of our lives are lived in this kind of automatic way.

HISTORY AND EXPERIMENTAL STUDIES

The vast majority of articles published on dissociation in the last decade are designed either to prove or to disprove the neodissociation theory of Ernest Hilgard. This theory of Ernest Hilgard's posits that dissociation is the essence of the hypnotic experience and that as it takes place, certain parts of the person's mental functioning remain outside of central awareness. These subparts, however, retain the knowledge and experiential base accessible during nonhypnotic states regardless of the dissociation present. This is referred to as the "hidden observer phenomenon" (Hilgard & Hilgard, 1994). With specific regard to the major hypnotic phenomena, Hilgard classified these as forms of "divided consciousness." Because of their limited focus, these articles have little direct bearing on clinical practice.

A couple of exceptions were found. Haule (1986) describes in some detail the contributions of Pierre Janet to our current understanding of the importance of dissociation in hypnosis. Whether or not you believe, along with Janet (and Hilgard), that the essential core of the hypnotic experience is dissociation, it is important to credit him for a multitude of discoveries regarding this phenomenon. For example, Janet was the first to describe somnambulism (very deep and dissociated trance states in which subjects appear awake) as a phenomenon within which dissociation—or a lack of awareness of what one is doing—allows one to later move through the world remembering nothing of what took place during the hypnosis. Janet also shed some light on a variety of other hypnotic phenomena, since dissociation was considered by him to be the foundation experience allowing many other types of phenomena to develop. One example is amnesia. He thought of this as not being a matter of psychogenic forgetting but rather a matter of information being in one part of the mind, dissociated, or kept apart from another part of the mind. Likewise, the experience often observed of the hypnotic subject perceiving and responding only to the hypnotist is thought of by many as involving negative hallucination. Janet, however, describes this experience as reflecting the subject's complete dissociation from others in the immediate environment.

Bartis and Zamansky (1986) also describe dissociation as being an underlying factor in other hypnotic phenomena. They chose to study amnesia and, in line with Janet, see it as actually entailing a dissociation of knowledge where different parts of the mind are unaware of certain information. In this fine piece of research, they demonstrate that at a conscious level, a person can forget having learned some information in a laboratory sorting task while he or she later performs the same task at a much better than average expected level. They convincingly demonstrate that unconscious and dissociated knowledge influences conscious performance unbeknownst to a subject.

In testing the neodissociation theory of Ernest Hilgard, Stava and Jaffa (1988) discuss some findings that bear on clinical practice. A corollary of neodissociation theory postulates that the extent to which a person dissociates in everyday life is indicative of how good a hypnotic subject he or she would be, as measured by scales of hypnotic susceptibility. Most practicing clinicians would assume this from their clinical experience. However, these researchers found that performance on everyday tasks entailing or necessitating dissociation (these tasks were converted so they could be standardly employed in the laboratory) did **not** predict how hypnotizable a person was.

INDICATIONS FOR USE

Dissociation can be indicated as a therapeutic strategy when a person uses it—typically unwittingly—as a mechanism that is creating the problem. This is the case with people suffering from a dissociative disorder. First of all, these individuals go into trance easily because they dissociate so naturally. The hypnotherapy can be organized around the idea of helping them *learn to control* the dissociation. You teach them how to begin the (controlled) dissociative experience, which in the context of the therapy takes the form of trance, then how to modulate it, and finally how to end it with associational strategies. Dolan's (1991) book on resolving trauma and abuse describes a number of ways to help clients turn the symptom of dissociation into a resource for healing. Capitalizing therapeutically on a client's dissociative tendencies for a smaller facet of the hypnotherapy can be useful as well. Gilligan (1990) used the dissociative method of ideomotor finger signaling with a woman whose symptoms of severe stomach pain had a dissociative quality to it.

Dissociation may also be therapeutically used when it is the *opposite* of the phenomenon that creates the problem. These are your clients who are **too** associative with the internal and external worlds. These individuals have great difficulty dissociating in natural and functional ways and remain too tied up in their everyday world. An example of this kind of person is one who is chronically worried about every unresolved aspect of his or her life. The ability to stop worrying unnecessarily requires a person to be able to dissociate on his or her own behalf. Other examples are people who have problems managing stress and complain that they can't leave their work behind them when they come home from the office.

Another opportunity to use dissociation in therapy is when it is a phenomenon that the person characteristically does effectively. For example, perhaps a surgeon comes to you because she is feeling overwhelmed by the sweeping changes in her hospital's administration and personnel that are affecting her work. You ask her, "How did you perform as a surgeon when you were going through that divorce of yours?" And she answers, "Oh, I just pushed it out of my head." This person becomes a perfect candidate for dissociation as a current strategy for a change.

There are a number of clinical groups that could particularly benefit from selecting dissociation as a therapeutic intervention. The dissociative disorders come to mind here. In addition to these, though, you can use dissociational strategies any time a person needs to separate two things in order to overcome a problem. For example, use it with an insomniac who can't keep his or her everyday worries out of mind. Use it with the athlete who gets easily distracted by the crowd or by salary arbitration. Use dissociation with someone who has taken reasonable steps to solve financial problems but is still worrying about money. Use it with the college student whose parents' divorce proceedings are interfering with her studies. Dissociation can be a helpful resource for the depressive who remains so stuck in his pessimism or sense of help-lessness that it threatens to seep into the core self-image of the person. In such an instance, dissociation functions as a *wedge* between the de-pressed client's self-esteem and his present feelings about himself, so that the latter ceases to compromise the former. An example of how we would use the phenomenon of dissociation in this way is the following:

> ....*You can bring to mind the idea of this wedge. It can come to you in the form of an image or of simply a concept, abstract to your conscious mind and exquisitely material to your unconscious. So that your unconscious can take this wedge, and begin to find the suitable placement, inside, softly, carefully resting the edge between that one part of you that has felt lost and hopeless, between this and that* **other** *part of you that has remained untainted by the sadness, left whole and hopeful still. And it can be* **this** *whole part that stays...operative...no matter what... ascending...separate and whole...allowing you to function, and to heal.*

Similarly, dissociation can be used with the depressed individual who has obsessive leanings, who cannot disengage from mental im-mersion into his or her shortcomings. In such a case, the person may repeatedly call forth proofs of personal or professional failure for ru-mination. Cognitive therapists have pointed out to us that depressed people often focus only on their failings. Using hypnosis, then, you can help these people to become more associated with their successes and somewhat dissociated from their shortcomings, thereby creating a healthier mental balance. Likewise, clients suffering from an anxiety disorder can often benefit from a dose of dissociation. It is very com-mon for someone with a phobia, for example, to take something that is, in reality, *somewhat* anxiety-provoking but remain too connected with it, too associated to it, "lost in it" so to speak. Dissociation is useful to help them regain distance.

I (JSE) used dissociation to help a woman keep at (mental) bay nega-tive statements she repeatedly said to herself that were undermining her confidence and professional functioning as a mental health coun-selor. Interestingly, the presenting problem at the start of therapy was an excessive, paralyzing degree of dissociation precipitated by anxiety. For this individual, the proclivity to dissociate was so much a part of her emotional functioning that trying to fight it head on would have been futile or, at best, a long-term course of action. Instead, it was better to utilize it, to find some way to have the presenting problem abate without attempting to restructure her psychological and characterological tendencies. In this instance, the client's dissociation was acknowledged in trance as an integral part of her personality, was *thanked* for its well-meaning but misguided attempts to protect her from overwhelming anxiety, and then offered a "different job." This new position would be *to keep the negative self-statements dissociated from the client's conscious awareness rather than to keep the client dissociated from her environment*. Thus, two problems were resolved by the simple redirecting of innate dissociative tendencies—the initial presenting problem and the secondary problem of toxic self-talk. Follow-up through several months indicated sustained positive results.

Dissociation in the body is a major means of controlling pain (see Erickson, 1980f, Vol. IV; Lankton & Lankton, 1983). It serves as a foundation for the development of anesthesia (Kroger, 1963) and can be used to separate a person from pain anywhere in the body. The physical dissociation can take place along many lines—upper body versus lower body, dorsal versus ventral, head versus body, above versus below the waist, right versus left. Women giving birth can benefit from a dissociation from their pelvic region; you can speak of *psychogenic epidurals* that allow them to push when necessary but escape any undesirable sensation. People with needle phobias can dissociate from their arms, and dental phobics can learn to dissociate from their entire bodies and "go somewhere else" for 20 minutes or so.

CONTRAINDICATIONS

Avoid using dissociative intervention strategies right off the bat with clients for whom dissociation (especially dissociation taking place outside of the therapy setting) has been associated with frightening, anxiety-arousing, or overwhelming affects or thoughts. This can inadvertently lead to the client's feeling panicked, depressed, or out of control in session. Until such an individual has developed an adequate sense of personal control and knows how to exit a bad ego state, or knows how to constructively use your presence and support as a therapist, it is better to spend more time building resources of control over the trance experience and over affects and then find a way to use hypnotically induced dissociation to help with the presenting problem of nontherapeutic dissociation. People who regress too far and lose the ability to use the therapy are better off staying integrated in the here and now during trancework rather than dissociating and risking a loss of ego control. Further, dissociation as a therapeutic intervention should be used judiciously with trauma survivors to avoid retraumatization.

Dissociation may also be contraindicated with the client who dissociates off into a withdrawn, autistic state that he or she is subsequently not able to process with the therapist. These contraindications are less absolute than they appear depending upon the hypnotic expertise of the therapist and the quality of the working relationship.

ELICITING THE PHENOMENON OF DISSOCIATION

Direct and Indirect Suggestion

You can **seed** dissociation as an intervention as soon as the hypnosis starts. This is ideally done by selecting conscious/unconscious dissociation for your induction strategy. You could say that *"your conscious mind can go down into trance slowly, while your unconscious mind goes down into trance quite quickly."* Other dissociative statements related to induction include, *"You can wonder with your conscious mind what kind of trance you'll develop today as your unconscious mind simply goes about the business of doing it."* (See Lankton & Lankton, 1983, for a full discussion of this strategy and numerous examples.) By using conscious/unconscious dissociation statements for induction, you have already begun the process of engendering dissociation without yet connecting it to the problem to be solved.

You can use **evocative language** to produce a dissociative reaction in a client, too. For example, you can incorporate the following phrases into your hypnosis: *divide up, get some distance, that part of you can become independent, disconnected from, apart from, you can put that aside.*

Consider inserting **presuppositions** to bring forth dissociation. These statements work by assuming that the phenomenon is going to happen soon. An example is, *"When you begin to really wander off in your thoughts, you can enjoy the freedom and go a bit further from those down into trance."* In this example, presupposition and deepening work hand in hand. Another example of presupposition is, *"As you notice a separateness beginning to take place, you might allow your unconscious mind to begin exploring how useful it will be when you are having your baby."* This latter example seeds the posthypnotic suggestion that would be given to this pregnant woman once she learns to generate and recognize dissociation in the form of separation (mind/body or upper body/lower body or excitement/discomfort, whichever is most suitable or personally preferable).

Double binds can also be used to evoke dissociation. You can say, for example, *"The dissociation that we're seeking can occur all at once or* *gradually"* or *"Dissociation can be complete or perhaps 90% involved"* or *"You can be totally absorbed in that one thing or just be utterly unaware of anything else but one important thing."*

Conscious/unconscious statements are especially useful here, as mentioned in the section on seeding, because the very structure of the language creates the desired phenomenon without any mention of the word "dissociation." Erickson's inductions were often characterized by methodical delineations between the different minds (or levels of mental functioning, really) without frank mention of what process or phenomenon was being sought (Lankton & Lankton, 1983). You can opt to directly mention dissociation as the phenomenon desired depending upon whether direct or indirect suggestion would suit the client better and be more effective. You might say, *"Your conscious mind can be fully absorbed in the exam as your unconscious mind keeps repeating 'you can take care of those other concerns later.'"* Or, *"Your conscious mind can choose to allow that other personality to come out now, while your unconscious mind begins a process of negotiation between the two personalities so that everyone's needs can get met together."*

Triggers for Constructive Dissociation and the Use of Mental Props

What is helpful to certain clients is the ability to dissociate quickly and suddenly, on a cue provided by themselves. Trauma survivors working in therapy are sometimes at risk for affective flooding or flashbacks as they confront their past, especially if they have not yet developed adequate new and flexible defenses to replace the crumbling repression, denial, and so on. Triggers that the person has at the ready in order to self-induce a stabilizing dissociation can be essential tools (Dolan, 1991; Schwarz, 1993). Athletes also can benefit tremendously from having a trigger that immediately helps them dissociate constructively from anxiety, doubt, external distractions, or (nonthreatening) pain.

One young show jumping rider I (JSE) worked with used to say the word *"later!"* to herself whenever intrusive worries came to mind right before going into the competition arena. That served to vanquish the thoughts for the next several minutes as she immersed herself in her performance. Other athletes I work with have used the following triggers to set in motion a dissociative process that carried them through their performances, untouched by irrelevant thoughts or unhelpful feelings: touching an earring prior to entering the performance ring; putting on one's helmet; and stepping up to the batting plate. With yet others I help them set up *mental props* that serve to deflect negative, intruding thoughts. Examples are mental fly swatters, cans of Raid, deadbolt locks, cavalry brigades, bouncers, or an Aladdin. They all serve to preserve the good head set, and these skills for the playing field can be of equal service on the performance stage or in life generally.

Naturalistic Examples of Dissociation

One of the easiest ways to bring forth dissociation is by reminding your clients of how they and others do this repeatedly in everyday life. As a matter of fact, dissociation is one of the easiest hypnotic phenomena to produce, in part because it is so common as an everyday experience, but also because it is almost always a part of the trance experience. Not only can you remind a person about how frequently it occurs day in and day out, you can also point out how it has probably been part of his or her trance experience already. The experience is usually recognizable to the person. A statement said by a client in trance to the effect of "This is interesting. I feel as if a part of me is listening to what you're saying and yet an entirely different part of me is daydreaming" is an example of a subject recognizing a dissociative episode even if he or she doesn't call it that.

As mentioned earlier, the other way to evoke dissociation in the present naturalistically is to remind the person how he or she has done it in the past. You can remind the client of how just about everyone has had the experience of getting into a car with the intention of travelling to a frequently visited place and then arriving there with little awareness of the trip itself. You can remind the person also of how one often doesn't remember the specific stop signs, the billboards, and the turns and yet realizes that these must have been observed and responded to or else he or she wouldn't be at the destination. There are endless examples of how we go on "automatic pilot" to our advantage in everyday life. Stories can be told of how to walk, drive a standard gear, fold our arms across each other, bathe ourselves, or scratch an itch without really thinking about what the sequence of movements is to accomplish any of these activities. Offering naturalistic examples to bring forth dissociation serves to validate Erickson's theory that healing or self-correcting resources often lie right inside the person. Your task as a therapist using hypnosis in psychotherapy then becomes one of reminding clients of this and of getting them to use these resources to resolve their current problems.

I (JSE) also like to use the image of a tennis player playing at the net, deflecting the ball out before it even gets into the home court. I tell clients (in or out of trance) that they can have their own net ball player inside their heads, ready to send back any thought, feeling, attitude, or self-statement that is unwelcomed. I also have clients imagining Plexiglas shields, or bubbles, with semipermeable boundaries around their heads or whole bodies, to reinforce their feelings of being able to be a part of and apart from their surroundings at the same time. With these two tools, people who need to dissociate from some internal stimulus and those needing to dissociate from an external stimulus can be helped.

Symbols

It can be very helpful to use tangible and manipulable symbols that are representative of dissociation. One way of doing this is to have dolls or animals whose parts come off. The therapist and the child or adult can toy with taking off an arm, putting it back on, taking off a leg, putting it back on. This can symbolize a dissociation useful for dealing with frightening or uncomfortable medical procedures or for achieving pain control directly, or as one aspect of a pain control intervention—that is, dissociation as a prelude to upcoming anesthesia for the dissociated part. The main contraindication for this is if the person has extreme body injury fears, wherein the disconnection of body parts on a doll arouses anxiety. Be mindful of individuals in developmental stages such as oedipal and preadolescent that predisposes them to these kinds of (unconscious) anxieties.

Another nice symbol for dissociation is the nested doll, like the traditional Russian ones. We have these in our office—when you open one up, there is another smaller replica inside. You open that one up and there is another inside, and so forth. This is a terrific symbol for a person who has ever deeper, dissociated facets to his or her personality (symbolized when you take all the dolls out and put them separately on the floor) that can be reintegrated (symbolized when the dolls are put back together in their nested state). Other symbols are limited only by the therapist's imagination.

Dissociation as a Symbol

Dissociation that is experienced in trance can be used in a symbolic way for other therapeutic goals. That is, it can function itself as a symbol. Consider, for example, a person who is very intellectual but totally cut off or dissociated from his or her body and senses. The idea here would be to put the client into trance and then suggest that his or her head remains in trance while his or her body comes out of trance. This symbolic use of dissociation indirectly suggests that the person's body *wake up and begin to feel.* (This can be called the "mindless body technique"!) A related strategy reverses the aforementioned procedure. Here, you have the person's head come out of trance while *"from the shoulders down you remain completely in trance."* This "bodyless mind technique" could be useful for someone who has not adequately developed his or her intellect, someone overly hysterical in personality, for instance.

SELECTED TRANSCRIPT MATERIAL

Dissociation, Conscious/ Unconscious

....I know that the last time that we worked together doing hypnosis, you had an experience ultimately of feeling very relaxed...you described it as feeling as if you were in a hot tub...and that even while all that was taking place, there was a part of your thinking that was absorbed in something else...that it was thinking about things that you had to do or might have to do later....And it's perfectly okay that this take place again at this time...that with your conscious mind you can continue to think about, even ruminate if you wish to, about what calls you need to make...about who you need to get back to...about what item of correspondence you need to get out in the mail this week...next week...and what errands need to be run...or what needs to be done around the house...and I want you to understand that there is nothing at all inconsistent with having those particular thoughts or ruminations and having a very solid, authentic and useful trance experience....

And there are even times, Anna, when I will encourage someone to think about those sorts of things...so that while that's happening at a very conscious level, at an unconscious level what can be happening is something altogether different...and you can be curious about the ways in which you can experience a dual level of awareness...as you maintain all the elements of control over your conscious experience as you wish to...your breathing rhythm can continue to slow, you can continue to pay bits of attention to the breathing...every once in a while coming back to that as you move down...the breathing rhythm that somebody might have if she were actually in a hot tub and that water was a very good temperature...as you sink downward, your conscious mind can attend to the sounds around you, the sound not only of my voice, but of clicks of machines and birds outside and even the generator....It can pay attention to all kinds of external stimuli and feel free to do so and even absorb itself in the rhythm of sounds outside you and the discrepancy between soft sounds and hard sounds...you can even think about the difference in decibel levels, between the sound of that machine, the sound of my voice, and the sound of this dictation machine next to me....

Dissociation, Mind/Body

....You might have been aware of a variety of things with your conscious mind...and your unconscious mind might have been aware of different experiences...this idea of there being a conscious mind and there being an unconscious mind parallels very nicely, Liz, the idea of your mind thinking about doing things and your body thinking about doing things...and the interesting thing about that is that the body really doesn't think about doing things, it just simply does things....Perhaps you've watched a child learn to ride a bicycle and you can remember that nobody ever really teaches anybody how to ride...a child simply gets on, straddles a bike...and allows the experience of being able to ride to evolve very naturally....I remember being at a birthday party...and there was a bicycle laying around and I had never had one that didn't have training wheels on it....I don't remember what the other kids were doing— maybe they were playing pin the tail or musical chairs or red light, green light, but I simply went over to the bike and straddled it...and allowed a sense of body knowledge to come out and so I moved in certain ways that either sustained balance, or didn't...and those muscle movements that were balancing were maintained, while those movements that made me fall I forgot about....I didn't really think about it, I simply just did it....

Dissociation, Mind/Body

....I think it can be important for you to trust that your body just has an enormous capacity in this regard...to separate from conscious awareness, to go off on its own...bye-bye...so long...see you later when it's all over....Bye!...

Dissociation, Mind/Body for a Woman Preparing for Child- birth

....Ultimately you will be the one and you need to be the one to find the precise way in which your body will so effortlessly allow you to drift off, for as long as you like between each contraction. It will take care of this while you take a break, rest up, there'll still be more work to do when you come back...so go ahead, when the time's right...as soon as you feel the swell of the contraction going away, you go rest...sleep....

Dissociation of Knee Pain During Staircase Induction for Pain Relief

So, now you can turn around and begin your ascent up the safe staircase...as you do, you can begin to bring most of you up and out of trance, you can leave your knees in trance, you can leave your knees in trance if you wish, you can leave them in the warm, comfort- able, numb way of trance if you wish...and the extent to which they stay in trance can be adjusted by your conscious wishes and your subconscious mind can respond...that's how the conscious mind can ask for co- operation from the subconscious mind...so, your knees can remain in trance and have that numb, warm tin- gling feeling to the extent that you need....You'll be able to walk fine, you'll be able to drive fine, the extent to which your knees are in trance will vary depending on situations, depending on context, but you don't need to have any pain, you can have comfort there—some numbness...loss of sensation, some adjustment to the situation...so, you can step up to step three, step up to step two...noticing again the plush soft carpet beneath your feet like a cushion...up to step one like a cushion....

Dissociation for Pain Control for a Psychologist

....T. X. Barber describes the experience of going to an ear, nose, and throat specialist and having some polyps removed from the upper portion of his nose...he was able to do it by separating the sensation from the per- ception. Now, as a psychologist you may be very inter- ested in this experience, that you can separate your primary sensory strip on your mind, on your brain, from the perceptual strip, secondary perceptual strip...and you can hypnotically create a secondary lesion in that part of the brain that controls head pain perception....T. X. Barber felt the sensation divorced from the perception...snip, snip, snip...cutting sensation, that's all...like many people in hypnosis, he just needed to convince the surgeon that everything was fine—that's where most of the work needed to be done...deeper and deeper down...so deep that, like many dental patients, you can have root canal work done and the experience of any discomfort would merely send you deeper down into trance....I have a patient who was claustrophobic...and who didn't like loud sounds...of course, you know she had to have an M.R.I....she was very panicky. She asked her subconscious mind for help. She was put in the machine and that's the last thing she remembers. The next thing was, she was out. And where did she go?...I don't know...perhaps you don't know...but your subconscious knows a lot more than you do...and you can respect that knowledge, that information....

Dissociation for Head-ache Pain Control

....You can have a headache and not be aware of it. Just about everybody's had the experience of cutting their finger while chopping vegetables and not knowing it until they see the blood and only then do you feel some pain...during wartime soldiers get shot, but they carry their friend back to safety and then and only then real-ize that they've been shot...and as you become certain that as long as everything that needs to be done medi-cally has been done, then you can ignore the pain...you can realize that as long as everything that needs to be done diagnostically has been done, you can ignore the pain, you can realize that if everything that needs to be done in terms of intervention has been done, you can ignore the pain...it's not important. It's a false signal, it's a signal that you don't have to pay any attention to...like a traffic light that everybody knows is wacky...like an alarm that goes off, but it's intended for somebody else and you sleep right through it....

Chapter 11

HYPNOTIC DREAMING AND DAYDREAMING

ABOUT THE PHENOMENON

Hypnotically induced dreams can be a useful and clinically significant phenomenological experience for a client. They manifest in the client as either pseudodreaming (akin to daydreaming), dreaming during trance, or responding to posthypnotic suggestions for dreaming at night during sleep. Dreams have long been recognized as a rich resource for personal growth, and Ericksonian psychology as a whole has capitalized on this productively.

When a therapist uses hypnosis to suggest dreaming in session, the range of responses can fall on a continuum. We have observed that more talented subjects, well-practiced subjects, highly motivated subjects, and good dreamers can have a full-blown dream, complete with REM activity. People falling at the opposite end of the continuum will merely see an image or, somewhat better, have a daydream. Posthypnotic suggestions for night dreaming often result in regular dreams that have some pertinence to the presenting problem or clinical issue at hand.

HISTORY AND EXPERIMENTAL STUDIES

The last couple of decades have not seen much research performed on hypnotic dreaming. The single good exception to this statement is the article by Albert and Boone (1975) regarding both dream deprivation and facilitation with hypnosis. The authors begin with a substantial review of prior research demonstrating that posthypnotic suggestion for dreaming can influence dreams and alter the content of dreams at night. In fact, this was the thrust of the active research agenda on hypnosis in dreaming that produced numerous articles in the 1960s. That hypnotic suggestion is the most powerful way to influence dream content was more than adequately documented, and perhaps it is because of this documentation that research is this area of hypnosis began to slow down. In any event, Albert and Boone demonstrate in the experimental part of their paper that hypnotic suggestion can induce dream deprivation such that experimental subjects experience a blocking of their dreams or a repeated wakening.

This bit of data can have some valuable ramifications for clients who are chronically disturbed at night by frightening dreams or frank nightmares. However, a caveat is that the subjects in this dream-deprivation condition often felt that their experiences were negative or aversive. There was also some suggestion of reduced REM activity as measured by EEG equipment for this condition. Aversion may not be the reaction in clinical applications where the dreams to be blocked are unpleasant ones; nonetheless, one should be cautious about the medium- or long-term effects of dream deprivation in general should suggestions for blocking the bad dreams impact upon a client's more general dream activity during the night.

The authors also demonstrate that hypnosis can facilitate increased dreaming, wherein subjects report not only more frequent dreams, but also say that they are more pleasurable ones. However, a corresponding finding of more REM activity on EEG was not found in the dream-facilitation group. The EEG results are suggestive only and are not as solid as the more central findings that both dream deprivation and facilitation can be elicited through hypnotic suggestion.

INDICATIONS FOR USE

Hypnotic dreaming should be used with people who are good at dreaming. These are the individuals who come into the therapy session reporting dreams even when no mention has been made yet of their use in therapy or hypnosis.

Another time to use dreaming can be when dreams are a part of the problem. Hence, hypnotic dreaming is strongly indicated for people whose presenting problems entail nightmares and sleepwalking. Used in this situation, hypnotic dreaming can lead the client's nighttime mental activity away from distressing material and toward more benign content. The person is already dreaming at night, and so it can be explained during a hypnotic trance that the task for the unconscious is only to switch channels or screenwriters or directors. "Same time, same place, different show" is much easier to effect than suggesting something completely different across the board.

Clients can also be instructed to make bargains with themselves in these instances, that is, to negotiate with the part that has been sending up these awful stories and pictures in the form of nightmares. By reframing the unconsciously driven mental activity as reflecting the client's inner wisdom regarding what issues/feelings/circumstances still need working through, the client can then simultaneously *thank* its unconscious/wise self for the tip and ask it to help out in a different way, perhaps by sending up *dreams with solutions, dreams with poignant symbols, dreams with hope or humor.* An excerpt from this kind of hypnotherapy might go as follows:

> *....Your unconscious mind has been working so hard at night, working overtime in a valiant effort to communicate something it thought important for you to know...you can appreciate that, and appreciate the fact that it thought it was doing the right thing, the helpful thing...but now you can encourage that part of yourself to change, to adopt a new way to be helpful....It can know now that you are aware of those other things, and are ready for **new** pictures at night, **new** sounds at night, **different** people with a **different** and **gentler** message, **softer**, more subtle, perhaps more inviting, these dreams, **peaceful** dreams, dreams you can learn from in a different way...tonight is OK to have that kind of dream, whenever you're ready...your unconscious mind understands now the difference, and how it can easily lend a hand....*

Hypnotic dreaming is also indicated when it serves as a symbol, metaphor, or idiom for the therapy. For example, depressed clients and clients without a feeling of hope can be engaged in hypnotic dreaming as a way of indirectly suggesting that *"you can have a dream for the future."* Likewise, a workaholic can be asked to have a hypnotic dream about being on vacation, an indirect suggestion to the person to go on a *"dream vacation."* Likewise, someone stuck in the dating and courtship process can dream about romantic encounters as a way of concretizing the notion of going out on a *"dream date"* and being out with a *"woman/man of your dreams."*

Another clinical situation in which hypnotic dreaming can be helpful is when the client requires the change process to be private and/or autonomous. Here, suggestions for the person to *discover answers, illuminate issues, lift amnesias,* or *integrate learnings* can all take place not in the immediate context of the therapeutic relationship but in the privacy of the client's own thoughts and psychology. It can subsequently be shared with the therapist if so desired. Erickson (1966/1980) described an exquisite use of in-session, hypnotically induced dreaming in the case of a hospitalized man diagnosed with catatonic schizophrenia who had been verbally and interpersonally unresponsive to staff for three years. The suggestion he gave to this patient in hypnosis was to "dream informatively about his problem" (p. 59). He had specifically chosen this intervention figuring that a dream, more than dialogue, would be an acceptable arena for change because, like the catatonia, it was an inner experience whereas direct communication was not. The man was able to respond to this suggestion for dreaming and worked with Erickson in an increasingly open and direct fashion with marvelous results.

Hypnotic dreaming can also serve as a means of imaginal behavioral rehearsal. A colleague of ours using dreaming with a 24-year-old bulimic female reported her client regularly having dreams in which she appropriately asserted her boundaries with an overbearing mother. The client would follow each of these dream experiences by enacting the very verbal assertion of which she dreamed. This seems illustrative of Rossi's belief (Rossi, 1971;1972 a,b;1973 a,b,c) that dreams provide us with opportunities to synthesize new phenomenological realities that become bases of new patterns of identity and behavior.

CONTRAINDICATIONS

One apparent contraindication to this technique is if, by virtue of the client's personality constellation, an increased degree of introspection and turning inward would be counterproductive. This includes some pain patients who are too focused on their bodies, and people who are excessively and unproductively analytical. On the other hand, the astute clinician will recognize when utilizing these traits through hypnotic dreaming is in fact especially indicated; for those clients who cannot or need not be bumped out of their characteristic way of mental processing, internal absorption through dreaming may be their ticket out of a mental rut.

Another contraindication is with clients who need a certain degree of structure in the therapy and/or relationship in order to maintain an adaptive level of functioning. Since this technique is relatively unstructured and uses a rather open-ended framework for hypnotic responding, clients who have structural vulnerabilities—either by way of generalized ego weaknesses manifested in severe character disorders, or who otherwise need lots of structure in the task or experience at hand—should generally not engage in this activity just in case the amorphous experience leads to maladaptive degrees of regression. This is not an absolute contraindication, but one that is well-heeded by the novice and intermediate hypnotherapy practitioner, lest they may find themselves in well over their heads.

ELICITING THE PHENOMENON OF HYPNOTIC DREAMING

Direct and Indirect Suggestion for In-Session Dreaming

Talking to your client about "dreamy" days, "dreamy" experiences, or "dreamy" desserts (remember *Dream Whip*?) can **seed** the phenomenon desired. Tell your client what you know about Morpheus, god of sleep. Introduce the hypnosis with a story, fairy tale, or song about dreaming or sleeping. Draw clients deeper into trance and seed at the same time by getting them absorbed in a favorite dream that they have. Invent any number of ways to naturally and fittingly hint to the unconscious about what is to come.

Direct suggestions for the phenomenon of hypnotic dreaming can be given as soon as your client manifests a state of responsivity following a hypnotic induction. Assessing clients' readiness to respond to your minimal cuing is an essential part of hypnotic work (Zeig, 1988a) as well as the therapist's way of knowing when to move from the induction phase of trancework to the intervention phase proper. Also, experienced hypnotherapists weave their interventions into all phases of a session and so the notion of rigid demarcations between intervention and nonintervention phases becomes a moot point. In any event, once a therapist knows that the client is in a receptive, responsive mode, he or she can go ahead with an induction something like the following:

...and as you remain in trance, you can begin to have a dream, right here, in this room, and it can be a very rich and full dream. It can be in color, vividly so, maybe one of the most vivid dreams

you've ever had or it can be a black and white dream, like a film noir, mysterious and telling, both. It can come slowly, in feathery fragments, or it can appear suddenly, surprising you with its clarity and wit.

Your dream can be one of three kinds. You can try out different solutions to your problems in the dreams, finding the alternative that's right for you. Alternatively, you can have a dream about yourself in which you're cured. Another possibility is just to dream about the problem in a way that will reveal new and useful aspects of the problem to you. And as you begin dreaming, you can let me know that you're dreaming by either allowing your right index finger to move or twitch up and down or your head to begin nodding slowly. After the dream comes to a satisfactory conclusion, those movements can stop.

There are a number of important aspects to the above statements. First of all, when you suggest dreaming activity, it's useful to have a way of monitoring the client's experience. That way you're not stuck sitting and watching a quiet person wondering if your suggestions have had any effect. In the example above, we give the suggestion for using either finger movements or head nodding. An alternative might be simply to suggest to the person that when a dream is over, he or she can come out of trance and describe the dream for you.

Hypnotic dreaming offers an ideal situation in which to incorporate talking trance; here the client describes the dream as it is taking place. It has the advantage of making the therapy more interactive and the client more of an active participant in the hypnotic process that is unfolding. However, even with the head-nodding and finger-signaling behavior, it is recommended that therapist and client discuss the dream. As Whitaker (1983) has said and researched, the hearing of a dream and the verbalizing of it with a caring person can be the most therapeutic aspect of dream work.

You'll notice also that the suggestions in the induction example above have a number of double binds contained within. **Double binds**, providing an illusion of alternatives, allow one to entice the client into responding in any of a variety of ways, each of which is desirable. Also contained within the direct suggestions to dream are indirect suggestions in the way of **presuppositions**. When you say "after the dream is over," the presupposed idea is that dreaming activity will indeed happen.

In addition, the induction offers alternatives for types of dreaming activity. Three major ways in which you can use dreaming in Ericksonian therapy are embodied within the suggestions above. One way offers the client a way to try out, from a distance, a variety of alternative solutions to problems. Another encourages an age-progression dream experience where the client dreams of himself or herself at a future time when the problem has been resolved. This serves as a point on the horizon to which the person can orient emotionally. And because the unconscious mind does not always distinguish between different temporal conditions or between reality and fantasy in a very definitive manner, the dream of being "cured" can, to some degree, take on an aura of reality for the client. He or she then orients toward that, not only as an imminent possibility, but also as a condition actually beginning to take place in the present.

The third possibility suggested is that the dream activity could provide ever more revealing insights into a person's condition or dilemma. This is particularly desirable when insight or self-awareness is important to the person or critical for change; this type of hypnotic dreaming tends to be favored by more psychodynamic hypnotherapists (Sacerdote, 1982).

Posthypnotic Suggestions for Night Dreaming

Clients who are not so responsive to suggestions to have a dream in session during trance may respond more readily to posthypnotic suggestions that the dream take place that night or the following night. Weitzenhoffer (1989b) comments that dreams taking place on the heels of posthypnotic suggestion are bound to be relevant to treatment even if no mention is made specifically to context, inasmuch as the client is in therapy and the suggestions take place in session. One suggestion could go as follows:

> *You can have a dream tonight or tomorrow night and it can be a dream about a solution or a number of possible solutions to your problem. You can try them on for size in the dream or dreams, or alternatively you can just have a dream about being over your problem, about what things will be like when everything is fine. On other nights you can dream about the steps that led up to being cured [note past tense, implying that cure has taken place], but perhaps this first dream can just be about that situation, when you know that your problems are behind you. Another suitable idea might be to have a dream that can be a symbol for the problem, helping your unconscious and conscious mind develop a new perspective.*

In analyzing the above suggestions, we find that here, too, we have double-bind suggestions (tonight or tomorrow night) as well as the three approaches to hypnotic dreaming (alternative solutions, age-progressed dreams, dreams as symbols). Including all these options has the advantage of appealing psychologically to resistive subjects and to those simply wishing to feel in charge of the processes of recovery. Postsession night dreaming can also be used as a prelude to in-session dreaming since it is easy to elicit and thus yields a success experience. Clients then feel considerably less pressure to have "something" happen on cue in session. In addition, because everyone sleeps, and most everyone dreams, therapists too can anticipate a response to their suggestions.

"The Rehearsal Technique"

Milton Erickson often used "the rehearsal technique" in working with dreams hypnotically. In his 1952 paper on creating deep trance states (Erickson, 1952/1980), he described the technique as follows:

> The rehearsal technique has been found useful in inducing deep trance and in studies of motivation, association of ideas, regression symbol analysis, repression and the development of insight. It has proven a most effective therapeutic procedure. This technique is primarily a matter of having the subject repeat over and over a dream, or, less preferably, a fantasy, in constantly differing guises. That is, he repeats the spontaneous dream or an induced dream with a different cast of characters, perhaps in a different setting, but with the same meaning. After the second dreaming the same instructions are given again, and this continues until the purposes to be served are accomplished. (1952/1980, p. 163)

Using this protocol, Erickson was able to help someone draw personal meaning from the dream. To the client, you can liken the process to a flower beginning to bloom, with the petals progressively becoming more and more open with each dream. Another metaphor for this approach is of an onion with the different layers being peeled off successively. Our understanding of this approach to hypnotic dreaming is that it embodies Erickson's belief that one important curative principle is making something that is static into something fluid and dynamic. Thus, we think it is safe to assume that Erickson believed that the meaning of the dream, and one's ability to understand it, was far less important than turning a frozen experience into something that could flow and evolve. The meaning of the dream was therefore probably a lot less important to him than the observations of significant changes in the dream over successive nights.

Provisions for Dealing with Resistance

With subjects who are not readily responsive to suggestions to dream you will need to find ways to have this hypnotic phenomenon become either more palatable or easier to experience. One way is to introduce a parameter that involves suggesting to clients that when they have the dreams on subsequent nights, they *"may allow themselves to remember the dream or not, and either way would be fine, but in either event, the dream can, if they wish, exert a significant influence on their being, and can have a very curative effect."* This is an effective double bind for slow starters or for resisters because it can never be said for certain that there was no response to the suggestion; this opens up the *possibility* that there was a response.

A second parameter for facilitating clients' experiences of hypnotic dreaming is to inform them that they can keep aspects of the dream private if they wish. The therapist says, *"You can have a healing dream, or a dream that is revealing in a way that's useful to you, but you don't need to discuss it in therapy. You can keep it entirely to yourself."* This can be especially useful for clients who are genuinely paranoid or for those who are self-conscious about what they are dreaming and thinking about. Encouraging privacy of dream content is also useful for people with a narcissistic character who may feel humiliated by revealing problems or personal parts of themselves to a therapist. Interpersonal disclosure is not always necessary for therapeutic progress and thinking about the possibilities for therapy in this (very) Ericksonian way can prevent a treatment from getting bogged down in a tug of war over talking for months or even years, which is what might happen in a traditional interactive therapeutic scenario. These parameters also underscore the (also very) Ericksonian idea that the presence of perceived resistance does not necessarily contraindicate a technique or the therapy itself.

SELECTED TRANSCRIPT MATERIAL

Hypnotic Dreaming and Age Progression for a Woman Who Wishes to Stop Smoking

....And when you were a girl, swimming...you probably dreamed about swimming...and those dreams could have been very vivid and very pleasurable...you could have a dream now, too...and your dreams can be about your future...they can be utterly pleasurable—so pleasurable that after you wake up, the pleasurable feelings inside can go with you through your day like a residue...you can dream about the future...you can

*Prior to
Getting
Pregnant*

dream about being utterly happy...and satisfied...you can dream about yourself as a mother, feeling comfortable, holding your child...and those dreams, vivid, they can be in bright colors...they can feel so incredibly real that after you wake up, you're not sure for a while whether it happened or it didn't....You're not sure whether, in fact, you're a mother...you're not sure whether it's not in fact 1998...the dreams can be so utterly convincing and real that their residue lingers with you through your day...you carry it with you, you hold it inside and the dreams can be about where you're going in life—the future...but the dreams can be so vivid, it's as if it's all happening right now in the present...so, they serve like a guiding light, guiding you into a comfortable port of safety.... They're like a lighthouse guiding you away from danger into a safe port, knowing where you're going, knowing how to navigate... incredibly vivid dreams, so vivid you'll be able to remember them years from now...turning point dreams, novel turning point dreams... dreams that signal a developmental milestone, a hallmark...markers, developmental marker dreams that take you in a certain direction... can be dreams about your personal life...could be a dream about a career move...your subconscious mind knows a lot more than you know it knows...it knows how to swim...it knows a lot of things that you put on cruise control....

*Hypnotic
Dreaming
for Hyper-
ventilation
Associated
with Panic
Attacks*

...so deep that you have a wonderful dream in trance now...dream of when you're cured and everything's all right. Your conscious mind might not even know what that dream is going to be, but your subconscious mind can produce it like a gift for you. It can happen momentarily...and your left pinky can lift if a dream fantasy unfolds for you...cured, breathing comfortably, easily...relating comfortably and easily...and you can wait, your conscious mind can wait, your subconscious mind can produce a vivid hypnotic dream of comfort and success and what it would take to breathe easily, take breathing lessons through the therapy, through the dream...deeply...and while you're waiting for your subconscious mind to produce that dream like a film beginning in a theater, you watch the screen and sooner or later the projectionist flips the switch and it begins automatically... and I don't know and maybe you don't know just what kind of situation cure that your unconscious has in mind for you...and you can wait for something to appear on that screen...perhaps eating your popcorn, perhaps munching on candy...perhaps with a friend, companion, comfortable, good choice of companion...and before the main feature, I can tell you some stories that can serve as sneak previews, shorts...and they can prove therapeutic in their own way and it's often quite enjoyable to go deeper and deeper down as you relax in the movies because it's a world apart—like hypnosis. You let go, you can focus on the pleasure and everything else just drifts away....

(after three metaphors have been told) Hypnotic Dreaming for Hyper-ventilation, continued

Has the feature started yet?...Or are they still waiting for people to come in?...If you don't have a hypnotic movie right now... you can have one tonight. You can have a most vivid dream of everything all right in a relationship with a man, comfortable, easy, secure...you can have a relationship in the dream and it can be a premonition that can foretell good things to come. On subsequent nights...you can have dreams that show the steps that lead up to the cured situation.

Hypnotic Dreaming (after numerous posthypnotic suggestions)

...and the only thing that you need to think about consciously is that next week when you come in, you'll tell me about the dream of your success, your cure that you had tonight or tomorrow night. It might be the third dream you have. It may have the most vivid, vivid color, the kind of dream where the feelings from the dream stay with you throughout the day. So positive, so full of joy, comfort, the feelings from the dream can travel with you through your day like a residue....

Hypnotic Dreaming in an Insight-Oriented Hypnotherapy with a Therapist-Client Who

...moving downward...further and further, deep inside yourself, allowing things to reorganize, now or later...doing it here in trance or doing it in the privacy of a dream that you have at night or in the trance experiences that you can have in the privacy of your own home....It doesn't matter where you do it, it doesn't matter when you do it...and you can allow yourself to be the only one who knows how and when those

Desires a High Degree of Autonomy in the Change Process	changes begin to take place....I know that dreams have always played an important role in your life...and they can be the sites where these changes begin to manifest themselves to you most apparently...it can be that those dreams become apparent to you...in a different way and that other things can become apparent to you in ways that allow you to really move forward....
Hypnotic Dreaming Suggested After the Hypnotic Session	One of the things that I forgot to tell you—I can tell you now because a person keeps their hypnotic receptivity for about 20 minutes after the trance experience—is that you can have a vivid dream tonight—it can be the third dream that you dream and you can remember it—it can be a vivid dream and you can remember it vividly in the morning when you wake up. So, you can watch for it—it will be the third dream—you can have it tonight or tomorrow night and then you can tell me about it. I'd like that very much.

Section D

Dissociated Movement

Chapter 12

CATALEPSY

ABOUT THE PHENOMENON

When a trance subject experiences catalepsy he or she feels immobile in one or more parts of the body. Muscles are felt as being in balance and comfortable, neither too tense nor too limp. More technically, catalepsy has been defined as an "involuntary tonicity of the muscles" (Kroger, 1963) or as a "suspension of voluntary movement" and "a condition of well-balanced tonicity" (Erickson & Rossi, 1981).

The whole body can be made cataleptic, with opposing sets of muscles all balanced against each other, resulting in what is sometimes referred to as a "waxy flexibility" or "flexibilitas cerea" (Kroger, 1963). It is because of this special state of the muscles that unusual positions can be maintained comfortably for incredibly long periods of time. Erickson (Erickson & Rossi, 1981; Weitzenhoffer, 1989b) viewed catalepsy as a sign of the presence of trance as well as a means of inducing and deepening the hypnotic state. In fact, he observed that it characteristically appears spontaneously, without direct suggestion, as a natural outgrowth of the hypnotic state.

Catalepsy can be both subjectively realized and objectively observed, depending upon how it manifests. It is frequently accompanied by feelings of numbness, analgesia, and/or anesthesia (Erickson & Rossi, 1981). Catalepsy is more visually evident when it manifests during arm levitations: a client may leave a hand suspended in air, *comfortably*, for 10 or 15 minutes. It is also evident when a hypnotized subject's hand slips

173

off of the lap, down to the sofa cushion and remains there, or in the collapse of head carriage during deep trance, when you see your client's head resting practically upon the chest.

HISTORY

The phenomenon of catalepsy has a long history in the psychiatric annals and has long been associated with both hysteria and schizophrenia as part of their symptom picture (Weitzenhoffer, 1989b). Its clinical use dates back to the work of Esdaile (1850/1957), who would induce catalepsy through "mesmeric influences" (believed to originate from the operator's inner organs) so powerful that surgery could be performed. Charcot (1882) also studied the phenomenon and, making the first bridges to a nonpathological understanding of catalepsy, defined it as one of three progressive stages of hypnosis (Erickson & Rossi, 1981).

The modern view of catalepsy is that it reflects a state of heightened sensitivity and receptivity to suggestion that is very adaptive for therapeutic work (Erickson & Rossi, 1981). Rather than the quiescent, unmoving body being representative of a fixed, rigid, or dull mind, the attention of a cataleptic individual is thought to be active and expectant. Suspended body movement is mirrored internally by a suspended awareness that organizes quickly around a new idea, perspective, or mental experience.

EXPERIMENTAL STUDIES

In a well-executed and original contribution to the medical hypnosis literature, Friday and Kubal (1990) successfully utilized hypnosis with 10 patients suffering from anxiety and claustrophobia who needed to undergo Magnetic Resonance Imaging (MRI). The procedure was successful in enabling these patients to complete the procedure with a minimum of stress. This reduced the degree of emotional distress, possibly reduced the use of tranquilizer medication and allowed studies to be completed that might otherwise have terminated mid-stream. (Uncompleted MRI procedures are emotionally, medically, and financially problematic for patients, doctors, and hospitals alike.) The authors mainly used relaxation and deepening suggestions just prior to and during the MRI procedure. In the article, however, they do allude to some beginning use of hypnotic phenomena, although they do not label it as such. Although the extent to which the patients experienced catalepsy is questionable, we can nonetheless assume that *some* degree of the phenomenon likely manifested for them while hypnotized, given catalepsy's tendency to appear as a natural outgrowth of the hypnotic state. Catalepsy, specifically induced, is usually a good and natural intervention for precluding panic.

In one section of the article, Friday and Kubal discuss their use of dissociative statements. They comment that these statements were designed to encourage dissociation from the enclosed space and noise that are part and parcel of the MRI procedure. In another section, they discuss having the patient visualize a "safe place," which could, if sufficiently realized, become tantamount to a positive visual hallucination. This is a good example of when increased attention to the contribution of hypnotic phenomena is warranted. All three of these hypnotic phenomena could have been enhanced and used more productively; there are other hypnotic phenomena that could have been utilized as well.

In fact, one of us (JHE) had a patient undergoing a hypnotically based therapy for reasons entirely unrelated to medical procedures. Upon learning about the task demands inherent in completing an MRI that she was going to need, this client spontaneously chose to put herself into a hypnotic state at the hospital and experience a deep catalepsy. This was followed by what seemed to her to be a deep sleep with hypnotic dreaming. It is also possible that she experienced negative auditory hallucinations, inasmuch as the loud noise from the shifting magnets, which would have awakened anyone, did not awaken her from this deep sleep.

Our literature review showed little in the way of clinically relevant research on catalepsy. It probably is one of the more overlooked hypnotic phenomena in terms of application to psychotherapy, but it does have many uses, especially in the areas of behavioral medicine and sports performance.

INDICATIONS FOR USE

Catalepsy has value in therapy applied both directly, as a vehicle of intervention itself (e.g., body stillness during medical procedures), and indirectly, as a means of communicating something relevant but tangential to the therapy proper (e.g., drawing a subject's attention to the body's ability to mobilize a variety of responses such as coolness, warmth, tingling, and other sensations that can be used obliquely toward the therapeutic goals). In the spirit of the latter is Erickson's idea of using catalepsy to help clients become more aware of how they are in fact readily responding to suggestions on the therapist's part; this is especially good for the overintellectualized client who tries so hard to "make" hypnotic trance happen in his or her head that he or she remains unaware that his or her body is already there—responding! (Erickson & Rossi, 1981). Related to this is another of Erickson's thoughts about catalepsy: since physical receptivity to input from a therapist is believed to mirror a mental, or psychological, receptivity, this phenomenon becomes an excellent tool for gauging a subject's state of readiness for whatever therapeutic inputs are forthcoming. Thus, in addition to conventional uses, which are described below, catalepsy can be used to seed receptivity and gauge its development within any individual.

Some clients will be so "good" at catalepsy, naturally, that the therapy becomes a matter of finding some way to direct this talent at the presenting problem—if it is focal enough. In instances like this, you can coach an easily agitated person to use catalepsy to feel more settled in the body or help an anxious public speaker use it to becomes less fidgety while presenting in front of audiences.

There are some clinical situations, however, that are so exquisitely appropriate for catalepsy that you work to enhance your client's ability to generate, at will, and richly experience the phenomenon more readily. Just such a clinical situation is in pediatrics: a hyperactive child can be taught, for instance, to remain relaxed and less active. Another situation is with an impulse-ridden, action-oriented adolescent who can use the cataleptic response to learn to just sit tight and wait. A sample trance segment of such an application might be as follows:

> *Well, look at that, Jason, can you tell how quiet your arms and legs have become as I've been telling you these stories in trance? I can tell by your expression that your mind's been kept busy and active but your body has become real quiet and still—hasn't moved for over 3 or 4 minutes—not one visible movement. Like a deer by the side of the road, or back in the woods, captivated by the light of a car's headlight. Thinking, wondering, yet still—you can do that, too; think and wonder and be still, **until you've had a chance to think through and wonder through all that you need to before you do anything**. Mind active, body quiet—just like this…it's that easy. Like a martial arts master—aware, mind active, **body quiet, until it's told by the mind what the smartest thing is to do**. Your body waits, like the National Guard, waits until called, always at the ready but intrigued by the patience it requires, feeling special because of how well it waits…in reserve…quiet body… mind thinking things through first…body waiting, listening, comfortably on hold….*

Catalepsy is also a natural antidote to overactivity in sports performance work whenever the athlete's overactivity compromises the efficiency and effectiveness of physical motion. Examples include equestrians that impair their horse's performance by making leg and hand movements that confuse the horse, billiard players whose hands shake, and archers and trap shooters whose arms vibrate.

A number of months ago, I (JHE) heard about an interesting potential application for catalepsy in the area of sports and recreation. One of my trainees was teaching relaxation techniques to professional dog handlers for their use during competitions. These handlers had to signal their dogs in the field from many yards away. The signals were tiny, minute finger and hand movements. In the heat of competition, some of these handlers would get so nervous that they would make inadvertent movements, to which the dogs responded. This would have been a perfect place to teach the handlers self-hypnosis oriented toward catalepsy (in addition to relaxation techniques) so that they could stay in better control of the signaling process.

We have also used catalepsy when working with pregnant women for natural childbirth. Whereas most of the labor and delivery work focuses on anesthesia and other tactics for pain control, we have suggested the use of catalepsy to counteract the annoying restlessness that these women experience late in their pregnancies. Whether it be while they sit during the day or while they sleep at night, they can thwart the incessant urge to shift position by going into trance and developing a comfortable stillness, an effortless immobility. Many women have been surprised to find themselves in our office for an hour in trance while remaining nearly unmoving. They laugh and say that they have not been able to do that in months, and their amazement in session creates a positive expectation about what else trance can do.

We have already spoken about the excellent use of catalepsy to help individuals undergo MRI procedures. In another behavioral medicine application, Kroger (1963) reports that catalepsy produced by light stroking of the skin frequently minimizes capillary bleeding secondary to vasospasus (spastic contractions of the vessel walls). There are many other situations in medicine where immobility is highly desirable or even essential. Consider removing splinters or broken glass, getting injections, or engaging in opthamological procedures.

CONTRAINDICATIONS

The only contraindications for catalepsy are when it would make the problem worse rather than better because of what it might directly or indirectly communicate to the client. You probably want to avoid enhancing or drawing much attention to the experience of catalepsy in trance when a person suffers from psychogenic fatigue or is characterologically lethargic. This could be found in cases where depression is the core problem and it is accompanied by a similar psychomotor depression or inactivity. Using similar logic, clients who are too passive in their orientation to the world would be poorly served by being taught catalepsy, except by therapists who are skilled at utilizing the catalepsy to pace and lead the person away from a mental complacency.

ELICITING THE PHENOMENON OF CATALEPSY

Direct and Indirect Suggestion

There are a number of words already mentioned in the chapter that reflect the **evocative** language that can facilitate the cataleptic response. These words include "motionless," "stillness," "unmoving," "frozen," and "immobile." "Paralyzed" is another possible evocative word; however, like the word "frozen" above, it needs to be used with caution because of a possible negative connotation. Planting these kinds of words in the beginning of your induction can **seed** the idea for catalepsy for later on in the hypnosis. You can say something like, *"Can you notice the heavy summer air pressing down on your shoulders, reminding your unconscious to begin its descent down into a **warmly** received trance experience, any residual tension melting away, maybe your conscious mind noticing first, your unconscious too absorbed already in its comfortable experience...."* You can also use **presupposition** to encourage the development of catalepsy, as in the following statements:

- *"...**as soon as you begin to notice that you don't even want to move**, you can take an even deeper breath and go another little bit into trance...."*
- *"**when you first start wondering whether it's warmth or numbness you feel** in your hands, you can smile with pride at how well your body responds to hypnosis...."*
- *...**whenever you feel more heaviness in one side of your body than the other**, you can begin to let your conscious mind settle on the most important issue at hand...."*

Double binds can be used to elicit catalepsy as well. The therapist could suggest that a person begin to develop a cataleptic response *slowly* or *quickly*. Another possibility is suggesting that the person *"allow the lower half of the body to become immobile, while the upper half followed later, or perhaps it will be the upper half that develops immobility first and the lower half the second part to experience it."*

As with other hypnotic phenomena, **conscious/unconscious dissociative statements** are useful. The therapist could, for example, express to a client that *"your conscious mind can be quite active in thinking, while your unconscious mind promotes physical stillness."* Alternately, one might say, *"Your conscious mind could intend the stillness to take place since it will be so useful to you, while your unconscious reviews experience after experience of times in your life where you've been unmoving for long periods of time."*

Metaphor, Anecdote, and Naturalistic Examples of Catalepsy

There are a number of stories and real life accounts that work well to encourage the development of catalepsy in hypnotized subjects. One is Tchaikovsky's *Nutcracker Suite*. In this ballet, toys that are unmoving all day in the toymaker's workshop begin to come to life at night. All night long they play, dance, and romance, only to scurry back in place and freeze once again in the morning when the door to the workshop is opened. Other relevant storylines include the recent movies entitled *Mannequin* and *Mannequin II*. In these movies, a man falls in love with a mannequin who comes to life when she is with him. If you are familiar with these films, you can detail the elements of the story to show your client how to move in and out of that cataleptic state, depending on circumstances. There are also the mimes who stand motionlessly on the steps of the Metropolitan Museum of Art in New York City or the Library of Congress in Washington, D.C., prior to performing an act, after which they once again freeze. There are wax museums where people are hired to remain cataleptic. Visitors think they are part of the wax displays, only to see them move at some point.

Therapists can draw upon a number of naturalistic examples of the cataleptic response from childhood, refamiliarizing clients with experiences long forgotten that can be drawn on as resources in the present. One is the children's game of Simon Says. Most American children have played this game where a leader commands a group of kids to make specific physical movements (i.e., stand on one foot, put your hands on top of your head). The kids are only supposed to respond if the command has been prefaced by the phrase, "Simon Says." Any player responding to a command that is not prefaced by "Simon Says" is eliminated. Most of us played Simon Says as children and, apart from those of us who were hyperactive, learned to remain immobile for extended periods of time until we heard "Simon Says." By reminding clients of their childhood ability to play this game (absorbing them vividly in that memory), you remind them that their unconscious mind already knows how to do what it is you are about to ask them to do. Interestingly, in another case, Simon Says could be a useful reference experience for the therapeutic idea of choosing either to respond or not to respond to another's idea or suggestion, *depending on context.*

Another example of naturalistic catalepsy from childhood is the game of Red Light, Green Light. This involves a leader who has his or her back to a number of players who are standing about 10 or 20 yards away. The leader yells, "Green light!" At that point the players begin to move toward the leader with the goal of being the first to touch him or her. However, the leader can at any time whirl around and say, "Red light!," whereupon everyone must stop immediately. Anyone seen still moving by the leader is sent back to the starting line. So, you can go fast, and risk not being able to become immobile quickly enough, or you can move slowly, making it easier to get still more quickly, but risking not being the first to tag the leader. Reminding clients of this childhood play helps them to recognize innate abilities for catalepsy long forgotten. This example is particularly useful for people who have to develop their cataleptic response in a flash but will then want to drop it quickly as well (e.g., surgeons, athletes, detail artists, photographers).

One can also talk to clients in trance about sprinters, posed motionlessly in their starters' blocks prior to a race or divers motionless on the edge of a 10-meter board. Consider the gymnast poised motionlessly for a few moments on the rings. Or the stillness for those few seconds after landing off of the uneven parallel bars. When talking about these situations you should repeatedly use the words "still," "motionless," "poised," or "balanced" as a way of interspersing the suggestion for catalepsy, even while using anecdotal or naturalistic material. When it comes to hypnotic work, what is important is not just *what* you talk about but *how* you talk about it. Emphasize and highlight, through tone, pace, and intensity, essential words or phrases that move the subject in the direction of the desired response. In hypnosis, the expressive qualities of communication are as important as the content.

You can also talk (in or during the inductive phase of trance) about how animals become immobile when they are startled. Related examples of catalepsy can be about animals that are injured or otherwise vulnerable to predators. These animals "play dead" in the hope that they will be overlooked and not further attacked. In fact, this animal response so resembles the cataleptic state that in the literature of comparative psychology it is referred to as "animal hypnosis"! Albeit a more morbid scene, certain clients with a taste for the macabre can be told about soldiers during war time who are injured, lying next to dead soldiers. They tried to escape the killing intentions of the enemy by pretending to be dead like the other soldiers around them. This kind of response required one to remain cataleptic for long (and surely miserable) periods of time.

Erickson would often guide a subject's arm and hand to a cataleptic pose during the induction phase of trance and leave the limb suspended in mid-air. The Handshake Induction (see Erickson & Rossi, 1981) is a relative of this technique and well known for its ability to elicit both catalepsy and amnesia. See the excellent chapter on catalepsy in the Erickson & Rossi (1981) text for exercises on eliciting catalepsy in clients.

Therapists may not actually need to use any of these stories, examples or symbols of catalepsy, nor might they need to use any of the earlier linguistically based suggestions. This is because of the tendency for catalepsy to emanate naturally from the trance state so often. Erickson (Erickson & Rossi, 1981) wrote that the phenomenon of catalepsy can be facilitated by any procedure that arrests attention, leads to progressive body immobility, and then leads to an inner attitude of inquiry, receptivity, and expectancy of more input from an operator (therapist). There is probably no other hypnotic phenomenon other than dissociation that presents itself so readily—just as part and parcel of even neutral hypnosis. In fact, there are likely to be times when you become aware of a client's catalepsy after the fact, without ever suggesting it or even thinking of it as a hypnotic intervention. However, as you notice and then ratify its presence as indicative of hypnosis taking place, you can then begin to think of ways to utilize it for the therapy.

Symbols

A few wonderful cataleptic symbols that can be kept in a waiting room or office are dolls, toy soldiers, and stuffed animals. Consider scarecrows, too. Also a terrific symbol of that "waxy flexibility," coupled with immobility, is the green figurine, Gumby. Therapists can fiddle with Gumby toys prior to the start of the hypnotic work or give it to the client prior to formal trancework, playfully saying it's "a communication to your unconscious." This is the use of symbols for seeding, although symbols can really be used at any point through the therapy. That same Gumby, for example, could be given to the client *during* the trance state or put on the side of the couch while the client is in trance. The client could then be instructed to open his or her eyes and look at it. Or, the client could be instructed to focus on it as he or she goes into trance, defocusing his or her eyes and becoming ever more relaxed.

We have been talking about using symbols for intervention during the trance work but they could be used for intervention after the trance as well. Give your client the task assignment that he or she go out to a toy store and purchase a Gumby as a personal symbol to carry in a briefcase or purse. Either during trance, as a post-hypnotic suggestion, or after trance, as a part of a direct suggestion, it can be mentioned to clients that *"any time [they] hold or touch [their] symbol, or even think about it being with [them], [they] can immediately reexperience whatever aspect of the practiced cataleptic state [they] would find useful at that time."* The relevant aspect can be a motionlessness, a numbness, a heaviness, a sleepiness, an inner stillness, and/or a sensation of warmth.

SELECTED TRANSCRIPT MATERIAL

Catalepsy   ...and as I observe a stillness outside of you, you can perhaps locate an internal stillness, maybe characterized by warmth, and even an inertia....

Catalepsy   ...and perhaps now you can feel in your body an in-
for a Recre-   creasing sensation of relaxation, still in that hot tub
ational   perhaps...and somebody, somewhere keeps adding
Athlete   warm, warm water, keeping the right temperature...so
Learning to   that there's a nice, very dreamy feeling of inertia, set-
Relax   tling down, a relaxation, a warmth...and that can be coupled with a growing sense of comfort and confidence about the activity that you've chosen to do as recreation in your life...because it affords you such pleasure...and challenge....

....I'd like you to begin to think about creating again that sensation of heaviness somewhere in your body...on your left side...on your right side...could be half and half as you allow yourself to really move downward....

For instance, any type of sinking sensation, any feeling of heaviness....

Catalepsy   ...and I don't know if already your arms and hands are
and Post-   getting a little bit heavier and more relaxed. Sometimes

*hypnotic
Suggestions
for a Smoker
Worrying
About
Overeating
When She
Stops
Smoking*

in hypnosis people develop a sense of "oh, yeah, I could move if I wanted to, but I don't want to move because I kind of just want to leave things as they are right now."...You can have the heaviness develop, you can have a comfortable sense of heaviness develop in your hands, heaviness developing in your arms and hands and it might even be a certain warm, numb sensation— maybe even a tingly, warm, numb sensation...almost like when you're lying in bed at night and you're in a slightly awkward position—maybe your arm is falling asleep a little bit and you know that you probably should move so that you can rest more easily, but you really don't want to move, you want to just lay relaxed there, the inertia that takes over...sleeping at night...becoming more and more rested...letting go...so there can be that inertia...and then there can be something that's related to that, like trying to get back into where you were...like after you've had a very pleasurable dream...and you wake up a little bit and you try and recapture...deeper and deeper down...your conscious mind can recognize that there...you can allow yourself to develop altogether new habits and you can do new things altogether with your hands...now...they may develop the warm, tingly heaviness...you may notice it already...you might even allow yourself to feel as if your hands are weighed down with some sandbags...of a comfortable weight, not too heavy, just that they're there....

Perhaps you might want to give yourself the post-hypnotic suggestion that you can keep your hands still in this fashion by imagining this anytime you desire a cigarette, anytime you desire to eat....I'll never forget the feeling of being at the beach as a child...and that can be reestablished...the feeling of being at the beach as a child and playing with friends and having friends load up piles and piles of warm, wet sand on top of my arms...and pretending and playing at the idea of not being able to move...standing in a hole dug in the sand right where the ocean washes up and allowing the wet sand to fill in the hole so that it covered up to my knees and thighs....

*Catalepsy
Extending*

I don't know if you're experiencing a lot or a little of the warm heaviness that characterizes trance so very

into an
Anesthesia
Knee Pain

often....If you are, perhaps you can raise your thumb up a little bit...very good...now, that warm, heavy feeling can also include a numbish kind of feeling... and it can increase, Susan, as you get deeper and deeper relaxed...and later you'll discover how easy it is for you to move in everyday life while being a little bit or a lot in trance, feeling this heavy, warm numbness because it will have consolidated in your knees and the consolidation can begin to float and drift there...like a boat on a lake being taken by a current, the warm, heavy numbness...can float toward your knees and the extent to which it consolidates there...can be in direct proportion to the extent that you need it....If you're having an energetic, good day...then it doesn't have to be around at all or it can just float through your body, perhaps in your shoulders, perhaps in your mind, giving you peace of mind...calm inside...but if you're tired and your knees begin to ache, that can be the cue, this signal for you to allow your body to go into trance and for the numbness, the warm, heavy numbness to float and collect mainly in your knees....

Chapter 13

ARM LEVITATION (IDEOMOTOR MOVEMENT)

ABOUT THE PHENOMENON

One of the most interesting and frequently used hypnotic phenomena is arm levitation. Actually, arm levitation is an amalgam of a number of different subhypnotic phenomena: a true arm levitation involves the hand and arm lifting up into the air in a dissociated fashion and is characterized by a seemingly effortless and automatic movement (usually toward the face); it is then sustained by the phenomenon of catalepsy. We devote a chapter to it and treat it as a hypnotic phenomenon apart from the others because it is so often used that way; however, it might best be considered a metahypnotic phenomenon, a phenomenon that combines different subphenomena into a higher-order one.

INDICATIONS FOR USE

What does arm levitation have to do with psychotherapy? Most people experiencing or viewing an arm levitation for the first time wonder with curiosity and amusement just how this is at all relevant to quality clinical hypnotherapy.

185

One important reason for eliciting arm levitations in clients is to catalyze a change. Milton Erickson did pioneering work in the use of arm levitations in hypnosis (Erickson, 1961/1980; Erickson & Rossi, 1980a). His rationale for so often making it a part of the hypnotic session was his repeated finding that clients who manifested an arm levitation also allowed the hypnotic work to proceed more quickly.

It seems to us that the experience of arm levitation is valuable also because it lets the client know that something *different* could happen in *this* therapy. The relationship between arm levitation and change might also indicate that subjects who are responsive to arm-levitation suggestions would also be especially responsive to hypnotic (and thus therapeutic) suggestions in general. If this is the case, arm levitation becomes a useful diagnostic litmus test for responsivity.

Another reason to use arm levitation is that it gives the therapist something very observable to view during trancework. He or she can see the influence of each suggestion for the hand or arm to move higher and thereby assess degrees of compliance or resistance. With this taking place, the therapist can improve the effectiveness of his or her suggestions and at the same time diagnose the nature of the subject's responsiveness to interpersonal influence.

When you do arm levitation, it is as if you have created a laboratory and put the subject's response style under a microscope for the two of you to view. When the client responds, or does not respond, the *dialogue* inherent in the *process* of hypnotherapy begins. An interaction involving request and response has been initiated. This is quite different from the traditional conception of hypnosis as being unilateral and unidimensional—operator to subject. Indeed, the nature of clients' responses to requests for arm levitations give a wealth of information about them. One can safely, albeit tentatively, assume that their ways of responding in this situation resemble how they respond in other request/demand-oriented interpersonal situations, too; the astute clinician can learn about how they create and maintain their symptoms.

Using arm levitation in this way is actually conceptually similar to how the psychoanalytically oriented therapist views transference—as a palpable, in-session, interpersonal manifestation of the individual's personality with significant others. It is also conceptually similar to how the psychodiagnostic tester uses the Rorschach ink blot test—as an ambiguous stimulus onto which the individual can project aspects of him or herself so that they become "observable." Whether we are speaking of transference, ink blots, or arm levitation, what we have, in effect, is an equivalent to a "particle accelerator" in which aspects of nature otherwise elusive have an arena in which they can be isolated and studied far more easily and purely. And, with arm levitation, these contrasts between individuals certainly do shine through. To borrow from the common everyday idiom, a person can say "Jump!" and some people will respond with "How high, when, and how many times?," while others will quickly lie down on the ground.

In making a request for arm levitation, the therapist will see both of these responses and every response in-between on the continuum of characterological possibilities. Illumination of character, however, does not imply a need to *do* anything to modify it—we are talking here about discovering as much relevant information about your client as is available in your contacts and incorporating this into your treatment planning. This ensures that the therapy is "custom-fitted" to your client and his or her way of accepting help and making changes.

Another time to use arm levitation is when it can serve as a *symbol* to clients for what is needed in their lives. For example, you can use arm levitation symbolically, with depressed individuals. It serves as a symbol, or "concretized" metaphor, for overcoming lethargy (*"your hand can move **spontaneously**, almost as if it has an **energy of its own**"*); psychological heaviness (*"your arm can get **lighter and lighter**"*); or sobriety and humorlessness (*"and as your arm moves up, you can enjoy the **experience of increased levity**"*).

Arm levitation can also be used symbolically for individuals seeking to lose weight. You could say, for example, *"...and as this takes place, you can enjoy **the feeling of lightness developing**, your hand moving easily as **the feeling of lightness** becomes apparent."* This would be an indirect suggestion for weight loss or lightness, movement or exercise, and for enjoyment of the situation that is developing. For a weight-loss client, one could also have the arm levitation stop in mid-air rather than going all the way to the face—again as a symbol—this time *"for a fork that does not go all the way up to the mouth."*

In other cases arm levitation can be a symbol to people who are fearful of heights: *"and it can go higher and higher and as it does, you can be comfortable and relaxed, in fact, you can find yourself going deeper into trance and getting more relaxed the higher up it goes."* Arm levitation is a wonderful symbol for flying; people who have a fear of airplanes and of flying can benefit from using this phenomenon as a primary intervention. In such cases, the therapy is organized around the direct and indirect suggestions made about airplanes and flying while the client plays with a levitation. The client could also be taught to use self-induced arm levitation during take-off as a way to absorb him or herself in an internal experience and trigger the calming suggestions stored from therapy sessions. Finger, rather than arm or even hand levitations, go a long way to reduce the number of stares from curious folk who share your client's seat row. A snippet of possible in-session hypnosis follows:

*And it can lift off. As it does you can have a predominant feel-
ing of curiosity, or interest, coupled with ever-deepening relaxation. It goes up into the air. It moves easily, effortlessly, and even
if it wobbles a little bit, you know that it's going up and this is a
comfortable and safe experience, and as this experience continues to take place, and for its entire duration, you can be very deeply
relaxed and comfortable.*

There are many other ways in which arm levitation can be used as a
symbol in therapy, but a final one that we will offer is in the case of
impotence. Here, the arm levitation can be a special type, with a straight
arm, elbow unbent, and the client making a fist rather than leaving his
hand open. The phrasing of the suggestion for arm levitation based on
this kind of positioning can be as follows: *"And it can lift up and up
and up, straight, stiff, staying in the air for a really long time, pointing
up into the air, lasting and lasting and lasting."*

There are numerous occasions when arm levitation is the phenomenon of choice because it is the one that the client does best, or because
it is the complement to the phenomenon that is creating the problem,
or because it is the mechanism of the problem that can now become the
solution. However, as the examples above illustrate, most often arm
levitation ends up being used as a parallel phenomenon or symbol relating to the problem, or as a way of catalyzing the hypnotherapy, or as
a way of developing a concrete, microcosmic representation of interpersonal experiences found throughout the client's life.

CONTRAINDICATIONS

Contraindications seem to be few for arm levitation. One
contraindication for its use is with people who are working to master
involuntary muscular movement. Other approaches are probably better suited for these people who experience involuntary tics, spastic
movements, or difficulties in controlling body movements due to partial paralysis. Likewise, clients with multiple sclerosis, who have difficulty with smooth, directed body movement, should not be asked to
perform arm levitation. For these clients, ideomotor movements—that
is, movements that are dissociated and occur automatically without
conscious, volitional intent—can be all too frightening inasmuch as
they have spent much of their waking time trying to control and eradicate rather than experience these types of movement. Although having
an arm levitation may be therapeutic from a conceptual standpoint, it
is just too emotionally charged an area for them to yield to these kinds

of "automatic" movements. So much time and energy is spent daily in avolitional body movement, or perhaps in being embarrassed by them, or maybe even in viewing them as evidence of their deterioration due to advancing disease processes, that arm levitation is rarely the treatment of choice.

ELICITING THE PHENOMENON OF ARM LEVITATION

Direct and Indirect Suggestion

As is the case with all hypnotic phenomena, arm levitation can be more easily elicited if it is first **seeded**. Inserting words like *disarming, handy,* and *enlighten* into the induction phase of your trancework can really amplify the impact of later suggestions (Zeig, 1990c). Examples include:

- *"...you can be curiously expectant about what kind of delightfully **disarming** experience you'll have in trance today...."* [We especially like the word "disarm" because of the inherent suggestion for dissociation (dis - arm).]
- *"...you may not yet have even discovered just how **handy** some of your own inner resources can become today in solving your dilemma...."*
- *"...let your unconscious choose whether today or next week will be the more **enlightening** of sessions...."*

As a part of preparing for any therapy in which hypnosis is being used, it is important to set the stage for the phenomenon that is to take place. In the case of arm levitation, you want to make sure that clients have their hands flat on their laps or on the armrests of a chair. This will make it much easier than if their hands are lower than their legs or if their hands are tucked underneath their legs or clasped together. In these instances, simply ask the person to rest his or her hands on top of his or her thighs or on the armrest of the chair, and allow the person a moment to once again get comfortable with the position. It is important that when using hypnosis you stack the deck in your favor by making the preconditions amenable to what you wish to happen.

Use **presuppositions** to enhance the power of and receptivity to your suggestions for levitation. This refers to the phrasing of suggestions, wherein assumptions are made that it will happen. Here one says to a client, **"When your hand lifts up**, *you can begin to go deeper into trance."* The word "when" makes the phenomenon seem inevitable.

Another means to elicit arm levitation is to give the client a **double bind**. With this method you provide comfortable alternatives, either of which leads in the desired direction. For example, you might say, "*You can be curious about which hand will lift up first. Will it be the right or the left? You just wonder.*" Or you can ask, "*Is your unconscious mind aware that the movements can start as minuscule twitches in a left finger or as smooth elevations in your right wrist?*"

Conscious/unconscious dissociative statements can also be used. An example of this is, "*Your conscious mind can be curious about which hand will lift, while your unconscious has already chosen. Your conscious mind can wonder, really wonder, while your unconscious mind has a sense of certainty, having made the choice.*" Dissociative statements are particularly useful in creating the dissociative phenomenological trend, one that we hope would carry over into the arm levitation itself; an arm levitation requires not just lightness and the effortless, balanced muscle tone associated with catalepsy, but also a sense of dissociation so that the arm feels separate from the rest of the person, acting with automaticity.

One can choose words that are so **evocative** of the desired phenomenon that they engender an arm levitation by their very use. For example, you can say to a client, "*And, Carol, what follows can be a* **disarmingly enlightening** *experience, one that will no doubt* **lighten up** *your life, perhaps add an element of* **levity** *and all in all be one which will perhaps prove most* **handy**.*" This differs from seeding in that the terms are used here in the spirit of direct suggestion, rather than as cryptic foreshadowers of things to come or happen later on.

It is important to recognize that the idea of an arm lifting up into the air as if it has a mind of its own can be too abstract for a person, especially for one very deeply in trance and therefore responding to communications in a rather concrete fashion. Therefore, it can be useful to phrase the request for this phenomenon in ways that are less abstract. For example, you can talk about "*fingers beginning to twitch, the elbow bending, a hand moving up to your face.*" As we've said throughout this book, in general, with hypnosis it is a good rule of thumb to make a suggestion many different times in many different ways. The above phrases do that and, furthermore, break something large into something smaller and thus more manageable. The act of "finger twitching" is a preliminary way of getting a full-blown arm levitation and is one example of an Ericksonian "foot-in-the-door" strategy. It should also be noted that the more resistant the client, the more you need to make simpler suggestions—and ones with which it is easier to comply.

Regarding this foot-in-the-door strategy, consider the following: in one transcript, Erickson (see Erickson & Rossi, 1980a) requests at the start of the induction that the person become aware of the texture of his pants underneath his finger. This is a brilliant strategy of indirect suggestion, inasmuch as to comply with this request (and who wouldn't, it's so innocuous?) the subject had to move his finger ever so lightly across the material of his pants, *therefore lifting it a bit.* When you get compliance to the first step in a sequence, it makes it much easier for the client to comply with later suggestions that are more difficult. This is also an example of the "yes set," wherein Erickson gets the client to say "yes" to requests that are easy to comply with. Saying "yes" early on makes it easy for the momentum of compliance to continue and for "yes" to be the response later on as well (O'Hanlon, 1987).

One can also suggest arm levitation in a way that is both pretty concrete and yet indirect; you never even speak about the arm levitation itself. This is what we call the "back door" method. If an arm levitation doesn't quite go up to the client's face (a common experience), you can get it that last quarter inch by commenting as follows: "*...and as your arm moves up that last little bit to your face, you can cheat a little bit...you can help out...your head can move down to your hand.*" This is a suggestion that you can see in action in a training tape of Erickson's entitled, *The Artistry of Milton H. Erickson, M.D.* (Erickson & Lustig, 1975).

Metaphor and Anecdote

Many metaphoric images have been used to elicit arm levitation. A common one popularized by therapists using traditional hypnosis is that of a huge helium balloon tied by a string to someone's middle finger, pulling the arm into the air automatically. Another one is the idea of having the person imagine a garden hose pointed into the air with a strong stream of water coming out, and the person is cupping a hand over the stream.

Another, more subtle way to elicit arm levitation is to talk about an elevator attendant automatically lifting his hands into the air to punch a number on the board and saying, "*Going up!*" This is effective in two ways. First of all, you are describing an elevator attendant that moves his hands into the air automatically in a dissociated fashion. Second, the inclusion of the words "going up" fits the context of riding in an elevator, but also gives an indirect suggestion for arm levitation to the client listening to the story. Stories about drawbridges opening, tightrope walkers balancing, and ballerinas spinning could do well. The image of Morticia Addams getting her outstretched arm kissed by Gomez would also do quite nicely.

Naturalistic Examples

As we discussed in other chapters, in eliciting any of the hypnotic phenomena it is a good idea to point out how the phenomenon is already a part of everyday life and how the client him or herself has experienced it naturally, even if unwittingly. With regard to arm levitation, one naturalistic example that you can offer is of how children in elementary school press up on their desks forcefully with their hands for many minutes; after a while they pull their hands out from under the table and the hands "automatically" float up into the air. You can also include accounts of how children indicate their desire to answer questions or *respond to instruction* (an indirect suggestion for client responsivity) by raising their hands in the air. It might go as follows: "*And your conscious mind only has an intent to provide some information to the teacher, but your unconscious, using its own mind without you even thinking about it, raises the hand right up into the sky with an automatic effort that you don't even need to be aware of.*" Telling these stories not only encourages a levitation to take place, but it is useful as well in facilitating the development of age regression since the tales involve school days. Another naturalistic story describes how a person takes a spoon from the plate to his or her mouth without any conscious direction, automatically.

Movement and Other Noncontent Ways of Eliciting Arm Levitation

Expressive aspects of eliciting arm levitation refer to ways of making suggestions that do not rely upon the *content* of what is said, but the *way* in which something is said. For example, it's helpful when trying to get an arm levitation to speak in a lilting fashion with a high voice tone. This expressive aspect of language mimics the movement in the arm that you are trying to engender. Apart from using your voice, you can move your head upward as you speak in uplifting strokes.

Another noncontent way of eliciting an arm levitation is to help the person get started. Here, you actually take the person's wrist (after asking permission to come over and do that) and gently lift it slightly into the air, hesitating as you let go so that the person is never quite certain whether you are holding the hand in the air still or if he or she has begun to support his or her own hand. This method *gets the person started*, which makes the subsequent stages easier. This approach is useful with clients who are not responding to the suggestions right away. It is often **not** a matter of resistance, but more a matter of the inertia that seems part and parcel of many trance states. That is, people tend not to initiate motor movement, in favor of maintaining the status quo. This inertia, combined with the classical economy or minimalism of movement found in most subjects (not to mention occasional self-consciousness), sometimes results in clients not manifesting an arm levitation even though they feel quite cooperative with that goal. In these instances, it really is helpful just to get them started by lifting their hand into the air.

Note also that by getting the hand a little bit in the air, there are tiny movements that begin at once in terms of the arm floating up and down. This is due to gravity and a person's inability to remain absolutely still. Whereas a hand in one's lap can remain utterly still, once in the air there is no way in which at least a tiny movement does not take place. It is a lot easier for the person to move toward a levitation once he or she feels movement rather than an experience of feeling the hand and arm as fixed. Capitalize on these inevitable physical/physiological realities in your hypnosis. Inviting subjects to *pretend* to have a hand or arm levitation by moving the appendage upwards a bit volitionally is another good way to get the person started until the momentum of unconscious responsiveness takes over.

Points to Remember

Keep in mind that a really good arm levitation has an involuntary aspect to it. That is, not only does the hand feel light, uplifted, and dissociated, but all of this happens seemingly automatically. The subject should not feel as if he or she is controlling it at a conscious level.

Also remember to phrase suggestions in many different ways, say them many different times, and say them over and over. Persistence is perhaps the most important thing a therapist beginning to use hypnosis can keep in mind with respect to any hypnotic phenomenon, but with arm levitation it is especially important. A classic rookie error is to give up on an arm levitation too early. When you see films of Erickson eliciting arm levitations, you see that he goes on and on and on in his attempts to get it going just right. Since about 70 percent of all subjects can comfortably manifest some type of arm levitation even in the lightest trance (Bowers, 1976; 1993), you can afford to persist. It is another classic rookie error to take the lack of an arm levitation personally. Just bear in mind that the client is providing you with information and that the presence or absence of arm levitation often has little to do with your personal adequacy as a therapist using hypnosis.

In the transcript material that follows, you'll see many uses of arm levitation. You will notice that we do not just get the arm to go into the air but frequently hook on therapeutic suggestions to the arm levitation. Examples include saying, *"As your arm lifts into the air, you can go deeper and deeper into trance,"* or *"When your arm touches your face, you can discover another set of personal skills."* The transcript material will also demonstrate that arm levitation is not simply a static event but rather a process that unfolds in the hypnosis over time and throughout a session. Notice also how sequential arm levitations can be used.

SELECTED TRANSCRIPT MATERIAL

Arm Levitation

....And you may remember learning about hovercrafts as a child...hovercrafts are vehicles that can move on land, marsh or water—the air pushes them up from the surface so they hover just a little bit above the ground, seemingly in defiance of gravity, but just a little bit though, so that a cushion of air's just below the vehicle....Arm levitation is also a vehicle, a vehicle to...change, Matt....

....Your conscious mind can just wait for the response...your subconscious mind can be curious as to which hand will lift into the air and begin its movement toward your face...now...your subconscious mind can...do something entirely different, can fix its attention on that hover craft....I can remember seeing pictures on PBS, Channel 12, actually, as a kid it was Channel 13 in New York...11, 10, 9 was the station that the Mets played on...8 was blank, Matt, 7 was ABC, 6 blank again...static...5...WPIX I believe, 4...NBC, 3 nothing again, 2 CBS, and maybe 1 (one/once) again you can remember that day when you wrote the "A" for the first time in class and formed a slanty line one way and a slanty line another way and then the bridge between the two of those...seemed to float in mid-air...delicately hooked onto the slanty lines like a bridge for a ladder—you've seen that...like the support for a ladder...deeper and deeper down...and as a child the hovercraft would sort of puff itself and lift up into the air...right or left, going up...and it moved up almost as if it had a mind of its own, now, somewhere there was a button pushed...an intention was experienced, an automatic movement was made, a button pushed, an automatic response in an almost machinelike fashion... lifting, the hovercraft would like lifting and it did...slowly at first and there was some twitching that took place...it wasn't quite certain where it was going to lift up first, the right or the left...it was hard to discern exactly when the lifting took place, but it did take place, an almost imperceptible twitching became a lifting into the air, which hand will do it?

....It can be something quite handy to learn—there you go...lifting up and there's nothing that you need to do with your conscious mind, your subconscious mind can do it all...can do it all...and can begin its journey toward your face...and your conscious mind might be concerned about saving face, here and elsewhere, but your subconscious mind knows that in order to face the world, you can allow the arm levitation to develop up...almost as if there was a balloon, a huge helium balloon attached to your fingers...pulling them up into the air toward your face, a strong breeze has blown the huge helium balloon back and your hand moved up toward your face rapidly, automatically, almost as if it moved on its own....But you know about that experience, you know a lot more than you know that you know...you know about that experience...because you played a musical instrument where you had an intention somewhere in your mind and another part of your mind moved your hands faster, quicker and with greater skill than your conscious mind ever could....Your subconscious mind played the violin a lot better...there you go!...lifting...a lot better than your conscious mind...knows how....The hovercraft lifted up higher and higher...huge engines inside performing the work, pushing up and up...your hand and your knuckles begin to go toward your face...elbow can bend—that's right....

And you can enjoy with your conscious mind the cogwheel kinds of movements that are characteristic of trance...and you may be surprised that trance deepens as your arm levitation takes place and a very nice arm levitation, it is...your conscious mind can just enjoy because there's nothing that it needs to do....Your subconscious mind can also enjoy because it's having its way and its way is okay, allowing you to go deeper

and deeper down...letting go, go deeper and deeper...
the deeper you go, the higher your arm goes up, the
higher your arm goes up, the deeper you go....It's a little
bit like what I heard the other day when watching show
jumping horses jump up into the air—1500 pounds
jumping over five and a half feet, effortlessly, easy,
easy...that they rock back a little bit and lift up, they
have an intention and nobody, nobody, least of all they
themselves, says move this leg this way, that tendon
that way....Their subconscious mind also knows a lot
more than they do...and you have to be good to be
lucky...either way, you can recognize that your arm can
continue its journey higher...and how does all that steel
remain suspended way up high in the air? Seems so
improbable to fly through the air in a tin can with
wings...lifting...but the jet plane does in fact lift up.

Your hand can remain there, hovering in space and
that's okay...every plane might want to get to a certain
height, but it's okay to be at a lower height....Your subconscious mind can make up its mind for itself...now
you can be surprised that in a moment your subconscious mind is going to choose to allow that hand to
begin its journey back down to your lap. When it hits
your lap, two things will happen...you can go twice as
deep into trance, but then your other hand, your right
hand can automatically lift up in the air and it too can
begin to hover, suspended in space as if attached by a
wire...muscle tone so balanced...now...and when it
touches your lap, the other hand will lift up almost as
if it's a kangaroo...or a spring, a shock absorber on a
car...one goes down, deeper into trance...other comes
up, lifting...lift...that's it....It can be a most enlightening experience.

With this having taken place, your right arm can now
also begin its journey down...when it touches your lap,
you can reorient from trance and when you do, you can
become aware of just how much you've learned....You
can wake up feeling refreshed, rejuvenated, and actively
energized....

Presupposi-
tion, Double
Binds, and

....And I don't know, Susan, whether those experiences
of joy will dance around inside your heart first or
whether you first will feel minuscule muscle move-

Expectation for Arm Levitation/ Levitation of Mood

ments of your hand, whether your hands might feel light and happy in a way that's different...or whether you will feel the sensations of joy first across your forehead or in the corners of your mouth as you begin to find yourself smiling more and more....I don't know, Susan, whether it will be other people who will turn to you and wonder what secret you have that allows you to experience such levity of spirit again, or whether it will be you who first recognizes that things that had in the past been enshrouded in worry no longer need to be so and instead can be replaced with a confidence and an attitude of assurance and a feeling of such delight that you can move forward in your life now with all the fun that you want....

Chapter 14

AUTOMATIC WRITING
AND DRAWING

ABOUT THE PHENOMENON

The automatic written expression of words or art is a fascinating hypnotic phenomenon with greater clinical utility than the majority of therapists think. It refers to a person's capacity to write letters, words, phrases, numbers, figures, symbols, objects, and/or abstractions during the trance state. It is subjectively accompanied by a mind/body dissociation and, in its truest form, a suspension of cognitive, conscious examination and evaluation of the written product during the process. Its naturalistic roots are evident in the doodling on every grade schooler's notebook, the margins of our scratch pads, and the memo books by our telephones.

HISTORY AND EXPERIMENTAL STUDIES

The method of automatic writing actually originated in the studies of psychic researchers and subsequently caught on in the psychotherapeutic community during the late nineteenth and early twentieth centuries before going out of favor by the 1930s (Hilgard, 1979). Some experimentation on automatic writing was done way back then (Messerschmidt, 1927–1928 [under the supervision of Clark Hull and summarized in Hull's 1933 text]) and followed up on in later years (Knox, Crutchfield, & Hilgard, 1975; Stevenson, 1976); however, these experiments mainly dealt with the issue of interference between simultaneously performed conscious and subconscious tasks. This was to primarily test the extent and nature of any dissociation present as a vehicle for assessing the viability of neodissociation theory—automatic writing was just a means to an end.

Erickson and Kubie (1938/1980; 1940/1980) were really the first to explore experimentally the phenomena of automatic writing and automatic drawing as observable manifestations of the *dynamic relationship* between conscious and unconscious mentation. These experiments, conducted in the 1930s, were composed of partially structured clinical situations that permitted unconscious expression (via writing or drawing) found subsequently to be distinctly different in meaning from the conscious communications about the same matters. In this sense, automatic expression was likened to the technique of psychoanalytic free association and to manifest versus latent dream analysis where the same material has different meaning depending upon the level of analysis or interpretation. The reader is referred to Volume III of *The Collected Papers of Milton H. Erickson* (1980, p. 158–176) for a detailed and fascinating review of the use of automatic drawing in the treatment of a 24-year-old university student with an acute obsessional depression.

In his writings on automatic writing, Erickson underscores the important role of dissociation in facilitating the phenomenon. Its critical function is to break up into three separate parts what seems to the subject to be a unitary act of writing, reading, and being aware of what was written. This way it becomes conceivable to do—phenomenologically—one part, without the others in tow. Given the experience of dissociation, a hypnotized subject can now write without feeling it necessary either to read what was written or to be aware of having written.

Suggestions may be given for automatic writing or automatic drawing, or both in a single induction, the latter allowing the subject to choose the most befitting mode of expression. However, Erickson and Kubie note that automatic drawing may be preferable to writing in instances where writing would force a too-rapid realization of repressed material on the part of the client. Automatic drawing allows for a more titrated expression of unconscious thoughts, feelings, fantasies, and impulses. Kroger (1963), in a similar vein, makes mention of the need for judicious therapeutic use of automatic writing that may reflect previously repressed material for which the client is inadequately defended.

Surprisingly, there is not much in the general literature in the last decade on automatic writing that is applicable to clinical practice. You can always find examples of hypnotic phenomena used as an experimental rope in a theoretical tug-of-war amongst researchers bent on proving their theory of hypnosis. The sole exception that we were able to find in our extensive literature review entailed a case study that was reported in the *Australian Journal of Clinical and Experimental Hypnosis*.

In treating a woman with a case of vaginismus (an involuntary vaginal clamping reflex due to a real or imagined threat of penetration), secondary to a history of sexual and emotional abuse, Oystragh (1988) age regresses the patient and gains first indication of sexual abuse through an automatic writing strategy. The author has the regressed patient communicate using automatic writing such that her conscious mind remains comfortably unaware of the painful memories elicited through the trancework. This leads to a great deal of information being revealed regarding an initial episode of sexual abuse by a caretaker. This interesting use of automatic writing coupled with age regression is, however and unfortunately, tainted by the repeated use of hypnotic suggestion to encourage the patient to forever simply dismiss, override, or ignore important information of which she was becoming aware regarding repeated instances of physical and sexual abuse. Essentially the patient was told to no longer be bothered by the experiences she had in childhood.

This is a rather irresponsible use of hypnosis, and the patient clearly should have been allowed, at a conscious or unconscious level, to come to terms with these repressed memories in a more adaptive way. Instead, hypnosis was used as the "muscle" to accomplish dismissal rather than the reworking of affect and memory; this may account for why the patient terminated therapy following resolution of the vaginismus, but was still having vaginal anesthesia coupled with poor interpersonal relationships with the opposite sex.

INDICATIONS FOR USE

Automatic expressive phenomena can be used to recover repressed or otherwise inaccessible (i.e., preconscious) material (Erickson, 1939/1980; 1944b/1980); to deepen trance (Lankton & Lankton, 1983); to open up a dialogue with an uncommunicative client (Brenman & Gill, 1947); or to unleash creative expression. It has been used to interpret dreams (Weitzenhoffer, 1989b); to treat amnesia (Erickson, 1933/1980); to help resolve sexual abuse trauma (Dolan, 1991); and to heal refractory skin disorders (Kroger, 1963). We have used automatic writing successfully on numerous occasions to treat authors who get blocked, graduate students who choke on written comprehensive exams, thesis procrastinators, and dissertation phobics.

CONTRAINDICATIONS

We tend to avoid the use of automatic writing or drawing whenever we work with clients who are extremely self-conscious or controlling in session or who experience anxiety when acting or speaking spontaneously. The reason is that this type of hypnotic phenomenon requires an extraordinary capacity for dissociation and/or an ability to suspend conscious self-observation and so there's little use trying hard to have clients do something that is characterologically difficult for them to do. You are better off using other techniques that don't challenge their need to avoid looking silly or out of control.

PRINCIPLES FOR ELICITING AUTOMATIC EXPRESSIVE PHENOMENA

Direct and Indirect Suggestion

Words or phrases related to writing, drawing, or painting that are included in the beginning part of your hypnotic induction can effectively **seed** the idea of automated expression. For instance, you can mention subjects' "***drawing*** *their own conclusions about what will be most useful in the forthcoming trance experience.*" Invite your clients to "***sketch*** *out their own blueprints for change as they go deeper into trance, or give voice to the **artful constructions** of the unconscious that may later have something to say about the matter **at hand**.*" You can even do plays on the words right/write so that your induction makes references to "righting"…the boat, or "right" of way, or even the disguised direct command masked in the phrase "***right now (write now)**, [pause]—you can go deeper into trance and allow your unconscious to follow a tangent of its own.*"

Saying to a client that you're not sure whether it will be a finger or the wrist that makes the first movement toward the automatic expression of feelings, thoughts, words, or images is one way to **double bind** the client toward action. You can offer another double bind in the form of wondering aloud whether the letters will be written in capital or small case form.

> *Will it happen gradually, tentatively and with some degree of self-consciousness? Or will the movements on paper be a rapid, urgent feeling of liberty in the arm, wrist or fingers, allowing an awareness only of how free it feels finally to be expressing those*

*things? Will the words be in your native tongue, or will they be of
another language only your unconscious understands?*

This latter bind is good for the client who feels self-conscious about
what he or she may write; the opportunity to write in a cryptic manner
alleviates some of that anxiety and allows the person to become more
absorbed by the experience. Most automatic writings are cryptic, in
fact (Weitzenhoffer, 1989b), and require a fair amount of deciphering
before the meaning is apparent to either therapist or client.

Presupposition is being used whenever a therapist says to the client
that "*as soon as a first, sketchable symbol comes to mind, **a dialogue
between your conscious mind and unconscious mind can begin.**"* Another statement presupposing an experience of automatic expression is
as follows: "***When you first catch wind of that symbol marking the
beginning of your writing/drawing**, you can signal to me through a
blink, or a finger movement, or a smile, or even, if you choose, through
an utter and completely silent moment.*"

Conscious/unconscious dissociative statements are exemplified by
the following: "*Your conscious mind can determine the time for you to
begin drawing, while leaving your unconscious mind to determine the
format.*" Or, "*You can allow your conscious mind to be as aware, as
curious, or even as skeptical as it needs to be, while your unconscious
devises a means to playfully circumvent that in a way that's entirely
acceptable to you.*" Or, "*Consider allowing your conscious mind to direct the elements of style in your writing, while your unconscious mind
is charged with communicating what's really important.*"

Developing this into a *double* conscious/unconscious dissociative
statement (see Lankton & Lankton, 1983) allows for even greater dissociation in the subject, as well as an experience of cognitive confusion
that can then be utilized by the therapist to direct the hypnotic process
further in a therapeutic direction. Here you juxtapose the suggestion
that one's conscious mind can do A, while the unconscious does B,
with a second suggestion that maybe instead the conscious mind will
opt to do B, so that the unconscious mind is free to tackle A. An elaborated example of this is saying to your client that he or she

> *could consider allowing your conscious mind to direct the ele-
> ments of style in your writing, while your unconscious mind is
> charged with communicating what's really important, or you can
> of course simply allow your unconscious mind to get lost in its
> considerations of all the varieties of style in your writing, while
> your conscious mind is charged with communicating what's re-
> ally important, or you can of course simply allow your conscious*

*mind to get lost in its considerations of all the varieties of style,
while your unconscious mind simply **gets the message across**.*

Part of utilizing the confusion engendered is putting the most important suggestion at the very end of the statement, as the last injunction, inasmuch as the confused subject, grasping to make meaning of what you are saying, will often pounce on and absorb that as the only immediately meaningful communication.

Direct suggestion can and should be a part of your trancework when trying to elicit automatic writing or drawing. I (JSE) have found that for clients who harbor some degree of self-consciousness, allowing and directly encouraging the writing or drawing to be consciously effected at first gets the process going. Otherwise, such individuals are always waiting for "it" to "happen" automatically or wondering what the observing therapist is thinking. As one trainee said after being the subject in a group training session where automatic writing was being practiced, "It seemed so illogical to be writing with my eyes closed....I was saying to myself in trance why would anyone want to do this?!"

Sometimes a therapist will need to midwife the transition from the writing being volitional to it becoming increasingly avolitional. Use dissociation in particular as a wedge that can manifest itself between conscious and unconscious levels of functioning to promote the continuum of automation. Examples of this are the following:

> *....You really can simply start scribbling here, purposefully...you and I can both know that it is volitional, intentional, your conscious mind pushing the pencil across, while another part of you, a more latent part, can reflect and wonder about when to jump in and take over the reins, now or much later, maybe even the next time we work together....*
>
> *....Go ahead and start, don't wait for that...automatic part of you to start moving...just push that pencil around and see what happens. Another part of you can carry the stroke a centimeter further or put a loop on the end of the line. One part is doing one part, another part doing one part, one part doing another part....*

Interspersing the direct injunction to write in the middle of a permissive suggestion is a very effective way to catalyze unconsciously driven activity (Zeig, 1988a). One example of this is to say, *"You can...Steve, **right away, this afternoon**...remember this experience as one more resource for you to **draw on** in times of stress."* By pausing before the word "Steve" and after the word "afternoon," your communication effectively becomes "Steve, write away this afternoon."

Metaphor and Naturalistic Examples of Automatic Writing/Drawing

Lie detectors with the erratic and seemingly automatic movements of the wand are a great metaphor for automatic writing and can be built right into the hypnosis, making either direct parallels between the wands and the subject's hand, or indirect allusions through comments such as, *"Your conscious mind may not readily understand why I'm telling you about my observations and experiences as a psychologist for the courts years ago, but I trust your unconscious mind to pluck out and put into handy action the part that is most relevant"* (following some stories with obtuse references to such kinds of detectors). Heart monitors, albeit a bit morbid, also are good.

Doodling, dealing cards, talking in dreams are examples of natural activities that reflect automated behavior (Lankton & Lankton, 1983). Consider, too, talking to clients in trance about people who wake up in the middle of the night to write down a dream and have no memory of having done so by morning.

SELECTED TRANSCRIPT MATERIAL

Automatic Drawing   Your unconscious mind can begin to draw for you and begin to write for you....It can draw a drawing on your behalf, your arm can move as if it has a mind of its own, as if it's deconnected from the rest of your body, as if it's on automatic pilot...cruise control in a car... everybody's had the experience of waiting to write a note and writing it and not even being aware of what it is they wrote...everybody's had the experience of doodling while being on the phone...and not even knowing about it until after you look at the pad and you see that you've been drawing and it's revealing to yourself....Your arm can move...it can create—it can create drawings, it can create words, the words may be random words, they don't have to be a sentence, they don't have to be punctuated...they can just be a letter, a word, a symbol....

The drawing can be the first thing you think of...it can be whatever you want it to be, it can be a gift to you from your right brain, a gift to you from your unconscious mind...and your mind can go deeper and deeper into hypnosis as you draw and as you write...deeper and deeper down...and in hypnosis, the critical part of you can be put away, can be put aside so that you just create....You'll have plenty of time to evaluate it later on...for now, you can just permit yourself to create....Even now, your arm can move as if there's a control panel inside your wrist that makes movement start...up and down, side to side—it's as if there's a connection, a wire going from your unconscious mind right to your hand—it moves itself...slowly or quickly... whole movements...it's hard to keep your hands still on the paper—they're tiny shapes and they're close...nice...tiny shapes...movement back, pencil beginning to move like the arm on a recording device that records brainwaves...the EEG recordings, up and down automatically...and a certain flow can begin, a certain flow can continue....

It can be a secret symbol that your unconscious mind wants to break or it can just be random words, random phrases, random drawings...phrases of your hand, painting...drawing, creation...and as you draw and as you write, you can go deeper and deeper into hypnosis....

It can be as if the very act of writing or drawing takes you down deeper...and it can be as if your hand has a mind of its own...controlled by your unconscious only....Are you willing to be surprised? I think so...your unconscious mind can communicate something that's surprising to you...you can learn from it, but later on you'll notice what it is that your mind has written for you....It can almost be like a secret, hidden part of yourself that comes out and begins to express itself, because it knows you're ready....

Figure 14.1 is the automatic writing done by a woman seeking treatment for the lifting of childhood amnesia. John was the therapist. Neither the client nor John recognized the word "goodbye" in the upper left corner during the session, although John recognized it afterwards. Its significance, however, became apparent when the client did not show up at her next scheduled appointment, nor did she make any further contact. Her unconscious knew she was terminating the therapy before her conscious mind knew!

Figure 14.1. "Goodbye."

Section E

Modifying Perception

Chapter 15

ANESTHESIA AND ANALGESIA

ABOUT THE PHENOMENON

Anesthesia, hypnotically induced, refers to one's ability to lose sensation in one or more parts of the body. Analgesia, hypnotically induced, diminishes rather than eliminates sensation. These two phenomena are reminiscent of negative hallucination; however, they are used for tactile sensation in particular, whereas hallucinations involve all sensory modalities. Also, for some people the phenomenon of anesthesia is experienced as numbness, a close cousin to the absence of feeling but not quite the same sensation. Most of the time, the tactile sensation toward which the anesthesia or analgesia is directed is pain or discomfort. Hilgard (1987), in writing about hypnoanalgesia and anesthesia, notes that when these are applied, pain will still follow the same course but at a fraction of its original intensity. Kihlstrom (1985) writes that hypnosis can cause a dramatic reduction in both the physical aspects of pain (*sensory pain*) and the psychological aspects (*subjective suffering*).

HISTORY AND EXPERIMENTAL STUDIES

One of the most interesting journal articles on the topic of hypnosis and anesthesia is on the history of the hypnotic application of anesthesia and analgesia (Gravitz, 1988). This article reveals that hypnosis has been utilized for anesthesia successfully for over a century and a half. The first documented case took place in 1829 when a mastectomy was performed by Jules Cloquet in Paris. From there on, in Europe and in the United States, hypnosis was successfully employed as an anesthesia in other mastectomies, amputations, removals of tumors, and dental extractions. Hypnoanalgesia waxed and waned in popularity basically in response to the medical and political climate of the particular period. Those periods in which hypnotists were held in great disrepute by the medical and lay community resulted in marked reductions in the use of hypnosis for anesthetic purposes. This was probably due to the outrageous and inaccurate claims of some practitioners. Much of it was also due to the misunderstandings and hysteria amongst various groups. In any event, hypnoanesthesia allowed essential surgery to be successfully performed at a time when many patients were not surviving surgery, dying either from infection, bleeding, or other causes.

A good example of the impact of hypnoanesthesia in medical practice was in Esdaile's (1850/1959) report of his surgeries with several thousand patients in India in which he used hypnosis as the sole anesthetic (Gravitz, 1988). At a time when 4 out of 10 surgical patients were dying, Esdaile's mortality rate was less than 5% due to the patient's ability to tolerate pain (and hence the surgery), a reduced rate of infection, and reduced blood loss. The advent of the more reliable and more professionally acceptable ether and chloroform anesthesia in the twentieth century soon resulted in hypnosis no longer being used as part of surgery on a regular basis.

There are present-day exceptions to the use of conventional anesthetics in medical practice. Some of these occur due to the cultural popularity of childbirth with no or limited chemical anesthesias or to times when chemical anesthesia is contraindicated because of cardiac or other problems. In other cases, prospective patients have allergic reactions or are hypersensitive to chemical anesthesia. Sometimes, tragically, chemical anesthesia is in limited supply or unavailable because of war, poverty, or exceptionally rural locations (Jackson & Middleton, 1978).

One fascinating case on the use of hypnoanesthesia instead of conventional anesthetics is that of dental surgeon Victor Rausch (1980), who actually had major abdominal surgery done on him while he hypnotized himself! Rausch was able to control muscle relaxation, breathing, pulse rate, blood pressure, reflex action, bleeding, and the pain.

These days, most applications of anesthesia are for pain control in less extreme situations. In the last decade articles have appeared documenting the utility of hypnoanesthesia for plastic surgery (Scott, 1975), obstetrics (Werner, Schauble, & Snudson, 1982), dentistry (Barber, 1977), gastrointestinal endoscopy (Jackson & Middleton, 1978), and dermatology (Gallagher, 1974). The Gallagher article is of particular interest because it involved the removal of over 4,000 tattoos in 1,500 subjects who were part of a rehabilitation program for people with criminal records. The removal of tattoos was done with negligible amounts of chemical anesthesia because supplies and budgetary limitations in the setting precluded their massive use. The purpose of the tattoo removal was so that upon release from prison, the men, sans the tattoos that might potentially identify them as ex-cons, would be better able to mingle with mainstream society. The author used a modification of the glove anesthesia technique, wherein subjects were also given a tiny bit of chemical anesthesia. This way they had a reference experience of knowing exactly what it was they were to produce in terms of numbness. Hypnoanesthesia greatly helped with the tattoo removal procedures, and no gross complications were encountered at any point.

Gallagher also began to develop an interesting procedure for screening out poor candidates for tattoo removal by using future progression techniques; poor candidates were considered those men who would get new tattoos upon their release from the program. Gallagher's screening procedure involved future progressing subjects and discovering which ones in the age- progressed situation did not see themselves with tattoos. Subjects who saw themselves as having new tattoos were considered poor choices for the removal procedures. Unfortunately, the author's illness precluded him from gathering any follow-up data to confirm or disconfirm the accuracy of the hunches derived from future-progression experiences.

One article in particular reviews state-of-the-art pediatric applications of hypnoanesthesia (Kohen, Olness, Colwell, & Hieimel, 1984). The authors found that in children as young as 3 years old, self-hypnosis using imagery was so effective with 27 of these young headache clients, that 29% had more than a 50% reduction in symptoms, and 70% evidenced a complete cessation of headaches. For other types of pain, a sample of 36 children showed that all but one obtained either more than a 50% reduction, or a complete reduction, in pain. Parenthetically, we can add that this excellent article provides similar data on cases that included enuresis, asthma, habit disorders, obesity, encopresis, and anxiety.

Overall, the authors found that 50% of all 505 children and adolescents treated with hypnosis showed complete resolution of the presenting problem while an additional 32% received significant improvement, 9% showed initial or some improvement, and only 7% demonstrated no apparent change or improvement. Moreover, the extent to which hypnosis was going to be successful with a given child was evident in four sessions or less. These results were maintained for follow-up periods ranging from 4 months to 2 years. Though the article is not explicit about the specific hypnotic techniques employed, it appears as if the procedure exclusively involved mental imagery and relaxation in the hypnosis. In another study of pediatric applications, hypnotized children receiving chemotherapy treatments had significantly more pain reduction during bone marrow aspirations than did their insusceptible counterparts (J. Hilgard & LeBaron, 1982; 1984).

In his scholarly chapter on hypnotic analgesia, Barber (1982) elucidates a number of points regarding hypnosis and anesthesia/analgesia that are worth reviewing. First of all, he notes that hypnosis has been found to reduce or eliminate a whole variety of experimentally induced pain, including ischemic, cold-presser, electric, and thermal. He also notes that hypnosis has repeatedly been demonstrated to be superior in achieving pain relief compared with other psychological methods. In addition, Barber reiterates the point that hypnosis is uniquely valuable because it can be used for the alleviation of chronic pain when other medical procedures cannot be used or have not been successful with a given disorder. He mentions in particular certain ongoing pain syndromes such as migraines, trigeminal neuralgia, or osteoarthritis as often being refractory to medical interventions.

In his review of the literature in this same chapter, Barber also points out that, to date, the experimental search for the neurophysiological mechanism through which hypnotic pain control is achieved has been for naught. Independent researchers have found no evidence for the notion that our endorphins are involved in hypnotic pain relief. Similarly, researchers have been unable to confirm that acetylcholine underlies hypnotic analgesia either. Moreover, Barber points out that muscle relaxation is not the essence of hypnotic anesthesia; it has been found not to be a useful treatment for chronic pain *unless* the pain is specifically caused by a muscle spasm itself.

Barber considers hypnotic anesthesia a relatively difficult phenomenon to achieve. He finds greater success with other pain control strategies such as displacing the pain to a different part of the body and substituting other sensory sensations. Yet he discusses those other strategies in the same breath with hypnoanesthesia, contributing to some of the confusion in the literature about this phenomenon. That is, some refer to hypnoanesthesia not specifically as a matter of removing sensation from or numbing the painful area, but as being almost synonymous with pain control through hypnosis. We think there are important distinctions to be made in these areas. Differences in the conceptualization of hypnoanesthetic numbing, itself, add to the confusion. Barber, for example, describes it as a positive hallucination of numbness, while Hilgard (1977) sees it mainly as being a matter of dissociation. Others (Jackson & Middleton, 1978) see it as being produced primarily as a byproduct of relaxation.

Barber (1982) also discusses another important issue in the area of pain control and indeed in the area of hypnotherapy at large. This is the issue of whether individualizing the induction and working phases of hypnosis, and giving indirect suggestions, is useful or even preferable to giving direct and standard suggestions. He points out that there is a significant body of evidence to suggest that individuals who perform poorly on standardized tests of hypnotizability and suggestibility may benefit the most from indirect and tailored suggestions. If you read the literature on hypnotic pain control, you could wind up thinking that it is just for high hypnotizables; in fact, high hypnotizables do achieve a significantly greater degree of pain control when compared to low hypnotizables. But Barber's point is that the low hypnotizables could fare better if they were given the opportunity to respond via indirect and tailored suggestions. Bear in mind that even if you are using only direct suggestion, it means only that your high hypnotizable subjects would be *more likely* to respond. Hilgard, Morgan, and Macdonald (1975) found that 44% of low susceptible individuals were able to reduce their pain by 10% or more. Therefore the relationship between hypnotizability and pain control is only probabilistic and not absolute. Barber's point, with which we strongly agree, is that the extent of responding can be enhanced through the adjunct provided by using indirect and tailored suggestion, at least in some circumstances.

Barber checked out some of these assumptions about direct versus indirect suggestion with Donald Price (Price & Barber, 1987). They discovered that when indirect suggestions for hypnotic analgesia were continuously given to subjects, the subjects evidenced a 44% decrease in the sensory aspects of pain and an 87% decrease in the affective complements of pain. (Sensory aspects of pain referred to the actual physical sensations and perceptions, whereas the affective components of pain referred to the fear and anxiety that makes pain worse.) One experimental group did not receive continuously given suggestions but, instead, suggestions that were given just once; they did not obtain these same results. Perhaps one reason why some prior research on indirect hypnotic suggestion has not supported its effectiveness was because the suggestions were offered once, in a static fashion. In any event, this has important implications for clinical practice with pain control; the Barber and Price research implies that in order to maintain the analgesia, you need to intersperse suggestions over a period of time. As they pointed out, however, it may not just be that the suggestions need to be given continuously. Perhaps subjects need to have a continuous, ongoing rapport and relationship with the therapist apart from any suggestions that the latter gives.

The Barber and Price research also suggested that with all subjects indirect suggestion is not only effective in reducing the affective component of pain, but also in reducing pain that is close to the pain threshold (low intensity pain). However, high intensity pain and the sensory aspects of pain responded well to indirect suggestions, too, but only in high hypnotizables. This alludes to the idea that indirect suggestion may offer its greatest clinical and experimental contribution to low and moderate hypnotizables with near threshold pain in the affective realm, allowing them to benefit from hypnotic approaches to pain control where they had previously been thought to be insusceptible. Since direct suggestion wasn't used at all in this study, you can't really say much about it specifically.

This excellent study was limited by the fact that the individuals providing the interventions were not double blinded. Also, the inductions were not standardized, although the suggestions for anesthesia proper were. Based on what we've said above, nonstandardized trancework will probably be necessary to test some of these hypotheses, despite the fact that in terms of research rigor it can create some problems. It will be challenging to test some of these nontraditional positions with traditional research methodology.

The Barber and Price study had been designed to shed light on why it had been difficult for experimenters to replicate Barber's earlier research (1977), which had shown an outstanding response to hypnotic analgesia provided within what was called the Rapid Induction Analgesia (RIA) paradigm. This paradigm used continuously given indirect and permissive suggestions and was effective in controlling dental pain in 27 volunteer subjects and subsequently in 99 out of 100 dental subjects. These results were used to challenge the assumption of traditionalists, borne out of experimental work with direct suggestion, that only high hypnotizables could consistently produce hypnoanesthesia. The 1987 study, suggesting the need for ongoing and continuous suggestions, may have answered the question of why other studies that used only direct and standardized suggestion did not produce similar results to Barber's original work.

Barber's 1977 findings were also confirmed by Friction and Roth (1985). They went further though and specifically compared direct suggestion with indirect suggestion. Analysis of the data showed that the indirect technique was significantly more effective than direct technique in changing pain thresholds regardless of susceptibility. The direct technique was significantly effective only with those subjects who received high susceptibility scores. On the other hand, Van Gorp, Meyer, and Dunbar (1985) found traditional hypnosis to be more effective than either Rapid Induction Analgesia, or relaxation, or suggestion without induction. However, their study must be disqualified from serious consideration in terms of really testing the issues in question because of liberties taken with the RIA protocol. In the RIA condition, the suggestions were not given continuously and simultaneously with the testing of the pain experience but were instead given prior to 10 minutes of pain. They were also taped instead of given live and differed from Barber's original protocol.

Malone, Kurtz, and Strube (1989) contributed further to our understanding of hypnoanesthesia. Their research study showed that there are at least two dimensions to pain that are differentially responsive to suggestion. Their hypnoanalgesia condition altered subjects' perception of the *intensity* of the pain without changing their perception of how unpleasant the shock was. A different condition, hypno-relaxation, produced reductions in the *unpleasantness* of the shock but not in the perceived intensity of the stimuli.

The person who has done the most classic research on hypnosis and pain is Ernest R. Hilgard. Based on his neodissociation theory (see Hilgard, 1977), Hilgard has always asserted in his studies that relaxation is not necessary for hypnotic anesthesia or analgesia, and that these phenomena can be achieved mainly by dissociation. His theory posits that there is a dissociated part of the self, called the hidden observer, that is aware of everything that goes on throughout the entire hypnotic procedure. Therefore, although a person may consciously report no feeling of pain when his or her hand is immersed in a bucket of cold water, when the hypnotherapist or the experimenter asks the same question of the "hidden observer," he or she gets a quite different answer. This dissociated part of the self is aware of the pain and, moreover, often experiences annoyance towards the experimenter for putting him or her through the procedures! Yet the part of the person reporting the experience talks in terms of feeling no discomfort. Whether or not you agree with this theory of hypnoanalgesia, or this theory of how hypnosis takes effect, Hilgard's research and his ideas are important. Dissociation may be but one of a few vehicles by which anesthesia takes place through hypnosis. It is possible that one type of pain control is achieved in this way and yet another is achieved through relaxation.

INDICATIONS FOR USE

Indications for using anesthesia or analgesia are when they are the phenomena a person does efficiently in natural settings. This includes people who, when asked how they manage to stay functional on those days when their back (or headache or stomach) acts up, respond with examples of how they get their bodies to feel numb. Some may do it unwittingly through self-hypnosis. Others may have developed a personal trigger or mental cue that elicits the numbness. Find out how the client generates the sensation and capitalize on that existent resource. A seamstress who would likely have learned to anesthetize her fingers to pin pricks should be asked what her "method" of doing that is. Most of the time people aren't aware that they do any such thing as self-anesthetize and don't know where to begin to describe their method. Ask your client to "walk you through" his or her technique or strategy; once articulated, the client may have a better sense of just what it is he or she does and how to do it at other times.

Another indication for using anesthesia/analgesia in therapy is when they are the complement to a problem-causing phenomenon. Perhaps a man has been so (tactually) sensitized to tickling that he cannot fully enjoy his wife's touching him around his neck, belly, or back. Analgesia that is posthypnotically induced to kick in whenever the man's wife begins to touch him romantically is a viable antidote.

Look to see if with certain clients the inadvertent use of anesthesia or analgesia is the mechanism of the problem. It is difficult to imagine a clinical situation where this would be a relevant guideline for use. One, however, would be the utilization of a spontaneous, hysterical loss of sensation as a way to discharge or circumvent the resistance from which it developed in the first place. Erickson did this in a demonstration of hypnosis to a skeptical medical audience which is shown in the film *The Process of Hypnotic Induction: A Training Video Tape Featuring Inductions Conducted By Milton H. Erickson in 1964*, narrated by Zeig[1]. In it, Erickson works with a young woman of seemingly pleasant nature who resists him through *overcompliance*. When asked to come up out of trance, she remarks that she can't—her arm is numb and cannot move. Erickson immediately sets about describing the ways

---

[1] This film is available through the Milton H. Erickson Foundation, Phoenix, AZ.

in which such a development can be of use to her in the future whenever undergoing medical procedures or dental work or childbirth. In doing so, he has disempowered the resistance symbolized by the anesthetized, cataleptic arm by reframing it as a useful, even special phenomenon. Interestingly, this very clever woman continues their repartee (and her resistance) by remarking that she doesn't ever experience much pain anyway.

Clients may frequently report the development of a spontaneous anesthesia in trance and it is rarely representative of resistance as in the case above. In these more benign situations, you can simply suggest to the client that *"anytime you have a muscle ache, or a headache, or if you're in labor about to give birth, you can remember and redevelop for as long as is necessary this very same experience."*

There are particular client populations for whom anesthesia and analgesia are naturally indicated. Pain clients are the most obvious. These include people for whom medication is not working or works partially, those with medical conditions that preclude pain medication, or those for whom medications are not viable because of the nature of their work (those who deal with sensitive material, operators of high-tech equipment, or competitive athletes). Others are allergic to pain medication or have histories of, or current problems with, substance abuse. Local and general anesthetics are contraindicated in approximately .5% to 1% of the general population (Jackson & Middleton, 1978) because of allergies, risk of respiratory or central nervous system depression, and interaction effects with other medications.

The use of hypnoanesthesia and hypnoanalgesia for pain has been documented extensively in the literature on clinical hypnosis. They have been used for headaches, burns, back pain, childbirth, the setting of fractured bones, pain from metastatic cancer, and many other situations (Hilgard, 1987). Surgical and dental applications have also been widely documented. As mentioned earlier, major abdominal surgery has been performed using hypnosis as the only anesthesia (Rausch, 1980). Kay Thompson, D.D.S., dentist and renowned teacher of the use of hypnosis in dentistry, shows a film in some of her workshops of a patient undergoing plastic surgery. Hypnoanesthesia is the sole agent of pain control. It isn't until the film is over that you learn that the patient is Dr. Thompson herself.

Kroger (1963) estimates that hypnoanesthesia would be effective in no more than 10% of prospective surgical patients, and then only with very careful patient selection and training. He adds that the greater use of hypnoanesthesia and analgesia in hospital settings is with minor surgical and pre- and post-op management and gives as examples the following: facilitating aspiration through relaxation (enabling patients to cough without discomfort); decreasing pain during the changing of surgical dressings (especially for burns); and the general management of pain. Kroger, however, cautions clinicians about the risks of reducing or eliminating pain to the extent that there is no longer any natural warning system in place for limiting damaging physical movement and activity on a patient's part.

In our discussion of pain patients we have been referring to physical pain. Hypnoanesthesia and analgesia can be used metaphorically to deal with emotional pain or hypersensitivity as well. Clients can be helped to develop *focal psychological numbing* for a past, wrenching trauma if too overwhelmed with mental pain to deal directly with it at the moment. Phobic clients can learn to raise their thresholds for tolerating anxiety by becoming increasingly *"insensitive" to their anxiety response*. Clients full of self-reproach can learn to become *numb to their own self-flagellations*. Clients in mourning can sometimes make use of an *inner analgesia* to take the edge off of a particularly crushing and eviscerating grief reaction. I (JSE) remember using hypnosis in this way with an engineer who was still grieving the stunning, sudden loss of his 5-month-old son one year after his death. Hypnoanalgesia was effected through making an analogy, during the trancework, between how a soothing agent like Maalox coats the stomach to protect it from disturbing things, and how an internally created soothing agent can move through the body, coating the *heart* to protect it from something too overpowering. Since Eric and I had worked together earlier on his somatic problems (in particular, gastric), I was able to segue very easily into this analogy. He found this to be very helpful.

Certain types of depressed clients may also be able to benefit from an emotional analgesia. These are the ones that are very emotionally sensitive, perhaps oversensitive, interpreting events in ways that support their depressive or self-denigrating perspective more than they accurately reflect the transpiring events. We have heard such individuals describe their experiences of sensitivity as if they were moving through life as third-degree burn victims. Such a case nearly calls out for the use of hypnoanalgesia. One of us (JHE) worked with a 17-year-old boy who was ultrasensitive interpersonally and who experienced social interactions as horribly painful, especially when they involved any possibility of criticism. Bart experienced significant relief after I induced a glove anesthesia and then had his hand levitate until it touched his forehead. As it approached his forehead, I suggested that when it touched, all the numbness could transfer to his brain and hence his mind. I then suggested that the level of numbness could vary depending on the circumstances and his need. In subsequent weeks he also developed, in hypnosis, images of his brain packed in either the plastic bubble wrap or Styrofoam "peanuts" that valuables are shipped in. The above methods have also been employed by us using a client's heart instead of brain, especially when the person has been hurt in romantic relationships.

Other people for whom hypnoanesthesia or hypnoanalgesia seems a natural intervention are those who have sought things out in life that will numb them or dull some emotional pain. Some recovering substance abusers may be able to use self-hypnoanalgesia or anesthesia to get relief from internal agitation in place of drugs or alcohol. These phenomena can also be helpful in the context of stress management, where people will complain of feeling burned out by the demands of work, life, and so on.

CONTRAINDICATIONS

Good clinical sense about the management of pain in therapy is really the best guideline for using anesthesia and analgesia in practice. Obviously, you do not want to override medically or emotionally significant pain. All our pain patients are medically cleared for the psychological removal or diminishing of physical pain. Caveats can be given to clients both in and out of trance about being *sensitive to medically meaningful pain*. Similarly, grieving clients need to grieve, and analgesia to assuage inner pain should only be used to enable people to function as they need to or to get some temporary respite from overwhelming pain, and never to interfere with the bereavement process itself.

Another instance where you might avoid using these phenomena is when a client had experienced paralysis earlier in life or some other type of loss of sensation (e.g., diabetic neuropathy). In these instances, the loss of control that they painfully and traumatically had experienced could make it difficult for them to comfortably use these hypnotic phenomena. Whereas from a utilization standpoint it could make sense to teach them how to use the experience of loss of sensation in some constructive way, or master it, sometimes an experience is so emotionally charged that it cannot or should not be done.

One of us (JHE) had a client suffering from multiple sclerosis who was having great difficulty controlling her muscle movements. To help her achieve weight loss, I had her experience an arm levitation that I described as being *light* and as taking place *outside of awareness*. Since she was a sensitive woman, I was also suggesting anesthesia—numbness as a way of decreasing her emotional sensitivity. However, after experiencing the arm levitation, she seemed panicked and, indeed, despite a number of phone conversations, wouldn't come back to me for more therapy. I speculated that it was the too-rapid induction of dissociation, automatic movement, and numbness that scared her. These were her adversaries with the multiple sclerosis, and she struggled with them day after day, hoping that such *involuntary* movement would not appear on a moment's notice. Having that happen hypnotically likely elicited an anxiety that overrode her interest in therapy. It may be that more preparation would have enabled her to utilize, even befriend, something that was a part of her life, but that's difficult to say for certain.

Just be mindful of being sensitive to your clients' needs apart from what you yourself may consider to be therapeutically useful. These cases remind us of the importance of watching clients for minimal cues of comfort or distress. However, it is also important to remember the adage "nothing ventured, nothing gained"; so that we can tolerate making mistakes, it is important to recognize that in clinical work it is often better to venture forth a benevolent effort at intervention than it is to sit and passively listen session in and session out.

ELICITING THE PHENOMENA OF ANESTHESIA AND ANALGESIA

Direct and Indirect Suggestion

Like all hypnotic phenomena, these are is best produced if some groundwork is laid in advance. Alerting clients' attention during the induction of trance to how they may be experiencing *"subtle, curious alterations in their senses"* or *"an absorption in sound or memory to the exclusion of other* (inferring tactile) *senses"* can be subtle yet effective ways of **seeding** the phenomenon of loss or changes in sensory perception. Alluding to naturalistic examples of body anesthesia or analgesia early on during trance induction also serve to seed the forthcoming interventions. Interspersing the words *numb, dull, unfeeling, insensate, laughing gas,* or *callous* early on in the trance seed as well.

One of the major principles of hypnotic pain control is for the client to get a toe hold on comfort and then expand that territory, and **presuppositions** can be used to facilitate this very thing. For example, you can say, *"Feel free to be aware that **when that dime-sized area of numbness expands,** you will find yourself moving more deeply down into a comfortable hypnotic state."*

Double binds can be employed to differentiate aspects of the pain, thereby "dividing and conquering" the client's universal experience of discomfort. Erickson often took this kind of divide-and-conquer approach in order to deal with chronic or acute pain. This was because the most difficult pain clients are the ones who experience their pain as unchanging and omnipresent. Examples here include, *"You can alleviate the discomfort in the center of the hurt or perhaps you'll begin by alleviating the discomfort somewhere else"* and *"You can experience alternating minutes of relief with minutes of the same old pain or perhaps relief will just increase in a linear fashion over time. That is, there may be a bit of a roller coaster ride at first before this ride is over or perhaps there will just be a straight line to recovery."* Another example is, *"Maybe the throbbing part of the pain will diminish before the dull ache dissipates, or perhaps, instead, the ache will diminish while the throbbing altogether disappears."*

Conscious/unconscious dissociative statements are useful here, too, in eliciting anesthesia and analgesia. Since another major principle of pain control is that the client learn to notice small changes in the pain, conscious/unconscious dissociative statements can be employed for this specific purpose. For example, you can say, *"Your conscious mind can keep track of each little bit of progress, while your unconscious mind can simply begin to increase the magnitude of the changes."* Or, *"Your conscious mind might develop a rating scale and notice that the pain is going from a 90 down to an 80, down to a 78, while your unconscious mind doesn't care about the quantification and just enjoys the quality of comfort."*

In fact, the SUDS (Wolpe & Lazarus, 1966) scale is frequently employed with pain patients so they can rate levels of pain and comfort and turn something that is subjective into something that is semi-objective. Typically, the scale runs from 1 to 100, with 1 being no pain and 100 being the worst imaginable experience of pain. In conventional hypnotherapy with more standardized inductions, the scale is usually employed in a simple and direct way, whereas tailored, permissive inductions capitalize on the use of conscious/unconscious dissociative statements to separate out the different dimensions of pain into more manageable, manipulable facets of experience.

Metaphor and Symbols

Metaphors that can elicit anesthesia and analgesia abound and are most effective in helping to develop these phenomena. A classic metaphor is the glove anesthesia metaphor. Here one suggests to the client that a numbness come over the hand, up to the wrist, covering it just as a glove would. This is the therapeutic utilization of what manifests as a glove paralysis in cases of hysterical neurosis and underscores how hypnosis can be seen as a territory where mental mechanisms are explored for the possible adaptive use of what are often seen only as psychopathological states. Once a client has developed a glove anesthesia, the therapist then suggests that the hand can move to the area of discomfort and the anesthesia *can transfer out of the hand into the afflicted area.* Granted, this can sound magical, even hokey, to our conscious minds. Nevertheless, this technique has proved remarkably effective in a number of medical, dental, and psychotherapeutic contexts (Kroger, 1963).

Zeig once demonstrated a nonverbal strategy for inducing hypnotic phenomena at a workshop on pain control (Philadelphia, September 1988). He held out his arm, took his other hand, and made a sawing motion at his wrist of the hand that was outstretched. This was a way of using mime to induce a glove anesthesia. What Zeig actually demonstrated was *dissociation* of the hand at the wrist. Anesthesia, specifically, would be demonstrated were he to have pinched himself on the hand and shown no sensation in his face. Mime could also be used to show how the flow of anesthesia could move from the hand to the afflicted part of the body. It would be an interesting exercise for therapists to try to develop nonverbal strategies for inducing each of the phenomena.

Another popular metaphor, one used more in traditional circles, involves people changing their pain thresholds by imagining a dial with numbers ranging from 1 to 10. O'Hanlon and Martin's (1992) appealing term for these and other less literal metaphors are "control knobs of experience." The dial might read "pain" on the right side and "comfort" on the left side. The person notices where the dial is set and then experiences him- or herself reaching out and turning down the dial. As that happens, he or she is to experience more comfort. We like to enhance the sensory aspects of this to both enrich and empower the hypnotic experience. For instance, we have people *hear* the "click, click" that takes place as they reach each new numerical level. We also have them *feel* the knurling on the dial and the indentations at each number marker when the dial hits a bit of a rut and is overridden. We have even suggested that the person *smell* the odor of the new electronic equipment.

Another metaphor that can be developed involves the client's developing calluses to the pain. We first heard Zeig use this metaphor in a workshop on pain control (Philadelphia, 1990). He also spoke about pain in some cases functioning as an alarm clock. This metaphor is useful for those people who need to experience pain as a signal to propel them toward medical treatment. On the other hand, for individuals who have already gotten all the medical treatment they need, reference can be made to an alarm clock when it needs to be shut off, as in the following quote, *"As long as everything that needs to be done diagnostically and treatmentwise has been done, you can afford to let go of the pain. It's served its purpose and it can be turned off, like how you press the button or tab when it's time to shut off the alarm. Go ahead, and turn it off, and feel the quiet now, that allows you to rest."* In either case, addressing the signal function of pain is often a critical component of hypnotic treatment of pain control.

Another useful metaphor is a circuit breaker. With this idea you talk about the nervous system in metaphorical terms, likening it to the electric wiring of a house controlled by a circuit box. Continuing with this metaphor, then, you suggest that a certain circuit breaker can be broken to the person's *advantage*. The suggestion might go like this: *"Like a circuit that's overloaded, your mind can switch off that neurological connection almost as if it's the circuit breaker in a circuit box flipping off to the side, stopping the flow of electricity. Of course, at another time and in another place you can flip the circuit back over so that the flow of electricity is resumed, but for now and for as long as you'd like, you can leave it as it is so that nothing gets through to that part."*

The metaphors above are ones you hear people use frequently because they seem to provide useful images. However, it is especially prudent for a therapist to tune into a client's own particular metaphor, and clients do commonly describe their pain in metaphorical terms. Consider such expressions as, *"It's a throbbing pain,"* or *"It's like a fireball,"* or *"It's like getting stabbed with a knife."* Go with these metaphors when you hear them in order to personalize your work and make it easier for the client to connect.

Take, for example, the last quote, in which pain was likened to a knife. Match the metaphor and talk about all the ways in which knives become duller and duller. Describe how eventually a knife can become so dulled that (here you don't want to say "it gets to the *point* that . . . " as that image counters the very one you are trying to project!) you can have the experience of *"running a finger over the edge and not being able to tell if it was a blade, or perhaps the rounded, smoothed edge of a spoon, or even a flattened coin."* Liken it to a butter knife, and move the image even further in the direction of dull by talking about *butter spreaders*, duller still.

The idea is that you can almost always find ways within the context of the client's own pain metaphor to attenuate the experience of pain. If a client doesn't offer up a metaphor spontaneously, ask the client to describe his or her pain (Zeig, 1990a) and see what he or she comes up with that may be of use as a working metaphor. If the metaphor is that *"This pain in my back feels like a burning red light, intense, bright and pulsating,"* the therapist can respond with,

> *And perhaps you can begin to notice the throbbing beginning to slow down, and diminish in pulse, slower still, like a metronome gradually winding down...and simultaneously you can also notice the edges of this red sphere, this red light beginning to show just a little bit of lightening, becoming just a little bit orange and the edges becoming irregular, breaking apart bit by bit like a giant pond of ice, melting, thawing, breaking up, and the orange at the edges begins to become a little bit lighter and begins to become yellowish and the yellowish becomes paler still, almost a whitish color and this activity around the edges begins to move inward toward the center, creating a kind of cooling trend.*

This response illustrates working within the metaphor itself to diffuse the painful imagery and shape it into something with the power to heal. It also illustrates how you can start with a toe-hold and then work to expand that. Illustrated here, too, is another principle of hypnotic pain control that we have not mentioned yet. This is working from the *outside in* while making gradual changes. It is easiest to get results starting with the *periphery* of any problem and then working toward the denser center (Zeig, 1990a). This is useful to keep in mind whether you are describing the problem metaphorically or treating it directly.

In sum, all the methods described so far in this protocol for inducing anesthesia or analgesia incorporate essential principles of pain control. These are (a) differentiating the pain, (b) taking a divide-and-conquer approach, (c) working from the outside in, (d) creating a little bit of comfort and expanding that over time to increase the degree of comfort, and (e) getting the person to appreciate tiny changes. All of these principles bespeak, once again, a *process-oriented approach* to pain relief, where you remain focused on what is happening within your client and how your client is experiencing the phenomenon of trance as well as the process of working together in trance. As therapist, you continually calibrate the therapeutic work at regular intervals to better meet clients' needs. It is important for clients to realize that they do have the skills to create body experiences of anesthesia and analgesia that can be implemented over time to a greater and greater extent. However, it is the classic misconception of many clients that hypnotic pain control is something that can be achieved immediately and remain enduring. Pain control techniques get better with practice and with repeated applications (Erickson, 1980a).

Symbols and Anesthesia

One powerful symbol for anesthesia for pediatric populations and even for many adults is any kind of doll or puppet that is either stuffed or has a soft body. Children can play with these, even as the therapist is making suggestions directly to the doll. Therapists can point out how

> *easy it is for that doll to be poked and pushed and pulled because it doesn't feel anything at all. Kids come in all the time and give it medicine and needles and shots and it just goes about its business of looking around and being curious about what's happening next and what the next thing is it'll be asked to play and it doesn't even know that there are any needles at all until long after any needle has been given and it can't believe how it felt nothing! Except curiosity and more curiosity and even some more after that! You see it's just all soft inside and you too can become soft inside and even curious, if you want to, about how you too can feel soft and nothing at the same time. There's just so much to learn about feeling soft and nothing, and curious....*

The fact that dolls and puppets have no apparent sensory nervous systems makes them ideal symbolic representatives for anesthesia and analgesia. For adults, we've playfully used Gumby as a prop to demonstrate the idea of having movement without sensation.

Naturalistic Experiences with Anesthesia

Anesthesia and analgesia can be induced by reminding clients of times in their lives when they experienced such things naturally. Remember that Erickson felt most hypnotic phenomena occurred in everyday life from time to time and that even hypnosis was a natural and everyday experience. Formal hypnosis, taking place in the therapy office, helps to enliven these phenomena in more predictable and manipulable fashions. If you let clients know that they have already done what it is that you are going to be asking them to do, it makes it a whole lot easier for them to do it again. There are just so many more doubts associated with something that is being done seemingly for the first time than with something that had once been successfully performed.

One naturalistic example that can be beckoned forth is that of children playing a long time in the snow and developing cold arms or legs or derrières that eventually feel sort of numb. This example may be developed as follows:

> *You might remember back to building that snowman and en-*
> *joying it so much that you stayed out too, too long. And you no-*
> *ticed your hands and maybe your feet, too, getting colder and colder*
> *and number and number but it was an okay cold and an okay*
> *numb because you knew that it wouldn't last forever but would*
> *last for a period of time that you could handle. Maybe you sat on*
> *the ground and built part of that snowman or built a snow fort and*
> *felt your bottom go cold and numb also. Later on you went into the*
> *house and you could feel the numbness to an even greater extent*
> *and it would feel like it was a cold/hot numb. Now, you can re-*
> *member that experience and recreate it for yourself.*

Another naturalistic example has to do with the way people's arms
and legs fall asleep while sitting or lying in bed at night. A therapist
might call this memory up in the following way:

> *And just about everyone has had the experience of lying in bed*
> *at night and lying on an arm and feeling it go numb, insensitive.*
> *Perhaps there's a sense of tingling or of pins and needles associ-*
> *ated with that, and sometimes a person might choose just to con-*
> *tinue lying in the very same way even though she knows that her*
> *arm is going to fall deeper and deeper asleep. Later when you go*
> *to move and you pick up that arm, it's almost as if it's someone*
> *else's—it's numb, insensitive, unfeeling, it doesn't feel like your*
> *arm. But you know this is amusing and it feels okay simply and*
> *mainly because you know that you have control over the situation*
> *and it will last for a limited period of time so that you can enjoy it.*

Because ideosensory experience is enhanced with hypnosis, having
the *thought* of numbness can begin a chain of mental associations to
the experiences being described, allowing it to be reexperienced spontaneously in the present. The person listening to the induction above
about playing in the snow is called upon to access the *kinesthetic
memory* of cold, leading to a sensation of tingling or numbness, and
then to project this *inner experience* onto a hand or foot or lower back
area. It is the accessing of the client's own resource (in the form of body
memory, in this example) that makes hypnosis used in this way potentially more powerful than the direct suggestion and superimposition of
numbness onto a hand by an external operator as is done in more standardized induction techniques (i.e., "*your hand is becoming more and
more numb as you count from 1 to 100*").

You can capitalize further on the ideosensory enhancement of
hypnoanesthesia by having the person recall experiences with chemi-

cal anesthesia. In recalling those experiences, some people can reproduce them quite effectively. I (JHE) once worked with a client who could think about being in the dentist's office, think about the smell of the dentist's office, think about the taste and smell of the liquid that numbs the spot where the Novocaine is going to be given, think about the feeling of the shot of Novocaine, the spray coming off the needle, the warm, mediciny taste, and then experience a full-blown mouth anesthesia. I also had a patient who smoked a lot of pot in college. Even after stopping drug use as an adult, he could vividly remember the sound of his favorite rock bands, The Grateful Dead and Pink Floyd, and begin to feel "high" again. This is another example of the power of thought and memory in drawing up phenomenological realities that are different from physical and contextual ones.

SELECTED TRANSCRIPT MATERIAL

Anesthesia for Knee Pain

Maybe as we go on, your knees can even tingle as they feel warm, numb...just about everyone's had the experience of an arm or leg falling asleep...that can be a fun experience because you know it will end eventually; it doesn't have to last forever, but in the meantime it's as if you've lost sensation in a part of your body...and you can let it be there, it can reside there to the extent that you need it, it can be variable...enough to get rid of any discomfort...but not so much that you can't walk because you can walk, it's just that there's a certain loss of sensation that you allow in your knees....

Anesthesia for the Emotional Pain of Anxiety Attacks

...and like a pain patient you can allow yourself to go into trance to escape the pain because pain goes away, softens when a person relaxes. There may be pain residing in your mind; there may be pain residing in your body; there may be memories residing in your body that are painful; but by going down into trance there's a certain natural trance anesthesia and that can come over you, can soften you, and provide a certain protective shield...can give you a certain physical numbness that keeps you safe and invulnerable and can give you a certain mental numbness that can be your shock absorber like the shock absorbers on a car. Some cars these days come equipped with adjustable shock absorbers, one setting for a hardier and sportier ride, another setting for a smoother, softer, luxurious ride. You can even walk around in trance, the depth of hypnosis can be calibrated to the amount of pain you're afraid of experiencing....

Anesthesia
&
Hyperesthesia
as Symbols
for Changes
in Emotional
Sensitivity

....Go out of your head into your body to avoid being out of your mind...and as these changes take place here and now, Dan, right hand becoming sensitized, left becoming systematically desensitized...as those variations take place, you recognize that you have the similar ability elsewhere, other ways, other times....Any time you begin to worry, anytime you get too intense, anytime you get too busy...go numb, mind, go sensitive, body...your mind can be as numb as that left hand of yours...feels some tingling perhaps like numb tingling, no sensation...it's like it's paralyzed....You vary this combination to suit your needs...your needs, the silence inside becomes more and more robust...and you understand that having these tools is incredibly handy...and just as you modulate the combination, juxtaposition, alternation, sequencing of sensitivity, numbness...so, too, do you learn to combine your busy schedule with relaxation time....You learn to dialogue and cooperate with Louise, you learn when to be available and sensitive to your parents and your in-laws and insensitive at other times...you learn to vary these things...and you appreciate your ability to be hypnotized because of how you can produce these phenomena in your hands...and then producing them, you go deeper still....They can be symbols for you...so that anytime you're out and about in the world or talking on the phone, you can feel the texture of your pant leg or not feel the texture of your pant leg...and know that you have the capacity to vary your reaction, your feeling state...now with this in mind, Dan...I'd like you to allow yourself, to allow your hands to become average, sensing again knowing that they can revert to this as you need them to...average sensing...before those changes are complete, though, take your right hand and touch your left hand...go ahead...notice some differences, some contrasts...and then put your hand back on your pant leg and when that happens, bring yourself out of trance, feeling anchored with a stable silence, a focus of attention, a clarity of mind, a peacefulness inside...you can then exit trance....

Interestingly, after this session, the client had difficulty opening his left *eye*; he said it felt numb and anesthetized. Also, he reported that there was an excellent discrepancy in sensation between his right and left hands and that on his right hand he felt much more sensitive. In addition, Dan reported having had the visual image of tiny fibers pointing upward out of boxes on his pant leg, similar to what one might see, or imagine seeing, if looking at blue jeans through a microscope. He reported that this experience came to him spontaneously and it wasn't something that he intentionally developed in order to get hyperesthesia.

Chapter 16

HYPERESTHESIA

ABOUT THE PHENOMENON

Hyperesthesia is the hypnotic phenomenon that is the complement to anesthesia. In this underused phenomenon the person experiences highly increased sensitivity to touch and other bodily sensations. Hyperesthesia is underused in part because its applications are more limited than other phenomena; however, there are still opportunities for use that have not been capitalized on by the therapeutic community.

EXPERIMENTAL STUDIES

In a wonderfully designed and comprehensive study performed by Arendt-Neilsen, Zachariae, and Bjerring (1990), it was found that for high hypnotizables suggestions for hyperesthesia could *decrease the sensory and pain threshold* of subjects by almost 50%. The stimulus in the experiment was laser stimulation applied to the hand. The 50% change in thresholds noted above manifested through reactions in the subjects to laser intensities that were far below what normally could be perceived in the normal awake state! Additionally, it was found that when pain-related evoked-brain potentials were measured, they consistently demonstrated the expected increased amplitude. Suggestions for analgesia resulted in even greater changes—*increases in the sen-*

sory and pain thresholds of a significant 316% and 190% respectively.

Amazingly, a number of the subjects who experienced total analgesia did not respond at all to laser stimulation that would normally be experienced as extremely painful and bordered on an intensity that would cause tissue damage. For analgesia, the brainwave-evoked potentials consistently and significantly decreased as predicted. Interestingly, in this experiment the magnitude of the change in the brainwaves was considerably less than the changes reported in the experiencing of the sensory stimuli and the pain stimuli. For example, subjects who subjectively experienced complete analgesia with no experience of pain still registered a diminished but present—and significant—pain-related evoked potential. This suggests that the experiences are still registering *physiologically* at some level, while psychological changes allow for a *perceived* difference. This observation, coupled with that of changes in the experience of sensation or pain related to laser stimulation being very rapid, has led the authors to suggest that it seems unlikely that the effect of hypnosis is due to changes in physiologically endogenous substances or hormonal/nonopiates and is, instead, due to other factors, presumably psychological/neurological.

In any event, this study is particularly significant because it is the first to make the observation that suggestions of hyperesthesia can simultaneously decrease the sensory and pain thresholds *and* increase the amplitude of the pain-evoked brainwave potential. Although with analgesia the authors could not definitively rule out the possibility that subjects were pretending to be numb and ignoring the pain, with hyperesthesia this could not have been possible. Subjects in that condition were reacting to stimulation that was well below what is normally perceived in a waking state and could not have been faked.

INDICATIONS FOR USE

Clinical applications for hyperesthesia are principally in situations where the problem has been generated by the client's inadvertent use of anesthesia. These situations include nail biters who do not feel the pain that others would, lip and cheek chewers, hair pullers (trichotillomania), and self-mutilators.

Moreover, hyperesthesia can be developed as a phenomenon that provides a hypnotic complement to a *psychological* rather than a physical state of anesthesia. This is a use of enhanced sensation as a *symbolic* antidote to a mental reality. For example, hyperesthesia can be cultivated to counteract a person's interpersonal quality of "insensitivity." Or a client in therapy who complains of being "emotionally numb" can be taught to use self-induced hyperesthesia symbolically as a means to learn how to "resensitize" oneself. Likewise, children who lack sensitivity and hit or say cruelties to others could be taught hypnotic hyperesthesia, again as a way of giving an antidotal, indirect symbolic suggestion to "be more sensitive to others."

Hyperesthesia can also be used in situations where the presenting problem or issue is not secondary to the maladaptive use of anesthesia. Perhaps a therapist sees it as a viable therapeutic course of action to enhance sensitivity in one of a client's senses or parts of body. An example is the smoker who would find smoking increasingly unpalatable were the therapist to use hyperesthesia to *enhance* the sensation of smoke in the mouth, bronchial tubes, and lungs. Some overeaters could similarly benefit from the induction of hyperesthesia to learn to feel more acutely the sensations of fullness in the stomach or to become more aware of how large the body feels.

Another good indication for the use of hyperesthesia is with women who are preorgasmic and men who experience retarded ejaculation. Hyperesthesia can increase sensitivity in each of these conditions, often making orgasm and ejaculation achievable or achievable more quickly. There can obviously be a multitude of factors involved in these two conditions, rendering the problem refractory to the singular or isolated use of hypnotic hyperesthesia; however, increased tactile/kinesthetic sensitivity at critical junctures in a sexual interlude can often be therapeutic. In other words, don't overlook the couples/marital therapy proper that may need to be done as a prelude to hypnotic hyperesthesia.

Another indication for hyperesthesia in the sexual realm is when a man or woman does not experience much sexual sensitivity even during Masters and Johnson-type pleasuring activities. These activities are often prescribed during sex therapy to increase sensory awareness and stimulation responsiveness. If these exercises are not accomplishing that, hypnosis can be used as an adjunct, wherein the tactile/kinesthetic sensitivity is increased via suggestion rather than through these ordered task assignments. A number of other sexual problems ranging from low sexual desire to low enjoyment of sex can maladaptively involve elements of psychological/emotional "anesthesia" and therefore be helped by the therapeutic use of hyperesthesia.

Erickson (1958/1980) described the seemingly paradoxical use of hyperesthesia for a man receiving dental treatment in whom hypnotic anesthesia was able to be elicited in all parts of the body except in his mouth. Efforts to transfer the anesthesia from his hands to his mouth were unsuccessful, as were all attempts to elicit even a bit of oral analgesia. Erickson decided to suggest to the man that his left hand become painfully sensitive to all stimuli (he was also told that care would be taken to protect the hand from any painful contacts). The man indeed developed hyperesthesia for the hand but also, and spontaneously, developed sufficient anesthesia for his mouth to permit the dental work with no other anesthetic agents. Erickson's understanding of this was that the man's fixed, psychological understanding of dental work was that it *necessarily* involves hypersensitivity, and so the anesthesia and analgesia desired would only be manifested as part of a hyperesthesia-anesthesia pattern. It is noted that other, similar cases have been reported as well.

CONTRAINDICATIONS

You cannot use hyperesthesia to enhance sensitivity in clients with neurological conditions where there has been nerve damage. You could consider the use of positive tactile hallucination in such situations, if it were thought therapeutic for the client to "feel," but for true hyperesthesia, the neurology must be intact. Therapists should also be judicious in their use of hyperesthesia with self-mutilators or not use it at all. A trainee once asked us about its use in counteracting the numbness her client felt when cutting up her arms. Only therapists who are very experienced in using hypnotic techniques should employ hypnotic phenomena so directly with so dangerous a symptom, should things go awry. Furthermore, the character pathology typically associated with self-mutilators and the inherent potential for acting out and regressing make this a poor choice of client for the novice hypnotherapist to learn on. In addition, some self-mutilators cut just *because* of the sensation of pain, inasmuch as skin wounds are the only things they believe that they can feel. Hyperesthesia, in these cases, would be strongly contraindicated in the therapy.

ELICITING THE PHENOMENON OF HYPERESTHESIA

Direct and Indirect Suggestion

You could **seed** the idea of hypersensitivity right from the beginning of your induction by focusing your client's attention on the "...*increasing awareness of the carpet underneath your feet, and of the feeling of the sofa cushion underneath your thighs, behind your back, supporting it **as you feel yourself touch** down at deeper and deeper levels of trance....*" Any noncontrived pretrance conversation about sensitivity, hypersensitivity, and the like could serve to facilitate the response of hyperesthesia later on.

Presuppositions such as the following should also be part of your induction: "***After you are more sensitive***," or "***When*** *the session is over and* ***you have that tactile responsivity***, *then....*" In both of these examples, you are assuming a reality that will be evident to the client later on.

Another method for eliciting hyperesthesia is to use **double binds**. For example, you could say, "*Your sensitivity could increase quickly or slowly/increase in a step-by-step fashion or all at once/increase and then stay that way, or increase a little bit and then you could take a step back and then two steps forward.*" These paired alternatives enchant the unconscious mind with the illusion of choice, wherein either one is fine—both will move the person in the desired hypnotic direction.

A third linguistic pattern used to elicit hyperesthesia entails the use of **conscious/unconscious dissociative statements**. In such statements, you attribute one aspect of the phenomenon to the control of the conscious mind and another aspect of the phenomenon to the control of the unconscious mind. Examples of how to phrase this include, "*Your conscious mind can allow the skin sensitivity to increase in a way that has happened to you before, while the unconscious mind can allow it to increase in a way that I suggest.*" Or, "*Your conscious mind can have your sensitivity increase in a way that you've experienced already in your life, while your unconscious mind has your sensitivity increase in a way that's new for you.*" Or, "*Your conscious mind can have your sensitivity increase by shifting your focus of attention to that part of your body, while your unconscious mind changes the physiological mechanisms internally such that sensitivity is increased.*" As this last conscious/unconscious dissociative statement illustrates, it is often best to attribute something to the conscious mind that is under volitional control while allowing the unconscious mind to take care of things that are normally outside of awareness.

Metaphor

One method of eliciting hyperesthesia via metaphor is to use direct images. You can suggest to your client that he or she imagine his or her tactile sense being regulated by a dial, perhaps a dial that resembles one on a fine stereo receiver. The following is an example of how this might be elaborated:

> *....And the dial can have little niches, little markings indicating levels from zero all the way up to 10 around the dial, and the*

little indentations have white paint inside, and you can wonder to yourself how they get the white paint exactly inside those little indentations and how they print the numbers on so precisely. While your conscious mind is wondering about that, your unconscious mind can just be moving the dial up to increase sensitivity, and it really can be experienced at each indentation....There's a sound, a click, and a little bit of a sticking point on the dial and you can stop there if you want to be exactly at 5 or 6 or 7, turning up the sensitivity, but you push through each one so that the sensitivity can be maximized. Your hand can become more and more sensitive to it as it presses, as the points press into your skin and you stop at 9 or 10.

You can follow this metaphorical use of a dial in trance with a direct suggestion for posthypnotic responses: *"Anytime you want to increase your sensitivity, close your eyes, put yourself into a light trance, and reexperience your dial being turned up gradually or quickly, whatever suits your needs best."*

Naturalistic Accounts of Hyperesthesia

Naturalistic examples of this phenomenon can fall into a variety of categories. We have outlined the following:

1. those describing everyday occurrences of acutely enhanced sensory sensitivity;
2. those describing the natural but gradual development of hyperesthesia;
3. those describing natural physical and physiological processes that lead to a hyperesthesialike awareness; and
4. those describing natural or honed hyperesthetic skill.

Everyday Occurrences of Acutely Enhanced Sensory Sensitivity

Stories in this camp include those describing how one gets a bad sunburn and is exceptionally sensitive to touch for days afterward. You could also talk about how it feels to have a blister break on one's hand or foot. Or just about everyone has oversensitized the tongue by eating very hot salsa or Szechwan chicken.

On more positive notes, you can talk about how people who are sexually aroused become exceptionally sensitive and responsive to touch. You can talk about the delicious feeling of one's romantic partner touching one's hair, or wrist, or shoulder blade and comment on how context and arousal levels enhance what could otherwise be a pleasant but romantically/sexually innocuous touch. Remember that stories of increased sensitivity can be tailored to the presenting problem. For example, the most relevant story for a person who bites her tongue or chews her lip is the story about eating salsa or one about sipping a too-hot beverage.

Gradually Developing Natural Hyperesthesia

This other category of stories illustrates situations where an increasing awareness of sensation develops over time. These examples are applicable for a person who is somewhat resistant or simply skeptical about hypnosis and who might not or psychologically cannot manifest a lot of increased sensitivity all at once. They are also very appropriate for the overly compliant client who tries hard to get a response and whose watchfulness interferes with its development. In such instances, you encourage the client's sensitivity to increase *imperceptively* over time so that it is more difficult for the individual to resist or analyze away the gradual increments. For example, you might describe having new shoes that feel fine when you first put them on but hurt unbearably by the end of the day. Another useful story begins by describing going camping and lying down comfortably at the beginning of the evening in a sleeping bag. It continues by describing how at 2:30 A.M. you begin to feel somewhat uncomfortable, and by morning you are unbearably uncomfortable, aware of every pebble underneath as if the pebbles were boulders. The tale of the princess and the pea would fit well here, too!

Sensory Quiescence Changing Over to Sensory Hyperesthesia

There are several natural physical and physiological processes in which a person goes from a relatively unfeeling state to one of acute awareness of sensation. Accounts of these situations are useful because they *pace*, or *mirror*, the current unsensing situation of the client and then describe the processes leading to the desired state of ever increasing high sensitivity. An example of this is how a woman's breasts increase in sensitivity during her menstrual periods and during pregnancy. Another physical/physiological process that you could describe to the client to pace and lead him or her toward hyperesthesia is how a person doesn't urinate for 4 or 5 hours and then begins to feel the increased sensation of fullness in the bladder: "*...the increased pressure on the bladder that increasingly dominates one's awareness...you may not have been aware of it before, but you are now, or can be soon, aware of the* *sensation that's most relevant for you, now and later, to the degree that's correct and helpful, rejoicing in that new-found sensitivity (in your fingers/cheek/scalp) that tells you something has already changed...."*

Talk to your hypnotized clients about how children and teenagers grow bigger and how clothes that once were loose and baggy begin to feel tighter and tighter each time they are put on: *"...each time feeling them against your wrist, against your upper arms, your shoulder blades in a way that is different, and the sensation is different, noticeably so, more acute, feeling the snugness, perhaps reminding you of the snugness of a favorite sweatshirt, the kind where you really feel the inside of the fabric lumpy-soft, cushy, against your skin...."* Another story that falls in this category is one describing Thanksgiving dinner and how one typically moves from an absence of awareness of one's insides to the very acute awareness of being stuffed.

Natural and Honed Hyperesthesia

Don't overlook instances of naturally developed hyperesthetic skill. Consider, for example, professional wine tasters and perfume developers. Think about cats with their enhanced night vision, eagles and hawks with their acute visual senses, and the compensating and enhanced auditory sense in individuals who are blind.

Focusing Attention to Heighten Sensitivity

Another indirect method of eliciting hyperesthesia is to shift the client's attention to a part of the body usually ignored so that the person suddenly becomes aware of some physical sensation. For instance, the therapist can describe to a client how he or she can

> *become increasingly aware of your feet in your shoes, the feeling of comfortable, flexible enclosure, surrounding each foot...you're not usually aware of this, but you can be now, especially aware, and feel your nervous system become especially alive with that perception of sensation...and the feeling of that watchband against your wrist, the leather smooth, the coolness of metal laying like a coin on top of your wrist, weighs as much as would a quarter, don't you think, or is it closer in weight to a nickel?...What do you think?...Take a moment to really allow yourself to detect the precise weight of that watchface resting on the outer part of your wrist...and then I want you to get ready to feel the earring in your ear, and to begin to feel the distinction between the weight of*

that pearl there, resting against the front of the lobe, and the weight
of a larger earring, how it would pull down a bit, perhaps a big
bauble of an earring that you'd wear to an evening out, or to a
holiday party, the kind that you feel delightfully every time you
swing your head around to see who just touched you on the shoul-
der to say hello....

Along these same lines, you could talk about hearing a faucet drip
when you're trying to sleep, and the way one becomes "...*hypersensi-*
tive to that sound, as it begins to sound larger than life, and becomes
too, too prominent in relation to all other sounds...." The same could
be said for a clock ticking, or a spouse snoring, and so on. The essence
is to capitalize on those instances where people do or can (with a little
help) become acutely aware of otherwise benign sensations.

In relating these situations, it is often best to appeal to the person's
own history of having had these or similar experiences. It is useful to
start by saying, "*Just about everyone's had the experience of...*" (listening to a clock tick, hearing a dripping faucet, etc.). Ericksonian therapy
is very naturalistic, and for the reader's work to become more naturalistic he or she wants not only to have the stories appeal to, and have
meaning for, the client, but more importantly, wants them to function
like *keys opening doors* for clients to their own extensive histories of
accomplishing the phenomenon at hand. It is not so important if there
has been a time when the client has become very aware of faucets dripping or clocks ticking, and it is not even so important if at the time that
the story is being told the client develops that awareness. What is most
important is the possibility that the client might hear the story and
then remember how, as a teenager, he or she once went to a slumber
party around the time that digital watches came out, the kind that beep
on the half hour, and was kept up by the sound and the anticipation of
that sound, or kept up by the muffled barking of a neighbor's dog. When
it comes to hypnotic phenomena, the specific content of your story is
less important than its ability to potentiate the client's accessing resources by virtue of triggering useful memories, ideas, feelings, and so
on.

SELECTED TRANSCRIPT MATERIAL

Hyperesthesia   ....And as you begin to let go more and more you can
for a   hold on to certain pleasurable sensations that you are
Depressed   already experiencing inside...so, you allow yourself to

Woman with Bodily Numbness and Diminished Sexuality

feel good and those feelings become accentuated, you focus in on them very clearly...and you become more and more absorbed in the pleasurable sensations inside and on the boundary of inside, which is your skin...your skin is the outer boundary of inside...so the good feelings of comfort that you begin to identify—I don't know exactly where—perhaps you could begin to absorb yourself in a comfortable feeling in your shoulders right now...muscles letting go...relaxing more and more...or a comfortable feeling in your stomach, a feeling of satisfaction...a feeling of sensitive comfort...and isn't that an interesting idea...a feeling of sensitive comfort...and those feelings like a balloon being blown up begin to expand...and go all the way from the top of your head all the way down to your chest, your stomach, your diaphragm, legs and feet...radiating, rippling out, all over...because of the depression, parts of your body once felt deadened...and heavy...now your body can feel alive and how will it happen?...Will it become alive, sensitive, so sensitive to touch...or will it become alive...all at once or will it become alive gradually over the course of this session, over the course of days?...

Just about everyone's had the experience of putting on silk and noticing how their skin feels next to it...just about everybody's had the experience of closing their eyes and running their fingers on some sand at the beach and noticing the texture, the sensuous texture...of the sand....You said a couple of moments ago that you haven't much noticed how your body is beginning to wake up, how your body is beginning to reexperience and rediscover certain feelings inside...but you have said that you've noticed more bouncy, more lightness, more happiness, more pleasure...now you can discover more sexuality coming back...just as joy is dampened in depression, so are sexual feelings...that's right... and as the heavy and deadened feeling leaves parts of your body, it can be replaced all at once or slowly by some very nice sensitivity, except it may be that the sexual parts of your body have an increased sensitivity...increased sensitivity...and as your body transitions from being numb-er to being more and more sensitive and receptive to touch, you might also use words to describe how you feel...so as the heavy and dead part of your body begins to reawaken, the depression begins to lift, you can use words to describe your feelings, what you're thinking and what you're feeling and so your body will no longer need to be the container for the sadness and it can reawaken...and whether or not Nathan notices it, you can notice it, you can be sensitive to touch and then you can get Nathan to notice it...and you have experience with this kind of thing....

Every teenager experiences rushes of sexual feelings as those hormones kick in...and we've described you at this point as discovering your identity so you can discover pockets or reservoirs of sexual sensations and feelings that can become alive...and muscles that are used for sexuality can also become very strong and in tone...it can be as if they're wired with energy from your mind, from your heart, direct wires being run now hypnotically from power sources, energy sources in your body right to those sexual parts of you....It can be as if the threshold has been lowered greatly and now, where as once it would take a certain level to get you going, the threshold has been lowered and now it all begins to happen in a very pleasurable way much more easily....It's like going from an electric stove to a gas stove and all of a sudden things heat up much more quickly...and it can be as if there's a dial in your mind controlling sensitivity of your inner body, tone of your muscles...and the receptivity of your skin to touch, how much it feels the touch, the touch of leather as your jacket is over your body now...you can touch the leather of the jacket, you can feel the texture of your pants...you can notice the gentle pressure of your earrings in your ear, the gentle tug...can notice sensation of your shoes around your feet...and how the feet feel supported and helped by the shoe...so it can be as if there is a dial in your mind and you turn up the sensitivity as it goes from zero to 10, controls the ability of your muscles to respond and the ability of your body to respond...and the sensitivity that you have to touch and you can move it from a 3 to a 4 and as you move the dial, you hear click as each number is met and then passes...you see the numbers painted in white with little notches below the numbers and as you feel the dial it has a kind of pleasant knurled rubber around it...and it feels so good against your fingers, your fingers become more and more sensitive…and you turn the dial to 5 and 6—maybe you leave it at 6…but when you're with Nathan, maybe it goes, maybe you turn it up to 8 or 9….

Hyperesthesia and Anesthesia for Weight Control

You can allow yourself as a prelude to closing your eyes to begin to go down into trance…in a moment you'll be closing your eyes so that you go down deeper still into trance and you can close your eyes just as you will soon close your eyes to irrelevant things in your environment and close your eyes to one relevant thing, your mother-in-law, so that your wife-to-be can open her eyes to situations that exist, that have existed that need to be changed. So, as you allow yourself to respond in ways that are alright for you, you can begin to recognize that there can be a certain blindness of sorts that can occur in certain areas while heightened sensitivity can take place in others…as you begin to head down deeper and deeper into trance, I'd like you to become aware, for example, of certain textures….You can, for example, notice the texture of your pant leg on your right hand…your left hand can go numb-er and numb-er…as if it's received a shot of Novocaine, your right hand simultaneously can become more and more sensitive…so that the texture on your right hand, the texture of your blue jeans can seem, can be sensed at a very, very subtle and refined level….Variations of touch that you didn't think you could be aware of and all the while your left hand becomes numb-er and numb-er, perhaps from the wrist down…almost as if you slept on it all night and it's gone to sleep…no sensation left hand…and these processes, Dan, can develop and they can snowball…as the hypnosis proceeds…and you go deeper and deeper into trance as these phenomena develop…you go deeper into trance to produce the changes that I just mentioned…and then, as those changes—sensitive, loss of sensation—take place, you go deeper into trance still having experienced them…so there's a very nice mutuality, reciprocal movement, complementarity…and you're really, really learning a lot as this take place and you want to learn, so you allow it to develop and your conscious mind lets itself be distracted so that right now your subconscious mind effects the changes....It knows how to do these things...everybody's had the experience of feeling utterly sensitive...perhaps...too little sleep, perhaps when you've had a lot of sleep, your senses wake up wide awake...sensing....

I'd like you now to allow your right hand to move up to your stomach and when it does, you'll go deeper still into trance and the sensitivity in your hand can be transmitted to your stomach so that you'll know when you're full, you'll know when you're hungry and you'll be like the Buddhist who says when I'm hungry, I eat; when I'm tired, I sleep...well, fat Buddha has an out...the fat Roshis say, this isn't fat, it's consciousness...this is the wealth of consciousness that I have...and so if you wanted to be big, you could do it, but you also need to develop just the kind of silence, quiet inside...and when you go inside, you can be aware of silence...and simplicity...like the Buddha who says, one day it's cloudy, the next day it's clear and sunny...and what does that mean—your conscious mind can wonder, your subconscious mind can take it....There you go...and the sensitivity can be transmitted and your conscious mind can be curious, your subconscious mind can know that from now on, you will have a heightened awareness...of that entire area, your left arm goes numb-er or deader because there is time—there's a contrast here—your left hand, numb...almost like when you've immersed it in snow—as a boy perhaps you played in some of those Rochester snows—and it got numb, very, very numb...and then your right hand can be like later on, when you get back inside and your hand warms up, it can become very sensitive in a different respect....Your right hand very sensitive...you were touching the leather on your belt a moment ago...now your jeans again...it can seem as if every tiny ripple in your jeans is just right there to be sensed! And it's very important for you to understand, very important for you to understand...that you need to develop the right combination of left and right and there's no one—and sensitive and numb—there's no one right way to allow these handy changes to develop, there are many right ways...sometimes you can make a left turn, for example, by making three righthand turns...and sometimes you can make a righthand turn by making five righthand turns and if you make the same thing in a left-handed way, does it come out the same?...Deeper and deeper down...your conscious mind can become evermore still, your subconscious mind releases yourself to the depth of trance that is right for you....Your left hand can have a sort of waxy flexibility...insensitive, deadened...you know that you're hypnotized and that these special things are happening because you can press, gently press down your left and right hand into your pant leg now and notice the contrast, the difference, left hand— loss of sensation, right hand—highly sensitive....

I'd very much like it from a clinical perspective if you'd allow yourself to become more sensing with Louise and less sensing otherwise....I'd very much like it...if your senses would open up...in those situations with her...when you go inward, you can go to silence...the deeper you go, the more profound the changes in the sensory threshold of your hands...the left hand, the threshold...is increased so that nothing can be sensed, the nervous system doesn't get triggered, nothing registers...and the right hand goes way down so that anything can be felt....Everybody's had a little burn on their fingers, an abrasion that creates an utter sensitivity, an increased sensitivity...some people have had the experience of closing their eyes and going way deep down, relaxed, shutting off their other senses and depriving themselves of sensory input only to then touch with your hand and, boy, does it feel rich!...does it feel rich!...you know, everybody's had the experiences of their senses coming alive...you have a cold and your ear gets blocked up or you're swimming...in water navigating your way through a pool...but you get out and there's water in your ear and you can't hear...it pops six hours later and all of a sudden it's as if all the sounds in the world are rich, vibrant and alive....Most of us have had that experience...or you have a really bad cold and you can't smell and you can't taste and your appetite goes way down and you really don't want to eat so much...you have a bad—it's as if someone turned off the switch for your nose—can't smell anything...and then the cold breaks and you smell and taste...the healthy food...and darned, if a celery stick never tasted so good before...the crunch, the juiciness...um...this carrot, very rich flavor...wonder where it comes from...the cold has broken....

Chapter 17

ON EXPERIENCING WHAT IS NOT THERE: POSITIVE THERAPEUTIC HALLUCINATION

ABOUT THE PHENOMENON

In a positive therapeutic hallucination a person perceives (or semiperceives) something in the physical environment that is not there in reality. These hallucinations, like the negative ones, can involve any of the senses—visual, auditory, tactile/kinesthetic, olfactory, or gustatory.

HISTORY AND EXPERIMENTAL STUDIES

There are discrepant opinions among those who have studied positive hallucination regarding whether the phenomenon reflects true neurological activity or is simply vivid imagining. As far back as 100 years, Binet and Fere (1890) were trying to figure out the psychological foundations for induced hallucinatory experiences. More recently, Weitzenhoffer (1989a) writes that it is unlikely that the sense organs

245

per se are affected to such a degree as to produce the phenomenon in question. His understanding is that evoked visual images, as in the case of positive visual hallucination, come from memory stores but appear more vivid than old memories for two reasons. One is their being unhindered by normal reality testing processes and the other is their enhancement through increased psychophysiological reactivity presumably due to the hypnotic state. Weizenhoffer's studies of the reality of hallucinations (1961, 1963, 1964) in sum led to a belief that they are forms of imagination and not manifestations of neurological activity.

Kroger (1963) also questioned whether or not induced positive hallucinations elicit organic reaction patterns and added two other possible explanations for the phenomenon: simulation and role playing. On the other hand, Erickson (1980d) conceptualized positive hallucination as manifesting neurophysiological changes. One of several experiments he conducted to explore the phenomenon of positive hallucination involved inducing hallucinatory color vision, which was then accompanied by pseudonegative after-images (Erickson & Erickson, 1938). In a later experiment designed to factor out the variable of subjects' desires to please and accommodate the operator (Erickson, 1943/ 1980), Erickson was able to elicit salivation experimentally (a wholly involuntary response) in response to visual hallucination.

Irrespective of this debate, hallucinations are pseudoreal experiences for the person having them, or at least real enough so that they can serve as a cue or trigger for other emotional reactions. We conceptualize the hallucinations as being *superimposed* upon the real sensory experience. For instance, an ex-lifeguard feeling anxious about an upcoming performance in a play can "hallucinate" a beach scene that becomes superimposed over the audience. The "sea of faces" can become a "sea, and faces," which can trigger a response of confidence and authority (resource retrieval from lifeguard days) to supplant the anxiety response anticipated. Gilligan (1987) advises therapists to ground suggestions for positive hallucination in a utilization of the client's real memory bank, associative knowledge base, and experiential knowledge base. Just as it's better to elicit a glove anesthesia by rekindling the client's own memory of "*playing in snow so long that the hand got cold and numb*" than by repeated dry and unassociated suggestions of the "*hand going number and number*," it's better to mobilize a client's resource of positive hallucination through relying on association and experiential reserves. Refer to the section on naturalistic examples for more ideas on doing this.

Although they are not experienced in the same way that reality is, positive hallucinations are more than just daydreams. Several research subjects, asked to distinguish hypnotic hallucinatory activity from dreams, described it as more organized, real, directed, controlled, and sensible (Cooper & Erickson, 1950/1980). In other studies, hallucinated images are described as diaphanous (Hilgard, 1987). In fact, Orne (1959, cited in Hilgard [1987]) has commented on the *overplaying* of the hallucination in experimental simulators—that is, these simulators do not report the transparent quality of the images hallucinated. True hypnotized subjects, on the other hand, experience a trance logic that allows them to tolerate perceptual inconsistencies and maneuver simultaneously through two discrepant realities.

INDICATIONS FOR USE

This is a good phenomenon to apply to the principle that we've cited throughout the book—of making a solution out of the mechanism that is generating the problem. For example, in one of Erickson's training-tape transcripts (with commentary by Rossi, in Erickson & Rossi, 1979), Erickson works with a man who is experiencing phantom limb pain in his foot. This type of pain refers to uncomfortable sensations taking place in the area once occupied by a limb that has been amputated. The sensations feel real even though there is no limb present. In this case, Erickson and the patient exchange anecdotes about people relieving phantom pain itches by scratching the "affected area." Erickson then said, very directly to his patient, "Now if you have phantom pain in a limb, *you may also have phantom good feelings. And they are delightful*" [our italics] (p. 107). When a positive hallucination is the cause of the problem, an alternative positive hallucination that is therapeutic can be encouraged. A variation on this theme of utilization is Zeig's work (1974) with psychotic residents in a treatment center. He taught several schizophrenic patients with auditory hallucinations to assert greater control over their voices by having them *move* the voices through their bodies and subsequently shake them out through their hands.

Another example of using this principle with positive hallucination is the case of a young man who was hearing voices and could no longer be maintained on his medication due to the development of tardive dyskinesia. I (JSE) was working with a severely disorganizing paranoid schizophrenic teenager of 18 years at a residential treatment center for emotionally disturbed adolescents. Ray repeatedly complained about the voices from passing cars in the driveway and parking lots, which were saying horrible things to him. Among the horrible things said were instructions to kill himself and harm others. Using direct suggestion and naturalistic trance (elicited by changing to lower voice tones, a slower speech rate, and hypnotic language patterns), I was able to help him begin to experience the voices as saying more innocuous things, such as "Have a nice day," or "It's raining out." Had there been greater plasticity in his paranoia, I might have been able to have him experience the voices as saying positive things such as "You're safe here," or "You can trust those guys." However, in his state at that time, doing so would have run the risk of triggering even more paranoia.

Positive hallucination can also be used therapeutically with people who have never developed the ability to sooth, comfort, or support themselves via internal, positive, self-statements. Such individuals typically have never internalized the comforting and supporting functions of the nurturing parent or, because of extreme self-reproach, have been unable to effect that. These people can use the phenomenon of positive hallucination to imagine a benevolent voice saying comforting or supportive comments that would be appropriate for an adult. Examples include, "*Settle down, and breathe easy*" (for someone in an anxiety-provoking situation); "*You're doing OK*" (for an obsessive worrier); "*These feelings will eventually end*" (for the hopelessly depressed or for someone in the midst of a panic attack); and so on.

I (JSE) have used this phenomenon extensively in my sports therapy work, in situations where the athlete needs reminding while competing to "*Concentrate*," or becomes disorganized without his or her coach's confirming voice to say, "*You're doing fine*," or needs some extra external support to remain task oriented, "*Eyes up, shoulders back, pelvis tucked underneath you.*" The voice in the hallucination can be the trainer's voice, the athlete's voice, or some combination of the two. In-session hypnosis, posthypnotic suggestion, and the athlete's practice with self-hypnosis are used collectively to ensure the individual's ability to subsequently generate the phenomenon in a reliable and rapid manner.

Another good use of positive hallucination is for adding a dimension to a situation that subsequently changes it. In this context, positive hallucination serves the purpose of pattern interruption, wherein a fixed pathogenic sequence is interrupted by something quite startling or positive. It can be used in any of the sensory domains. Changing one element of a sequence or of an experience can often be sufficient to set in motion a change in the entire experience. We sometimes find it useful to do this in the direction of adding humor to a somber or uncomfortable situation or in humanizing a painful situation.

Let's say you are working with a couple and part of their complaint is (from her), "all he ever talks about is work!" and (from him), "all she ever wants to talk about is the kids!" A way to use positive hallucination here as a form of pattern interruption is to hypnotize the couple together and suggest the following: Anytime the two of them are sitting down for a meal together by themselves (if the couple aren't at least sometimes doing this, you may have to first redirect some therapeutic attention to their anxieties about prioritizing their relationship and being along together) and he begins to discuss work, he is to have a positive olfactory hallucination of roses. She, on the other hand, is to have a positive olfactory hallucination of a *dirty poop diaper* anytime she begins to talk about the kids. Now, he is at liberty to talk about the kids, and she can talk about work without anything happening but not the other way around.

In this example, positive hallucination works to interrupt a behavior pattern but in two different ways. For him, the hallucination works as a cue/reminder to *"stop and smell the flowers."* In a sense, the hallucination is working almost as a symbol. He may or may not heed the metaphorical message, but at least he can no longer segue obliviously into the topic of work. Awareness can be enough of a first step in breaking up the integrity of automated behavior.

For her, the hallucination functions as a noxious stimulus; again, she may or may not change the topic away from the kids but she'll sure know that she's broached it! We could have given him the noxious stimulus and her the cue or have given both of them noxious stimuli, or we could have suggested other hallucinations appropriate for this couple's situation. Rapport and a sense of humor is what makes this technique work, plus good hypnotic work with lots of imbedded suggestions and a few good posthypnotic ones, too. Using hypnotic phenomena with couples is a good way to move them through impasses that might otherwise have caused them to become mired down in therapy for a long time (see Kershaw, 1992). Once the tension over a couple's impasse itself has dissipated, they can usually go back and figure out for themselves relevant ways to improve their relationship.

An example of using positive hallucination for pattern interruption both to add humor to and to humanize a painful situation occurred with a woman who was feeling extremely anxious about a series of doctor appointments. These doctor appointments were scheduled monthly and were to take place across the state line into Connecticut. Dr. Jeffrey Zeig was the therapist and he suggested to this patient, with whom he had a very good rapport, that when she crossed over the state line and saw the sign that said "Welcome to Connecticut," she could visualize Dr. Zeig waving and smiling beneath the sign. This left her the options of waving back and driving on or stopping and mentally picking up this roadside traveler, thus maintaining the positive visual hallucination, much as a child uses an imaginary friend. Since the sign had been a trigger for anxiety, adding this positive hallucination changed it into a trigger for laughter and whimsy and/or for the comfort and emotional support that came from the therapeutic relationship.

Another example of adding a hallucination to provide humor in a situation occurred with my (JSE) father. Leon, a retired physician, has forever waged war with modern technology. Photography cameras, video cameras, VCRs, automobile dashboards, and the like have historically caused him great consternation and not a few lapses in decorum. During one particularly difficult bout trying to get the VCR to record, we suggested to Leon that he call upon his benevolent hero of *Kindergarten Cop*, Arnold Schwarzenegger, to hang out with him and help him stay patient and calm. Silly as Leon thought this was, he began to play along (initially, we're sure, just to appease us). We did however need to keep reminding him that Arnold was not a technical advisor but rather a supportive pal! A few months after the introduction of Arnold, we received the following letter:

Dear Janet:

I thought that Arnold had deserted me. The day you left I spent about 4 hours trying to reproduce the latest video of Casey [our son]. I tightened connections, I changed circuits, I reread the manual, I brought the other VCR from my bedroom down to the "family room" and tried to copy on that, I disconnected the new UHF antenna to see if that was causing interference, I pondered and smoked cigarettes, and finally considered that the problem may be in the original cassette you brought. What was happening was that each time I put on the camcorder and then tried to record the video on your tape, the cassette would eject! But it didn't happen with a new cassette! So the problem was not with my technique but with the faulty cassette! It was behaving as though the "tab" was broken as one would do to prevent accidental superimposition on a taping one would like to preserve; yet the tab had not been broken! I then hooked up the two VCR machines in order to transfer your original video of Casey to a new cassette, but the result was a poor rendition. Fortunately, I still had the original tapings on my camcorder and so I made a new taping on a new cassette. I hope you and John enjoy it. Tell John that as I completed it and began to clean up the mess in the family room, I believe I felt a soft touch on my right shoulder and a distant voice saying, "Leon, you are a good man."

Love,
Dad

Using certain figures within the context of positive hallucination can serve as a repairing function for clients. To the extent that they have been unable to feel as if caring individuals from their earlier life go with them in the form of mental representations, hypnotic hallucinations can serve to begin to correct that experience. The protocol here is rather simple. You suggest to your clients that they pick someone from their current or earlier life from whom they were able to experience unconditional love and support. You then suggest that this person, with whom they felt prized, can be made "mentally available" to accompany them into troublesome, difficult, or anxiety-provoking everyday situations. Clients can experience the person as being there with them if they like and, depending on clinical indication, they can invite the special person to either talk to them about the experiences and help them process them or the special person can touch them in a way that is comforting. The touch may be a hand on the shoulder, a hug, or a rub on the back. In this instance we are referring to having the person with them in everyday current life to provide companionship or support during trying times. However, if you do this with a client's past, that is, with memories, you can be providing a corrective emotional experience in an age-regressed fashion. Please refer to the chapter on age regression where this was discussed.

CONTRAINDICATIONS

One important consideration in deciding whether or not to use positive hallucination in treatment is the client's capacity for manifesting it. Some people will simply be better than others at suspending select cognitive faculties and superimposing a mentally constructed visual, auditory, or olfactory experience onto reality. People with disturbed reality testing may not be good candidates for this either, unless one could be sure that the utilization of positive hallucination would not compromise those adaptive ego functions that are keeping the individual stabilized.

Furthermore, those people whose characters require structure in their environments and interpersonal relationships may find this experience too disorganizing, too abstract, and/or too frightening. This could include those diagnosed with borderline, paranoid, or schizotypal personalities or features, as well as those who function best when ambiguity is minimized.

ELICITING THE PHENOMENON OF POSITIVE HALLUCINATION

Direct and Indirect Suggestion

In line with our process-oriented view of hypnosis, we think it is important first to **seed** this intervention of positive hallucination during the early stages of hypnotic induction. Let's say, for example, that you are encouraging a person to move more deeply into trance by noticing the spots of light on the area just inside his or her eyelids (Zeig, 1990): *"...and those spots can begin to move and shift, and the shifting patterns of light could continue, as you continue moving downward...."* Here, the phenomenon of positive visual hallucination has been seeded in the idea of those specks of light on the area inside the eyelids which, of course, don't really exist.

Evocative language can be used to elicit this phenomenon as well. The therapist can talk about *seeing*, *imagining*, or *visualizing* the changes beginning to take place. Alternately, one could anticipate the client's soon *feeling* a ticklish sensation of change beginning deep in the belly or anticipate the person's *feeling touched* by a story soon to be told. Words like *perceiving, sensing, realizing, becoming aware*, and the like, are useful too.

Presuppositions are also useful in eliciting positive hallucination. The therapist can say, *"**After you begin to hear the sound of a voice**, you can begin to become curious about what it could be saying."* Or, *"**When you begin to see a shadow off to your side**, you'll know that the details of the person will soon flesh out, at a pace that's consistent with your needs for accompaniment."* The therapist could also use **double binds**, saying, for instance, *"Instead of the tinnitus* (ringing, clanging, crunching in the ear), *you can, Joe, begin to hear either beautiful classical music, or perhaps the pleasant hum of a dishwasher, turned on, late at night after the kitchen's been cleaned and closed down."*

Conscious and unconscious dissociative statements are useful too in fostering the development of positive hallucination. Examples include: *"The conscious mind can have doubts, while your unconscious mind can generate the experience of your friend standing right next to you on a moment's notice,"* and *"Your conscious can expect it to happen in one way, but your unconscious mind might manufacture that sound [odor, touch, vision, taste] in a way all its own,"* and *"Your conscious mind might hallucinate one grandparent by your side as you go through the medical procedure, while your unconscious mind surprises you by choosing to hallucinate in addition your other grandparent."*

Metaphor, Anecdote, and Naturalistic Examples

There are a number of metaphors and naturalistic anecdotal stories that can be used effectively to elicit positive hallucination. The concept of childhood imaginary friends works well. Go into great detail about how real these made up companions are to children, how children actively engage in regular and ongoing "dialogues" with their playmates, how children ask that food be set out on the table lest the playmate (or animal in many cases) go hungry, and how children will often take the time to make sure the playmate has been properly introduced to family members. By talking to your hypnotized client about this, you are indirectly inviting the person to think about whether or not she/he ever had an imaginary friend and did those things, too, or perhaps remembers a friend's child or a nephew who had an imaginary friend and made his parents set a place for the friend at the Thanksgiving table. This is retrieving the resource of a natural developmental process that is universal and that has the function of allaying anxiety. There's no reason why, as adults, we can't borrow this bit of our own history to allay fears in the present.

If you are working with a client who responds well to direct suggestion, you can overtly articulate the connection between the story about imaginary friends and the client's current and future use of positive hallucination to overcome a difficulty. In such an instance you would simply say something like the following:

> ....*And you too can do this imaginary friend business, right here and now, as a grownup, whether or not you had two imaginary friends as a kid, or five, or none. You can learn how to create the sense of your father's (grandparent's, coach's, teacher's, sister's) presence with you when you rehearse (feel frightened, are training alone, take the exam, need company). You can do it now, or in the privacy of your own home. Go ahead and ask your unconscious mind to open up those memory stores and show you again how easy it is to drum up whomever you need, whenever and for as long as you like....*

Now, let's say you are working with a client who does not respond well to direct suggestion. You avoid the types of statements above and instead say something along these lines:

> ....*Go ahead and let your conscious mind wonder about my choosing to talk to you about imaginary friends. In fact, your conscious mind can keep wondering for as long as it finds the ques-*

*tion of interest, and the longer it wonders the more time your un-
conscious mind has to rise to the occasion of figuring out the answer and providing you with a new ability, a new idea, a new
experience that can really wipe away those tears of your depression. A certain creative part of you knew what to do back then as
a child and still knows what to do. Let it conjure up now for you
exactly what you will find pleasing, comforting, rewarding....*

Here the use of confusion, dissociation, and obtuse suggestion work
to indirectly promote the experience of positive hallucination. This
alone is probably not going to be enough, but it serves as an important
part of a hypnotic session that provides several dozen subtle prods
toward the development of the phenomenon.

Another way to use anecdotal examples therapeutically is to describe
how someone you know successfully used positive hallucination to
overcome a problematic situation. John worked with an individual who
had a terrible fear of failure, which became especially manifested during speeches. One of this man's biggest fears was that the audience
would have frowns on their faces while listening to his speech and
look very critical and judgmental. This client was able to use hypnosis
to develop a capacity to see in his audience the smiling and nodding
faces of family and friends.

Janet worked with an auditioning concert violist who was able to
substitute cabbage patch dolls for the somber, stone-faced judges sitting in the front row of a theater at auditions. Hallucinated groups of
homeless people, eating popcorn on the bleachers, substituted for the
(really present) family members of a first baseman Janet worked with
who was made so anxious by having his family watch that he could not
effectively throw the ball.

Any of these examples could be told to clients in a confidential fashion to help them evoke their own hallucinatory phenomenon. This is
especially useful to do with the clients (and there are many!) who are
skeptical that anyone can mentally develop this kind of an experience;
telling of others' experiences suggests the possibility and lets clients
know that the phenomenon can really happen to them.

For more storytelling, consider the following naturalistic examples:

*Just about everyone's had the experience of hearing a song on
the radio and then having it go around and around in one's head
all day long, or even for days at a time, almost as if it's actually
there. The distinction between real and not real becomes minimal
and you experience it as if the music is actually present, playing
over and over like a broken record.*

Everyone's had the experience of looking up at clouds and imag-ining just what the shapes look like, and as you look at the clouds for a longer and longer period of time, the objects or the faces that you decide that they look like become evermore obvious and ever-more real, detail after detail being shaped and seen.

Many people, as children, played at night at looking at shad-ows and patterns on the wall in their rooms and began to imagine that they formed certain objects. It seems [note the change of tense from past to present, implying an experience for the hypnotized subject in the here and now] that as you look longer and longer, a certain tunnel vision develops and your range of vision narrows and what was once shadows on a wall becomes a friendly dragon or a batman or whatever. The longer you look, the more real it becomes!

Another naturalistic example drawn from later in life is the follow-ing story:

The stars in the sky appear to be random at first, but then when you begin to know where to look and what patterns to look for, what was once apparently random begins to look like something real. Once you've identified the Little Dipper or the Big Dipper or the Archer, each time you look, it becomes more and more appar-ent; it is as if it jumps out at you. It's almost as if it's carved in the sky and becomes ever more obvious. And it's easy for you to allow your mind to forgive certain mistakes in the pattern so that the reality of the vision can become evermore apparent, three dimen-sional, your mind can fill in lots of other details. And it doesn't matter that what you're looking at is apparently just stars, because to you it has become a Big Dipper or a Little Dipper or a lion in all its reality. It's common for people to even colorize these images in the sky.

Lankton and Lankton (1983) mention using such images as heat mi-rages, fire watching, and crystal balls, as well as the psychological phe-nomenon of the Zeigarnik illusion in order to elicit positive hallucination. Gilligan (1987) offers such examples as seeing oneself in mirrors or pictures and hearing one's own voice on tape or video. He also mentions the cooperative endeavor of "shared visions," where thera-pist and client together manufacture and simultaneously participate in a visual hallucination in session. Gilligan (1990) also writes of the interesting use of both positive hallucination and future progression together in therapy, which involves the client hallucinating his or her future self. This future self serves as an image of achievement around which the unconscious mind can orient and weave constructive patterns of thought and behavior. The hallucinated figure is also said to serve as a "third party" in the therapy, stabilizing the therapist-client dyad and preempting potential countertransference reactions that would slow down the therapy.

Note that the examples above had incorporated into them the idea that a positive hallucination can develop over time. It is important to include this idea—one great error of the novice hypnotherapist is to assume that the positive hallucination either will or will not take place immediately. Experienced practitioners know however that it either can evolve over time, begin after a lag period, or simply differentiate on an ongoing basis. In one of Erickson's training tapes (Erickson & Lustig, 1975), you can see Erickson work with Monde, the subject, helping her to develop a positive visual hallucination. At one point where she stares off to the side, looking a little perplexed, Erickson tells her to take her time, that it's all right, that it (meaning the vision) will become clearer over time.

The metaphor Erickson used in this case was of a crystal ball becoming clearer as you stare into it. A metaphor that we use is of a fog beginning to lift so that the outlines of the objects to be seen become increasingly clear and their colors more apparent. In any event, what is important to remember is that you should persist, and persist, and persist; the development of a positive hallucination is a process that takes place over time. You will need to be respectful of that process.

Symbols in Positive Hallucinations

Whenever you have the client hallucinate something, that "something" can have symbolic value. For example, in the film, *Symbolic Hypnotherapy* (Zeig, 1978), Erickson has a female subject (who had been somewhat resistant) hallucinate a dog next to him—Erickson's dog in fact. For this subject the dog became a symbol of companionship, loyalty, fidelity, and protection. Since she had presented in a somewhat regressive, girlish manner, the dog constituted something that a young girl could naturally form a relationship with without resistance. And since she had been resistant to Erickson's efforts to help her through the development of an arm levitation, the presence of this dog between the two of them formed a symbol of the kind of relationship that Erickson wanted her to begin to develop with him and with people in general.

SELECTED TRANSCRIPT MATERIAL

Positive Auditory Hallucination with an Equestrian, Allowing the Client to Select What It Is She Will Hear

...wondering how that compares to the imagined sound of water rushing in and out of your hot tub...the rhythm of sound is an interesting concept...because it leads one to think of the sound wave...and the symmetry of the sound wave....If you were to look at it from one perspective, it might appear in the shape of a sine wave...but in certain diagrams one sees sound as a radiation...moving out from its origin in concentric circles....So, while the visual representation of sound waves can be different depending upon illustrator or the scientific discipline studying the sound waves...you can experience sound in a way that's useful to you....There can be particular occasions where you find you can hear sounds...that can be used in a very constructive and supportive way...and these sounds that will be useful for you to hear can be soft and distal or they can be closer to you and apparent in a much more defined way...and while I know, Valerie, that there are certain sounds that you've been hearing and continue to hear, I also know that later in your day or later that next time you ride, you'll also hear sounds...of different people, of horses, of the outdoors, of the leather of the saddle underneath you...of your boot against the stirrup...but perhaps also you can allow for other sounds as well...that it can start as if coming from afar or you can become curious about whether it's really from afar or just inside your own thinking...or even mix the distinction between what's an external sound and what's an internally generated sound...so that what you might be delighted to experience...is an innocuous hallucination of sorts...the perception of sound where none might exist...so that you can have such a sound say to you any variety of things that will be useful to you on any variety of occasions....

Positive Auditory Hallucination with a Golfer

...you find yourself hearing somebody, somewhere reminding you of *rhythm and stroke, rhythm and balance*, all the way through....

Positive Visual Hallucination for Shy Bladder

...and it would surprise you, I think so, if the next time you went into the urinal, you went into the bathroom, and you were able to fully hallucinate your home bathroom with the door closed and locked and all the time in the world...the same kind of rug on the floor, the mirror right there, the sink the way that it always seems to be and I do not know whether you'd want it to be the main bathroom or your own private bathroom....

Chapter 18

ON NOT EXPERIENCING WHAT IS THERE: NEGATIVE THERAPEUTIC HALLUCINATION

ABOUT THE PHENOMENON

Negative hallucination refers to the hypnotic phenomenon wherein something present in the environment is not clearly perceived by the person. The word "negative" here refers to the fact that the presence of something is perceptually removed or negated; it does not refer to anything as being unpleasant or unproductive. The sensory facilities involved in negative hallucination include visual, auditory, tactile, somatic, olfactory, and gustatory. Like the other hypnotic phenomena discussed in this book, negative hallucinations can be elicited during trance, applied to everyday life, and used for therapeutic benefit.

HISTORY AND EXPERIMENTAL STUDIES

Amongst the handful of relevant articles on negative hallucination is an interesting article containing research, along with a review of the literature, demonstrating that there are striking similarities between hysterical blindness and hypnotic blindness (Sackeim, Nordlie, & Gur, 1979). In both these situations, subjects report not seeing anything, while their performance on tests measuring visual stimulation demonstrate that they have, in fact, been influenced by the visual input. Test performance tends to be above chance levels when there is little motivation for blindness, but when secondary gains are high, performance is *below* chance expectations. This means that the negative visual hallucination is manifesting itself through a deteriorative influence on performance. This study suggests that in these conditions of hypnotic and hysterical blindness, both the sensory input and the perceptual awareness remain; however, they are experienced outside of conscious awareness, as subjects sincerely denied having any visual input! The authors cite evidence from studies on psychogenic deafness that comes to similar conclusions.

Erickson's studies on this topic (1938/1980), however, came to different conclusions. He had ingenious means of testing for hypnotic deafness and blindness. In these relatively undiscovered articles, Erickson experimented with these phenomena as a way of testing for the outer limits of what could be accomplished with hypnosis. An experimental "acid test" was created to prove that hypnosis, and particularly this specific phenomenon of negative auditory hallucination, was real and **not** a by-product of a person's wish or need to be helpful or cooperative in the experiment.

He first had subjects become classically conditioned to respond to a tone in the same way they had earlier responded to a mild electric shock (muscles jerking). Erickson subsequently induced hypnotic deafness in each subject and then sounded the tone. The vast majority of experimental subjects did not, at this trial, have a muscle twitch take place. What is especially interesting about this piece of research is that it rules out faking the nontwitching response; since a classically conditioned reflex like this takes place at a subcortical level, it is impossible to control it at a conscious or volitional level.

Despite mixed research results found elsewhere and subsequently, this study seems to support the validity of hypnotic deafness. Sometimes, varying results are obtained because of the use of methodologies that are poor at eliciting a hypnotic response there for the finding. For example, Erickson often hypnotized subjects over a long stretch of time so that they were able to respond fully. Contrast this with a study that might use a 5-minute induction read by an undergraduate psychology major. Negative research results may say more about what methods are needed to obtain a result than they do about the nature of hypnosis and its possibilities.

Experiments like Erickson's above help to disprove theories that describe hypnosis as a phenomenon of social cooperation or role playing. This kind of experiment also points out the inaccurate criticism that Ericksonian hypnosis is not supported by research findings. In his later years, Erickson's concerns turned much more to clinical matters, but there is a wealth of literature on Ericksonian's experimentation to be found in the *Collected Papers* (Erickson, 1980f). Parenthetically, we can mention that it is a shame that clinicians—within both traditional and Ericksonian schools—remain largely unaware of Erickson's research contributions. Critics of the Ericksonian approach who cite the approach for not being adequately research based cannot be speaking of Milton H. Erickson himself. However, there does remain a dire need for the rekindling of research efforts. The criticism in large part holds true for the more recent work among Ericksonian-oriented therapists and stands in the way of the Ericksonian approach from gaining prominence in academic and scientific circles.

In any event, there were other studies done on hypnotic blindness, too; however, these focused on color blindness. They include one by Harvey and Sipprelle (1978), wherein suggestions for color blindness reduced but did not eliminate interference on the Stroop color-word test and another by Cunningham and Blum (1982), which found that subjects receiving suggestions for color blindness did not mimic the performance of *congenitally* color-blind subjects on the Farnsworth-Munsell 100-hues test. They did find, however, that hypnotic color blindness is a genuine experience that actually occurs and that it is highly unlikely that it is a matter of the subject role playing or trying to cooperate. At a conscious level colors were not perceived.

Erickson's (1939/1980) studies in this area, however, were the first and they supported the *functional* reality of hypnotically induced color blindness. His experiments demonstrated that experimental subjects with induced color blindness responded to the Ishihara color blindness test as if they were color-blind. Erickson's findings were replicated and expanded by Harriman (1942), but his original assertion that hypnotic color blindness is like congenital color blindness has consistently *not* been supported. This same conclusion is common in other areas of hypnotically altered sensing/perceiving—real changes occur but they are not like those found in people born congenitally impaired. Color blindness itself doesn't have much application in clinical work except perhaps for someone who needs to overcome racial prejudice. In this case, inducing the phenomenon of color blindness in session would serve as a literal symbol for what the person needs to achieve in an abstract sense.

Other studies on the effectiveness of suggestions for hypnotic deafness besides the ones done by Erickson show mixed results. In a study by Spanos (1982), subjects given suggestions for unilateral deafness continued to show intrusions from the ear in question in a dichotic listening task. A study by Crawford (Crawford, Macdonald, & Hilgard, 1979), however, showed clear changes in auditory sensing following suggestions for partial hypnotic deafness. Jones and Spanos (1982), attempting to replicate an earlier study, had experimental results wherein suggestions for increased auditory acuity were shown to be effective but the suggestions for decreased acuity were not. This is reminiscent of Zeig's point (discussed in the chapter on amnesia) that direct suggestion is not as effective as indirect suggestion for hypnotic phenomena that negate or reflect an *absence* of stimuli; direct suggestion only draws more attention to that which is to be "ignored."

Dr. David Spiegel and colleagues have done some interesting research on the physiological correlates of negative hallucination. In one study (Spiegel, Cutcomb, Ren, Pribram, 1985) they found that in high hypnotizables, an obstructive hallucination—that is, a positive visual hallucination that would *block* the seeing of something else—was effective not only in achieving the negative visual hallucination, but also in significantly decreasing event-related evoked potentials. In a later study that expanded these findings into the area of somatosensory, or tactile systems, Spiegel, Bierre, and Rootenberg (1989) found interesting and similar results. Spiegel suggests that inconsistent prior findings concerning the physiological correlates of hypnotic phenomena, particularly negative hallucination, have been due to poor research methodologies. He also believes that research results have been inconsistent because of the ways in which researchers have attempted to produce negative hallucinations.

This has important bearing on clinical work. For example, clinicians and researchers who try to produce a negative hallucination by telling the person *not* to pay attention to something, or to ignore something, fail because one needs to pay attention to something in order to ignore it. This, again, is consistent with Zeig's (1985a) insights about the need to use indirect suggestion when trying to elicit phenomena that delete experiences from awareness (such as negative hallucination, amnesia, and anesthesia). Likewise, attempts to produce a negative hallucination by obliterating the stimulus—that is, suggesting that nothing is there—work only erratically; if there is any breakdown in the effectiveness of the suggestion, the person may actually wind up paying *more* attention to that which is to be negatively hallucinated, since they will be surprised by its presence. Thus, that kind of suggesting either works in toto or fails miserably—there's no in between.

There are other aspects of this research (Spiegel et al; 1989) that are interesting and deserve attention. When high hypnotizables were given the suggestion for an obstructive hallucination for painful tactile stimulation, they felt the stimulation only 38% of the time in contrast to other control conditions where the painful stimulus registered 80% to 86% of the time. This perceptual suppression was consistently accompanied by a reduction in amplitude of event-related potentials at two sites of the cortex. Both changes were statistically significant.

When these same subjects were told to pay closer attention to the stimulus, there were corresponding changes at the same brain sites. That is, amplitudes increased under the conditions of stimulus enhancement, considerably more so for the experimental group of high hypnotizables than for the control conditions. This is an interesting finding, for although paying closer attention to a stimulus (or stimulus enhancement as it is sometimes called) is not exactly the same as suggesting a positive hallucination, it is a bit like it and hence the findings of increased brainwave amplitude might correspond in some fashion to what happens physiologically under conditions of simply and straightforwardly suggesting positive hallucinations alone.

In this study, the subject experienced an obstructive hallucination of a "local anesthetic," in the limb that was to be painfully stimulated. The hypnotic anesthetic worked, like Novocain might, by spreading from fingers to hand to forearm. What this suggests is that Spiegel considers anesthesia not to be a phenomenon unto itself but a phenomenon achieved through a person positively hallucinating numbness to mask the pain. This is certainly a different conception of anesthesia and it has important clinical implications.

We are impressed with the above findings. We're especially impressed because they were obtained under conditions using very little hypnotic induction. The researchers don't say much in their methodology section about the induction itself; downplaying the significance of the induction is typical in research these days. They do however say that "the subjects were first led through a hypnotic induction exercise that involved closing the eyes and elevating the left hand in response to an instruction that it would feel 'light and buoyant.' These movements provided behavioral confirmation that the subjects were complying with instructions" (p. 751). One can wonder what kinds of findings would result from a more prolonged period of subject training in hypnosis and a longer induction period. Unfortunately, the science of hypnosis has become in many instances the study of what high hypnotizables can accomplish under hypnotic *constraints*, such as brief inductions involving only direct suggestion.

The authors also discuss how brainwave-evoked potentials for pain increase when the stimulus is novel or infrequent or is seen as being important to attend to and relevant. This provides physiological evidence that these factors, also discussed in the anesthesia chapter, are important to deal with. Suggestions for pain control through anesthesia then should be oriented toward new and novel pains as well as customary ones, so long as everything that needs to be done in terms of diagnosis and treatment is being done.

INDICATIONS FOR USE

When would removing or diminishing the perception of some stimulus in the environment or in the body be therapeutic? Going back to our major principles of when to use hypnotic phenomena, we can say that negative hallucinations are often indicated when they are a part of how a person creates the problem. An example of this is the now retired athlete-pain patient who developed a debilitating knee injury due to repeatedly ignoring the internal experience of pain while on the playing field. Negative somatic or kinesthetic hallucinations can now be used to help the person ignore the chronic discomfort in his or her knee (as long as this is not medically contraindicated).

A related principle involves using this hypnotic phenomenon when it is one that the person characteristically does in daily living. For example, the therapist of a teenager who habitually overlooks piles of dirty laundry in his room could use negative hallucination to help that same teenager "not see" his ex-girlfriend around school if such contact were to have become emotionally painful.

You might also use negative hallucination when it is the complement to the hypnotic phenomenon creating the problem. Here, for example, the therapist of an executive who has both a fear of flying and a habit of visualizing plane crashes taking place with such vividness that it has a hallucinatory quality can help the executive develop a *negative* hallucination so that he or she doesn't even notice the airport, or the sound of the planes, or the vibration of the plane taking off. When using complementary hypnotic phenomena, however, a clinician needs to be sure that there is enough plasticity in the client's "hypnotic repertoire" that the complement can be elicited. Otherwise the therapeutic complement may be too "overpowered" by the phenomenon already in place.

What is written above is a general review of indications for using negative hallucination based on the major principles outlined earlier. The following section goes through each of the sensory modalities to illustrate specific symptoms and situations that might call for the use of negative hallucination. This will give the reader a sense of the surprising breadth of applications possible.

Negative Visual Hallucinations

In the visual sphere a person can be given negative hallucinations for the very visual cue that signals the start of an anxiety reaction. It can be used for the sight of blood, certain pieces of medical equipment, a cemetery (for someone still mourning the loss of someone), and so on. In this way, a phobic individual or a person susceptible to disabling or undesirable degrees of anxiety, sadness, or fright can have a psychological tool that enables them to go through needed medical procedures or navigate through day-to-day living.

Hypnotic tunnel vision, a first cousin to negative visual hallucination, is another useful intervention for some. Here, the person begins to visually perceive as if he or she were looking through a tunnel: The peripheral vision blurs and whatever is being looked at becomes more sharply focused. Many people spontaneously experience this when doing an eyes-open trance. The astute therapist, picking up on the spontaneous development of tunnel vision, can elaborate on this and put it to good use in solving some aspect of a presenting problem. Hypnotic tunnel vision is useful for people who have concentration problems and who can learn to block out irrelevant visual stimuli.

In a similar vein, it can be used with hyperactive children. We have also induced tunnel vision to help athletes focus better on the task at hand and avoid distracting stimuli in their surroundings such as spectators, judges, and players on the sidelines. In fact, encouraging athletes to do this hypnotically simply puts them in line with what successful athletes do anyway. Uneståhl (1979) has noted that tunnel vision is one of several spontaneously manifested hypnotic phenomena characterizing the "ideal performance state" of elite athletes. Hypnotic tunnel vision and arm levitation were phenomena considered in a case I (JSE) supervised involving a shotputter seeking to better his record.

Tunnel vision may also manifest itself as a function of rapport during a hypnotic session. Gilligan (1987) reported this to have taken place between Erickson and subjects numerous times, augmented by interspersed references to "vacant" chairs in the room (actually, chairs in which observers were seated) and the presence in the room of "just you and me." In fact, I (JSE) have noticed that when working intimately with a client during hypnosis, and especially if the trance experience is deep, I develop a tunnel vision, too. The office blurs into a grey mist and all I become aware of is the person sitting a few feet away from me and myself.

An example of using negative visual hallucination to complement counterproductive positive visual hallucinations occurred in work one of us (JHE) did with a psychotic woman. This 25-year-old repeatedly saw flashes of light that would herald the transmission of thoughts into her mind. She was also seeing what she claimed to be people and "elements" from years past in her everyday life and felt that they were placed there purposefully by someone who had it in for her. According to this client, these people were "doubles." Negative therapeutic visual hallucinations were used in this instance, with the hypnotic discourses in session including such things as televisions that could be on in the background and be unnoticed (even though the picture would be constantly flashing and changing); televisions that can be turned off by remote control; and *people known to you in everyday life but who, lost in thought, you walk by unknowingly.*" These suggestions for negative visual hallucinations were designed to counteract the problem of positive visual hallucinations and were part of a successful therapy in which the client no longer "noticed" the flashing lights and other anxiety-provoking visual hallucinations.

Incidentally, eliciting negative visual hallucinations is something that Erickson experimented with in some depth (1944a/1980). Erickson would put the subject in a very, very deep trance over the course of a long period of time, perhaps even hours. He would then give the subject a rationalizing explanation for *why someone who was actually present in the room was, in fact, missing*; this explanation was offered to satisfy the person's conscious awareness or memory of the third party. For example, Erickson might have said, "*You thought he was here because you expected him, but at the last minute he couldn't come, so he's absent.*" Trance would be deepened even further, and other suggestions for negative hallucination for the third person in the room would be offered. Erickson would then sometimes have the subject become deeply absorbed in an irrelevant puzzle or task; he thought this useful in allowing the suggestions for hallucination to crystallize or "set." After some period of time, Erickson would have the "missing person" speak to the subject and try to interact with him.

The two experiments on negative visual hallucinations written up in this 1944 paper (reprinted in the *Collected Papers* and entitled "An Experimental Investigation of the Hypnotic Subject's Apparent Ability to Become Unaware of Stimuli") had groups present to observe the experiment and members of the group were able to observe the extent to which the hypnotized subject reacted to the attempts of interaction by the person for whom the negative hallucinations were targeted. The degree to which the subject did not respond reflected the success of the intervention. These experiments were in fact successful, with subjects oblivious to the third party despite this person being in the subjects' line of vision and talking to them.

Having a negative hallucination for a person or people can be useful in clinical work. We use negative hallucination when a client complains that he or she can't get an old boyfriend, girlfriend, husband, or wife out of his or her mind. In addition, those who have had romantic involvements at the worksite or who expect to meet up with a former lover around town or in church, and so on, often appreciate the capacity to develop a negative hallucination so they don't have to have unpleasant affects constantly dredged up by the sight of an old flame. In a more positive slant on coupledom, negative visual hallucination can be a *symbolic* intervention with a partner who wants to develop a "blind spot" for his or her partner's unpleasant but benign habit.

Negative hallucination isn't always a cut-and-dried phenomenon. People can experience it in modified and partial ways especially when they may *have* to deal or interact with the hallucinated figure (i.e., the ex-wife comes over to say hello at church). Another way of conceptualizing negative visual hallucinations in the awake subject is that they serve to break up the *integrity* of the percept so that there is a cognitive lack of recognition, so to speak. A beautiful naturalistic example of this phenomenon resides in the first chapter of Richard Adams' best-selling novel of 1972, *Watership Down*, where a den of rabbits become increasingly puzzled over the growing presence of short white sticks on the ground. The reader eventually experiences an epiphany once it is realized that the sticks are the scattered cigarette butts of a tree-downing developer.

We have an interesting and personal tale about the usefulness of negative visual and olfactory hallucinations. Jeffrey Zeig, obliging my (JHE) request to help me stop smoking, elicited in me negative hallucinations for cigarette smoking. Rather than smoke acting like a cue to invite me to smoke again, the smoke would have no effect; somehow, Zeig had discerned that I was responsive to contextual cues in this fashion. He also knew that my then-girlfriend (JSE) would still be smoking while I had quit. There is nothing in my experience with hypnosis that compares to the feeling of astonishment I had when I took someone's cigarette (I was such a difficult subject—I had to challenge everything) and held it underneath my nose, only to smell nothing!

Zeig also induced a negative hallucination for the cigarettes themselves. I experienced this as a kind of *visual agnosia*, where I'd look at cigarettes and not recognize them! To me, they looked like white paper tubes stuffed with dried plant matter that had brown paper to cover the cotton at the end of the tubes. For some reason, people would set the opposite ends on fire and then suck, so that the smoldering plant matter would go down into the interior of their bodies. They then held their breath for a moment and expelled this smoldering air. And for some reason, they were getting pleasure out of this. It was as if I were observing a different primitive culture engaging in a ritual for which I had no experience. Zeig had effectively severed my emotional history with smoking. In a dissociated way, a part of me knew what was going on, but I *allowed the larger part of me to participate in and go with this bigger experience.* It was quite amusing to me and very effective.

Negative Auditory Hallucination

Negative auditory hallucinations are frequently employed when they are needed as a complement to a positive hallucination in the auditory sphere that has proved problematic. For example, one of us (JHE) worked with an insomniac who reported that the ticking of the alarm clock and the dripping of the water faucet were the items that kept him from going to sleep. In his efforts to go to sleep, he inevitably wound up focusing on these sounds, enhancing them so much that they took on a hallucinatory quality of being "larger than life." (This is the familiar experience of sounds like ticking and dripping that seem as if they are at least 40 or 50 decibels. You wonder why everyone else in the house isn't kept awake by these noises as well!) Suggestions for negative auditory hallucinations were given to rectify the problem.

Another example of the use of hypnotic complements in the auditory sphere is with tinnitus. Tinnitus is a condition characterized by ringing/buzzing/clinking sounds heard internally ("ringing in the ears"), which is sometimes secondary to hearing loss. As with the insomniac, first permission is given to the person to ignore the sounds, and then numerous, sequential metaphors about overlooking sounds are delivered in trance. For example, a client can be told about how one often acclimates to the sound of an air conditioner so that it is no longer noticed. Giving multiple metaphors of this nature for negative auditory hallucinations can be extremely powerful when the problem, or part of it, is auditory. In fact, hypnosis is highly effective with tinnitus patients, and these are people for whom other therapeutic approaches—physical and psychological—are often ineffective.

I (JHE) employed negative auditory hallucinations in a case with a woman who had been verbally abused and berated by her parents when she was a child. She now had a very good marriage but would become unnecessarily frightened when the husband became loud and gestured in an exaggerated way. It brought back too many memories of the abuse.

I was able to successfully teach her to *"turn down the volume,"* so that his voice was heard by her to be soft even when it was, in fact, quite loud. The metaphor I used was of having a hearing aid in her ear, with a volume dial that could be turned down.

Negative Somatic Hallucinations

Negative hallucinations for somatic/kinesthetic stimuli are mainly indicated when there is physical discomfort. Most often this occurs with regard to pain control.

Negative Olfactory and Gustatory Hallucinations

It is possible to give negative hallucinations for the olfactory and gustatory senses. We have done this with cancer patients because of the unpleasant, often metallic tastes they have in their mouths from treatments. Also, chemotherapy patients often have an unpleasant smell pervading their senses as a result of the treatment; they also can experience nausea triggered by certain odors.

As we described earlier, people trying to give up smoking can be helped to develop negative hallucinations for the (sometimes enticing) smell of cigarette smoke (see p. 1265). Negative hallucinations in this sensory domain can also be *symbolic* interventions for a person who complains that a certain situation in life "left a bad taste in his mouth" or for someone who comments on a problem where "the situation really stinks."

ELICITING THE PHENOMENON OF NEGATIVE HALLUCINATIONS

Direct and Indirect Suggestion

Seeding the phenomenon of negative hallucination can be accomplished during your inductions by pointing out how easy it was for the client *"to have lost awareness, within even these first several minutes of trance, of the sensation of the sofa underneath your left thigh, and maybe, too, of the sound of the air conditioner...such things can really move out and in and out again of awareness....Later you can discover what you've been missing...go ahead and override your conscious mind's need to realize everything...your unconscious mind knowing all about the beauty and simplicity of absence...."*

The use of **presupposition** in session refers to the therapist making a statement to the client that references the anticipated hypnotic experience in a way that makes it sound as though it will definitely happen. An example is the following: "*And **when you find your perception modifying, attenuating**, your unconscious can begin to speculate about how best to apply that special, different experience of the world....*" One geared to the olfactory sense is this: "***Once your nose knows*** [indirect reference to noes, that is, denies] ***that something can be different, can be absent, missing**, you can begin to recognize how comforting such an outcome will be for you....*" Presuppositions prime the unconscious, prepare the client, pave the road, and set the context for the phenomenon in question.

Evocative language is another linguistic way to promote cooperation indirectly. For negative hallucinations, you can use words like "it can be *absent*," "you can allow yourself to be *unaware*," and "you can *delete* it." These are but a few examples of how you can choose your words so that they engender the response you are seeking.

Double binds are another way that negative hallucinations can be elicited, for example, "*You can lose your awareness of that stimuli while in deep trance, or lose it while still in a lighter one.*" Notice the specific stimulus itself is not named. Negatives don't register effectively in the unconscious; by saying "don't see," the concept left in the person's mind *is* "see." Another double bind is, "*You can lose awareness of it all at once or the awareness can fade over time.*" We're getting a little bit ahead of ourselves, but with a double bind like that, it might be nice to follow-up with a metaphor that illustrates how a gradual fade over time could take place. The metaphor in this instance could be of a person who lives in the country coming to sleep overnight in the city. On the first night she can't get much sleep because of the traffic noises. On the second night she only notices them a bit, and by the third night she no longer notices the noises at all.

Although the protocol section in each chapter describing how to elicit the different phenomena breaks down into separate categories of intervention, in clinical practice it is best to combine several and even dozens of interventions in order to elicit the phenomenon. Many therapists using hypnosis go straight to telling a story or direct suggestion and forget the value of including other "smaller" but empowering interventions such as seeding, presupposition, and the like. Other lesser known forms of suggestion that mark the difference between simple and sophisticated (and thus more effective) trancework include twisting, tag questions, conversational postulates, misspeak, word plays, and paraverbal techniques (Zeig, 1990).

Conscious/unconscious dissociative statements can be used to elicit negative hallucination as well, for example: "*Your conscious mind can*

choose to distract itself and focus on something else, while your uncon-
scious mind monitors that stimuli, outside of your awareness, and calls
it to your attention only if something needs to happen; otherwise you
can comfortably allow yourself to be unaware of it." Another example
is, "*Your conscious mind can focus on the fact that you have given*
yourself permission to ignore that situation, you've decided and cho-
sen to disregard it, you've decided that you can dismiss it, and all the
while your unconscious mind can be implementing that choice."

Metaphor and Naturalistic Examples

Metaphors and anecdotes about negative hallucinations taking place
are one relatively easy way to facilitate the development of this phenomenon. When you read the examples below, you'll notice that they
frequently draw on two principles, one physiological and one psychological. The first illustrates how the body habituates to everyday stimuli.
This physiological principle of habituation is the way in which the
body naturally experiences negative hallucination. Therefore, the natural phenomenon of habituation can be evoked anytime a client has a
need to obliterate something that is constantly present.

The second principle refers to the phenomenon that if the conscious
mind chooses to think of something as being irrelevant and unimportant, it gives permission to the unconscious mind to ignore it. Interspersed into the middle of any metaphor in this context then can be the
direct suggestion to the client to make the overt decision at a conscious
level so that the unconscious mind can "do its thing." Sometimes encouraging someone to allow that decision to be made becomes the only
intervention that is needed.

This was the case with a tinnitus patient that I (JHE) treated a few
years ago. He was worried that his tinnitus was indicative of a brain
tumor and therefore felt that it needed to be attended to because of its
supposed signal function. Once he got an MRI, at the suggestion of both
myself and his physician, he was able to trust that the tinnitus was
unrelated to any other physical problem. This enabled him to let go of
his need to attend to the tinnitus. By using hypnosis, I encouraged him
to make that decision at a very deep level. He was able to do that in
trance, and when he came out of trance, the tinnitus was already almost gone.

The metaphors and naturalistic examples you use can be divided
into the different sensory systems. For example, to encourage negative
visual hallucinations a therapist might tell a story about a teenager who,
out of an oppositional attitude, consistently overlooks the filled-to-the-
brim garbage that he's supposed to take out each evening. Another an-

ecdote to elicit negative visual hallucination might entail speaking about driving down the street and missing your turn: you just "overlook" it. The use of the word overlook is not incidental inasmuch as it is evocative of the process desired. You can also relate the anecdote of a person walking down a street and passing people without ever really seeing them. Or consider the example of a person looking for his or her keys and repeatedly staring at the table that the keys are on without ever really seeing them. The keys become obvious only after the person has finally spotted them.

In the auditory sphere we can once again go back to our teenager and tell a story about how he doesn't hear a parent calling him to come. Another example is how someone doesn't hear the phone ring when absorbed in a good book or intent on watching TV. In one of his hypnosis demonstrations for Rossi, Erickson tells a story to a patient suffering from tinnitus about his experiences in a boiler-making factory (Erickson & Rossi, 1979). He speaks at length about how, when he was a boy, he walked into this factory and couldn't hear anything because of the raucous noise. Yet, he noticed workers speaking to each other in normal tones of voice, hearing each other, and responding to one another. Erickson goes on to talk about how he got permission from the foreman to sleep overnight in a sleeping bag at the factory. When Erickson awoke in the morning, his experience was that the pounding and clanging were still there but was somehow *dampened*, and he could now hear the people speaking to each other clearly. This story is a beautiful illustration of the body's capacity to produce a negative hallucination adaptively. Erickson felt that if a person's body could do something under some circumstances, then it probably could do the same thing under other circumstances; hypnosis was viewed by him as the ideal vehicle to allow a person to gain control over that happening.

Another inviting story about negative auditory hallucination has to do with the mind tuning out certain sounds while focusing on others to permit care-taking functions. It may go like this:

> *Just about every mother and father has had the experience of ignoring all sorts of night sounds no matter how loud they might be and yet focusing in on their baby's tiniest cries. Even in the city, a mother might ignore the ongoing droning of traffic, as loud as it might be through an open window, and yet, let her baby whimper, and she's all alert, awake, and attentive. Even novel stimuli outside the window such as sirens from fire engines, people screaming at each other, and police activity, can be totally ignored by a mother while at some conscious and unconscious level she's chosen to selectively focus on other sounds such as her baby's cry. When parents take turns getting up to get the baby, some couples have had the experience of the "off-duty" spouse sleeping through*

the baby's cry when it is his or her night off while alerting very quickly to the first whimper when it is his or her night to attend to the baby. This can switch back and forth from one night to the next. The mind is quite powerful at implementing decisions regarding selective attention when it is programmed correctly.

In the tactile sphere it is easiest to prime the phenomenon by using examples of those things actually touching the client's body that are not being attended to. This gives the client an immediate awareness that he or she is *already* experiencing negative hallucinations. An example of this is as follows: "*You know, at the present time, you aren't aware of the glasses on your face. You could have been if you wanted to have been but, since you eliminated them on some level you decided not to be and so you weren't.*" The following would also work: "*You could have chosen to be aware of the tension of that belt around your waist, but you decided that that's unimportant, so, while it is in fact there, you're choosing not to experience it. Likewise, you could, but only if you really wanted to, feel your feet in your shoes, you could, if you had wanted to bother, feel your earring in your ear, you could have felt your hair resting on your head, all of those things are real and a part of objective reality. However, your mind has chosen to ignore them as being unimportant and irrelevant and you've implemented that decision wonderfully.*"

In the olfactory and gustatory modality you could talk about something burning on the stove yet not recognizing it for a very long time, or about a cigarette burning on a table and, again, not being tuned into it. Likewise, stories can be told about how a house smells a particular way, but after living in it you no longer smell it, or cooking with garlic and at first being very impressed with how strong the smell is and then over a course of hours you no longer smell it at all, only to be reminded of how strong the smell is when you go out for a period of time and then came back or have guests over. Stories for gustatory negative hallucinations can involve people with colds, and how it's difficult or impossible for them to taste anything and how all food tastes bland. Another example is people who have burnt their tongues and who temporarily can't taste food. Still another involves how people hold their noses to take bad-tasting medicine so that they have negligible awareness of the taste. A great story came from one of our trainees. He spoke about a recent big family holiday occasion where his mother was serving meat pie as the main course and an apple pie for dessert but got the two mixed up. He said, amusingly, that the entire family was significantly into the main course before anyone realized that they were eating the apple pie and not the meat pie! Because of the expectation for meat, everyone tasted the apples as meat!

SELECTED TRANSCRIPT MATERIAL

Negative Hallucination to Generate Tunnel Vision

You can notice changes in your eyes, they can de-focus a little bit...you might begin to get a little tunnel vision, almost as if you're looking through a paper towel cardboard inner holder, a little bit of tunnel vision like you're looking through a tunnel, right through to the other end—everything else is irrelevant, blurred, or misty, or grey/black....

Negative Hallucination for the Experience of Chronic Bad Taste and Bad Smell after Chemotherapy

...so deep that I can suggest to you that if you do smell the bad smell and taste the bad taste you can ignore it, distract yourself and ignore it...everyone's had the experience of that happening...reading a really good book and becoming more and more absorbed—that happened when you read the book *The Prince of Tides*...you became so absorbed in the book that you probably didn't hear the TV on in the background...you became so absorbed that you probably didn't notice the sound of the cars going by outside...and maybe there was a meal cooking or maybe the litter box needed changing....I don't know...but I do know that you might have become so absorbed in Tom and Luke that you could ignore and forget all sorts of things, and if you had been in pain, you could have forgotten about the pain too....

Everyone has the experience day in and day out of not noticing, but overlooking, things that are real nonetheless, but you don't have to notice them. The mind is trained to notice new things...you have an old thing—you can ignore it...like when you have furniture for many years...you stop seeing it, you stop noticing it. You walk into the room and you no longer see anything, you no longer notice the furniture...you take it for granted...you get used to things in a certain fashion...and you over**look** things [look is emphasized to try to indirectly encourage the use of the visual sensory system]...and so too you can oversmell things...just about everybody's had the experience of having the air conditioning unit go on and you notice it at first because it's something new—it's novel, there's a change....Because of that novelty you notice it, but then as the air conditioning's on for a period of time, you over**look** it, you forget about it...it just becomes part of the background....The mind is trained to notice changes and novel things; it's trained to notice that for survival....New things could be dangerous, so it's important to take notice of them...the smell you experience, and the taste you experience have been around for a long, long time. You know and I know that they are unimportant things and because you know they're unimportant, you can forget about them, you can ignore them. You know that they are just meaningless artifacts so you can choose to over**look** them.

How many times have you skimmed through a newspaper looking for something in particular and you know that you don't have to look at everything...so, you ignore that, you overlook it, you've given your mind permission not to notice certain things, you scan for what's important in the newspaper. You and I know that the smell and the taste you taste is unimportant, so you can get rid of it....I'm quite certain that at some point in your life, you've already had this experience...How many times have you or someone you know awakened in the morning, spoken to someone and then your friend or your husband has said, "Oh, you need to brush your teeth, your breath doesn't smell so good," but you don't notice it because it's yours....Over time you learn to take care of things like that, but not because you yourself notice it...your situation is even better because you don't even have to think about it because others can't notice it or be offended.

And my brother was just commenting the other day about a similar situation and he said, "Isn't it interesting, John, isn't it really interesting when you grow up as a kid, even as an adult, that you don't think that when you pass gas it smells bad, you don't think it smells bad, you don't mind it, but you know that other people do, so you make certain changes, but you certainly don't experience it as bad, it's there, but it's not bad for you like it would be if other people passed gas."

Every house has its own particular smell...it's a smell you come to know and love and enjoy...when you go over to a relative's house, you probably recognize a particular smell...that's their house, distinctive...and yet, isn't it interesting that after you're there a short while you no longer notice that particular smell...even if it's peculiar, you no longer notice the peculiar smell...your nose has the capacity to get used to something very different. The physiological process of habituation can help you get used to something very quickly and pass it out of your mind, just ignore it, it's unimportant, it's irrelevant...putting on perfume and at first you smell it, and it's easy to smell, because it's new. Did you ever think that perhaps at the start of the day you might only then notice the chemo smell and the taste and then you would get used to it....

Every school has its own particular smell...you walk into school...at the start of a day, at the start of a new year...things are going to be different...you know, the smell is going to be the same...at your old school, it smells the same...by the end of the first period, if not by then, then by the end of the second period, you quickly find out that you no longer smell it—you take it for granted, it's just there....

You can even imagine a faucet in your nose, you can imagine a faucet in each of your tastebuds and you can imagine yourself turning off the faucets automatically....

You know, you can even bake warm bread in your house or cook a really good stew and at first it smells really good—it smells really good...smells really good, but unfortunately after a while you get used to the smell and you can't smell it anymore—sure you could if you wanted to—you could walk outside and come back in, but after a while you just get used to the smell and you don't notice it anymore even though it's warm, fresh bread....

PART III

Apart from Intervention: Other Uses for Hypnotic Phenomena

Chapter 19

HYPNOTIC PHENOMENA FOR INDUCTION, RATIFICATION, AND DEEPENING

Up to this point we have been discussing hypnotic phenomena as they are used for intervention. This is their more common clinical use. There are as well other benefits to eliciting and utilizing hypnotic phenomena and those are the subject matter of this chapter.

INDUCTION THROUGH HYPNOTIC PHENOMENA

If you elicit the hypnotic phenomenon at the start of a hypnosis session, it will serve to accomplish much of the induction phase. This may seem like putting the cart before the horse, but consider that in order to accomplish the hypnotic phenomenon, you pretty much have to go into trance. Therefore, it is an indirect way of eliciting a hypnotic state because the client experiences it (via doing the hypnotic phenomenon) without ever being *told* to go into trance. Phenomena like catalepsy, time distortion, sensory alterations, and dissociation are the relatively simpler ones to achieve and can be experienced within the first several minutes of trance. Using catalepsy to induce trance, for instance, would entail orienting the client's attention to a heaviness or stillness developing in the body; once the client confirms that he or she is aware of that, you can absorb attention more and more in that phenomenon. The person is effectively hypnotized simply through exploring his or her experience with catalepsy.

Wicks (1982) describes the use of arm levitation as a rapid induction technique. By lifting a client's arm in the air and giving him or her imbedded suggestions that it remain there—cataleptic—the client is found to go into trance quite quickly. This is another example of how, when you elicit hypnotic phenomena in a context defined as hypnotic, that experience alone provides for an induction, creating a trance state.

Erickson, too, particularly with better subjects, sometimes induced trance with hand or arm levitations. He believed this to be useful in ensuring active participation on a client's part in the therapy itself. This is a good example of the symbolic use of levitation in hypnotherapy. Erickson's method was to raise a subject's arm and then release it, but release it in a way that was so gradual the person was never certain when Erickson had stopped supporting the arm and when the person, him or herself, was left supporting it in mid-air. Dissociation and catalepsy quickly followed, and then what Erickson would get is a genuine arm levitation.

A variant of this strategy is Erickson's handshake induction (Erickson, Rossi & Rossi, 1976). The strategy basically entailed Erickson shaking a prospective subject's hand and then freezing in mid-shake, allowing his own hand to go limp, and gradually stopping the support of the subject's hand. The procedure begins with an interrupted handshake, continues with an increasingly "dead fish" hand on the part of the therapist, and is followed by words that are hypnotic in nature. By this time the subject is in a hypnotic trance to some degree. Hypnotic intervention then follows. The "session" ends a few minutes later with the *resumption* of the handshake and the therapist asking the subject how he or she is, *as if they are still first greeting.*

There are actually two hypnotic phenomena being produced in this handshake induction: one is an arm levitation, elicited in an indirect and unsuspecting fashion, and the other is an amnesia, elicited through the technique of a structured amnesia (see Chapter 4 for a full description of structured amnesias). This "induction" has another trance-inducing aspect to it beside the arm levitation and amnesias—confusion. Any time an overlearned, socially produced movement is abruptly interrupted, confusion is created. The mildly disoriented state which then manifests can be easily guided toward trance. There is perhaps nothing more routine and overlearned in our culture than the process of shaking hands and exchanging greetings.

Incidently, this is one important objection to the use of simulators as a control group in experimentation in hypnosis. It is quite common for research designs to include a control group called "simulators." This is one type of control procedure where group members *pretend* to be in trance while hearing the experimental suggestions. Essentially, they fake being hypnotized. However, in the process of faking the experience of hypnosis, many simulators often inadvertently end up experiencing some of the hypnotic phenomena. The outcomes or results for this simulator group on the experimental task are then compared to the results for the experimental group who are genuinely hypnotized. However, you have a faulty design: by faking hypnosis and unknowingly manifesting some hypnotic phenomena as a natural outgrowth of this, simulators can, in fact, be going into various degrees of hypnotic trance through unwitting self-induction.

RATIFICATION THROUGH HYPNOTIC PHENOMENA

Ratification occurs when the therapist reports to a client in trance about which of the physiological, physical, and other nonverbal signs of trance are being manifested by him or her. It serves to affirm a client's experience of trance (especially for first timers), it differentiates trance from nontrance states, it often deepens trance further, and in addition it serves as a social reinforcement for the client's hypnotic experience. These signs of trance, known as the hypnotic constellation, typically include decreased motor movement, slowed swallowing reflex, alterations in the blinking reflex, slowed and deeper breathing, slowed pulse rate, tearing, and benign muscle twitches, among other signs (Zeig, 1984).

Hypnotic phenomena themselves can be used to ratify, too. Because they are typically so distinctive in the magnitude of experience compared with what happens in everyday life, a doubting or uneducated client can recognize that, indeed, something very different is happening. Hypnotic phenomena can be "impressive convincers" for clients who otherwise aren't sure that something out of the ordinary is happening. And it is important in hypnosis to impress upon the client that something out of the ordinary is happening because it sets up the positive expectation that (therapeutic) change will take place. There is nothing more ratifying than, say, an arm levitation where the arm feels dissociated and is moving autonomously toward one's face. Lankton and Lankton (1983) write that levitations in this context are means of proof to the conscious mind that the unconscious can alter the body in inexplicable, yet controllable, ways. We sometimes have clients open their eyes and look at the levitating arm so that they gain the visual conviction as well as a kinesthetic one.

It is not just arm levitation that can produce this sense of conviction. Recently, one of us (JHE) was hypnotizing a client who spontaneously developed a positive hallucination and then spoke of it upon coming out of trance. He said that he "saw this huge bowl of chicken soup in front of me and could smell it—it was as if it were real!" Surely the client figured that *something* different had happened, no?

DEEPENING THROUGH HYPNOTIC PHENOMENA

When clients initially produce a hypnotic phenomenon, whether it be an arm levitation or automatic writing or something else, the experience does tend to lighten the trance a bit; they feel somewhat self-conscious and have a kind of orienting response. This response makes sense since the mind is trained to orient toward novelty, and when a hypnotic phenomenon is elicited the first time, the experience is so new. However, this is merely an initial response. As clients become more familiar with a particular hypnotic phenomenon, they will not go to a lighter state of trance when it manifests but, rather, will go deeper. Also, even when clients do come out of trance a little bit initially, in a short while they will probably go right back down, often more deeply. As clients become more adept at hypnosis in general, apart from the particular phenomenon in question, eliciting any of the hypnotic phenomenon will customarily deepen the trance.

Perhaps you're wondering if an initial lightening of trance, is a problem. It is not. As clients go back down into trance on the heels of that lightening, they are effecting the process of *fractionation*. Fractionation is a technique of deepening, whereby a client is brought in and out of trance repeatedly. Each time the client re-enters trance, it is usually at a deeper level than before. Fractionation is an indirect method of increasing depth—clients are never "told" to go deeper. If you produce a hypnotic phenomenon and the client initially experiences a lightening of the trance state, you may simply consider this an indirect way of accomplishing fractionation. Fractionation is especially useful with the wary client who has seen too many movies where hypnotized subjects are implored by sinister-looking men with thick voices to "Go deeeeper and deeeeper into trrraaance!"

Any of the trance phenomena can be used to deepen the hypnosis. Lankton and Lankton (1983) talk about using dissociation in deepening techniques, and Erickson would frequently use catalepsy and arm levitation for the same effect (Erickson & Rossi, 1981). As clients become increasingly absorbed in their experiences of catalepsy, or dissociation, or time distortion, or hypermnesia, their attentions are drawn even more toward the internal. Their connection with external (irrelevant) stimuli diminishes further, and they increasingly suspend analytical faculties in favor of experiencing the hypnosis more fully. Again, nothing may need to be said directly to the client about deepening the trance to foster the process; clients will bring themselves further into the experience—if, indeed, they are comfortable with it—simply through your guiding their awareness to the changes taking place or by your allowing them to privately explore the hypnotic experience.

SELECTED TRANSCRIPT MATERIAL

Arm Levitation for Induction

....And I'd like you to allow yourself to just focus on the sensations in your arm, I'd like you to allow yourself to just consider that your arm might begin to allow itself to hover in the air, I'd like you to allow yourself to just begin to relax all the muscles in your arm...and allow your arm to begin to maintain a certain relaxation and tension simultaneously...allow me to hold your arm up and then allow your arm to hold itself up—that's right, close your eyes...that's it...that's it...your arm will begin to hold itself up, yes...and I can hold it up...and you can go into trance as this happens...you can go into trance to allow it to happen...as it happens you can go into trance, both can be true...that's right, allowing yourself to feel a certain...that's it, that's it...and your arm can support itself and I can help out a little bit and go down deeper and deeper into trance.

For More Induction

....As your arm begins to suspend just like a bridge being suspended in mid-air...effortlessly and your muscles get more and more relaxed, but they maintain enough balance, tension, that your arm stays in the air relaxed, and it can move in the air to a position that's even more comfortable...that's right, there you are...going deeper into trance and your arm can move anytime it likes to a position that's even more comfortable...notice how you go down into trance to allow comfort and it can suspend itself effortlessly, muscles relaxing more and more and as that happens, your mind can relax more and more and you're really learning an awful lot about how to maintain relaxation in your muscles while allowing for something to happen...you're learning about how to allow for a kind of muscle tone that can be relaxing from the tip of your fingers all the way up to your shoulders...you can even notice your shoulders and all the way down relaxing as your hand begins to move up towards your face a little bit and where it—yes, that's right—and you go deeper down into trance as that movement takes place...

For
Deepening
and there's no need to rush it, you can allow it to go as if it has a mind of its own...there's nothing that you even need to do, it just begins a journey up and you can feel yourself going deeper and when it touches your face, you can allow yourself to go even deeper down, five times deeper down into trance...

More
Deepening
that's right...and it stays there for a moment...it stays there for another moment...it stays there and you notice you're going deeper down into trance...that's right and it strokes your face and that feels good, it feels good to comfort yourself and that's very different. When your body moves, it can comfort itself...and that's an important learning for you to have....I don't know if it would surprise you or whether at this point, you could expect it, but your other hand can begin a certain journey toward your face also and as it does, the hand on your face can begin a journey to your lap...that's right...so one comes up and you go deeper down into trance...yes...and the muscles of that hand—that hand that just came up isn't yet as deep in trance as the hand that's going down and that's right—it can rest on your thigh...and you go deeper into trance and you notice that you're moving differently than you would otherwise...

Ratification
your mind relaxes more and allow the relaxation of your mind to just flow through—and I'm going to lift your cassette into the air and flip it over so that you have record of your accomplishments here and now and you can notice that things feel differently, you can notice that your hand moves—yes, that's right, you stroke yourself a little bit and that hand can begin a descent

down and your other hand can come back up to your
face and as it does, you go deeper down into trance,
learning how to relax while you move, moving while
you relax...

*(Note: This is an excellent symbolic experience for this chronic pain
patient who normally increases her pain by tensing her muscles against
it) (She also has had trouble walking ["moving"] due to muscle pain
and tension)*

and it's so interesting to learn to enjoy moving while
relaxing simultaneously...that's right, your hand can
begin coming up, so there's a certain synchrony of movement and the movement's different from how it would
be normally and that can tell you that you're in trance
and you can appreciate your trance response, more relaxation even in your shoulders—that develops more
and more and so by noticing changes in muscle relaxation, and differences in the movement, you can appreciate, really, really appreciate, Sandra, how you are
hypnotized and now you can go deeper still as your
hands come to rest down there...and they can feel increased pleasure, they can feel comfort, many people
think of their hands and arms as personal servants—
you can learn to think of your hands and arms as companions in pleasure—you can learn to think of your
mind as being coordinated with your hands and arms
for purposes not only of productive accomplishment,
but of the productive accomplishment of pleasure which
actually means that you allow yourself to feel joy and
can participate in the rejuvenation that comes from
people giving themselves time to do what they want to
do and feel what they are feeling and to enjoy themselves in ways that are right for them. And I don't yet
think you yet know how you wish to enjoy yourself because you've been told how to enjoy yourself and what's
right and what's wrong...when people think about
should and right and wrong, they don't often get around
to asking themselves, what would I like...and that's
where you are now...learning to ask yourself "what
would I like?" and it doesn't need to mean that you
wouldn't also ask yourself "what do I need to do?" but

there can be a certain balance just as there was a balance in your muscles a moment ago when your arm was moving and your arms both, two at a time, moving up and down with a balance between flexor and extensor muscles. And your conscious mind doesn't even need to know what those are and what they do, but your subconscious mind knows and demonstrated how to put them in such perfect balance that they could be in the air quite comfortably, suspended and moving...now I know that you had...that's right, that's right...they can go up again...naturally and effortlessly...and it can go where it wants to go...and your conscious mind can be suspended, your conscious mind can be out to lunch...your subconscious mind can move your body as would be pleasurable...and so anytime you want, your body can move without arm levitation, can move with your muscles being balanced and in tone, muscle tonus allowing for a comfortable freedom of movement ...and in the same way you can find yourself spontaneously breaking into dance...you can find yourself moving effortlessly and easily and comfortably...and with all of this in mind, you can allow yourself to begin to bring yourself out of trance, knowing that you went into trance, you deepened trance and you appreciated trance through movement, movement that was easy, natural and comfortable, so I'd like you to allow yourself now to take one, two, three deep breaths and wake up all over....

The client came out of trance and was thrilled with learning how to move this way; she continually said that she was *delighted, delighted, delighted*. She spoke about how it would help her with her new hobby of ballroom dancing because she had felt very tense and restricted. She said that she hadn't ever known she could move like this—being active and relaxed at the same time—and, moreover, she said that she had learned to move in very constricted and tense ways since she had hurt her back years ago and that learning how to do arm levitation would enable her to learn how to move safely and comfortably, but with relaxation and a fluid style.

REFERENCES

Adams, R. (1972). *Watership down.* New York: Macmillan.

Adler, A. (1927). *The practice and theory of individual psychology.* New York: Harcourt, Brace & World.

Albert, I. B., & Boone, D. (1975). Dream deprivation and facilitation with hypnosis. *Journal of Abnormal Psychology, 84*(3), 267–271.

Alexander, L., & Brady, P. (1985). Forensic hypnosis. In J. K. Zeig (Ed.), *Erickson psychotherapy: Vol. 1. Structures* (pp. 524–534). New York: Brunner/Mazel.

Araoz, D. L. (1983). Use of hypnotic techniques with oncology patients. *Journal of Psychosocial-Oncology, 1*(4), 47–54.

Arendt-Nielsen, L., Zachariae, R., & Bjerring, P. (1990). Quantitative evaluation of hypnotically suggested hyperaesthesia and analgesia by painful laser stimulation. *Elsevier Science Publishers B.V., 42*, 243–251.

Aristotle (1943). *On man in the universe.* Roslyn, NY: Walter J. Black, Inc.

Ashford, B., & Hammer, A. G. (1978). The role of expectancies in the occurrence of posthypnotic amnesia. *The International Journal of Clinical and Experimental Hypnosis, 26*(4), 281–291.

Barber, J. (1977). Rapid induction analgesia: A clinical report. *American Journal of Clinical Hypnosis, 19*(3), 138–147.

Barber, J. (1982). Hypnotic analgesia. In J. Barber & S. Adrian (Eds.), *Psychological approaches to the management of pain.* New York: Brunner/Mazel.

Barber, J., & Malin, A. H. (1977). Hypnosis and suggestion for fitting contact lenses. *Journal of the American Optometric Association,48*(3),

379–382.

Bartis, S. P., & Zamansky, H. S. (1986). Dissociation in posthypnotic amnesia: Knowing without knowing. *American Journal of Clinical Hypnosis, 29*(2), 103–108.

Baumann, F. (1982). Hypnotherapy with children and adolescents: Some Ericksonian ideas. In J. K. Zeig (Ed.), *Ericksonian approaches to hypnosis and psychotherapy* (pp. 310–314). New York: Brunner/Mazel.

Beahrs, J. O. (1982). Understanding Erickson's approach. In J. K. Zeig (Ed.), *Ericksonian approaches to hypnosis and psychotherapy*. New York: Brunner/Mazel.

Beck, A. (1983). Negative cognitions. In E. Levitt, B. Lubin, & J. Brooks, (Eds.), *Depression: Concepts, controversies, and some new facts* (2nd ed; pp. 86–92). Hillsdale, NJ: Erlbaum.

Beck, A., Rush, J., Shaw, B., & Emery, G. (1979). *Cognitive therapy of depression.* New York: Guilford Press.

Berrigan, L. P., Kurtz, R. M., Stabile, J. P., & Strube, M. J. (1991). Durability of posthypnotic suggestions as a function of type of suggestions and trance depth. *The International Journal of Clinical and Experimental Hypnosis, 39*(1), 24–38.

Binet, A. (1886). *La psychologie du raisonement; recherchers experimentales par l'hypnotisme.* Paris: Dentu.

Binet, A., & Fere, C. (1890). *Le magnetisme animal.* Paris: Felix Alcan.

Bishay, E. G., & Lee, C. (1984). Studies of the effects of hypnoanesthesia on regional blood flow by transcutaneous oxygen monitoring. *American Journal of Clinical Hypnosis, 27*(1), 46–49.

Bornstein, P. H., Pychtarik, R. G., McFall, M. E., Winegardner, J., Winnett, R. L., & Paris, D. A. (1980). Hypnobehavioral treatment of chronic nailbiting: A multiple baseline analysis. *The International Journal of Clinical and Experimental Hypnosis, 28*(3), 208–217.

Boscolo, L., Cecchin, G., Hoffman, L., & Penn, P. (1987). *Milan systemic family therapy: Conversations in theory and practice.* New York: Basic Books.

Bowers, K. E. (1976). *Hypnosis for the seriously curious.* New York: W. W. Norton.

Bowers, K. S. (1993). The Waterloo-Stanford Group C (WSGC) Scale of Hypnotic Susceptibility: Normative and comparative data. *The International Journal of Clinical and Experimental Hypnosis, 41*(1), 35–46.

Brende, J. O., & Benedict, B. D. (1980). The Vietnam combat stress response syndrome: Hypnotherapy of dissociative symptoms. *American Journal of Clinical Hypnosis, 23*(1), 34–40.

Brenman, M., & Gill, M. M. (1947). *Hypnotherapy.* New York: Wiley.

Charcot, J. (1882). Note sur les divers états nerveux determines par l'hypnotization sue les hystero-epileptiques. Paris: C. R. de l'Acad des Sciences.

Cheek, D. B. (1975). Maladjustment patterns apparently related to imprinting at birth. *American Journal of Clinical Hypnosis, 18*(2), 75–82.

Cheek, D. B. (1976). Short-term hypnotherapy for frigidity using exploration of early life attitudes. *American Journal of Clinical Hypnosis, 19*(1), 20–27.

Cheek, D. B. (1982). Some of Erickson's contributions to medicine. In J. K. Zeig (Ed.), *Ericksonian approaches to hypnosis and psychotherapy* (pp. 281–286). New York: Brunner/Mazel.

Churchill, J. E. (1986). Hypnotherapy and conjoint family therapy: A viable treatment combination. *American Journal of Clinical Hypnosis, 28*(3), 170–176.

Clay, W. (1990). A program for self-hypnosis and age regression. *Individual Psychology Journal of Adlerian Theory, Research and Practice, 46*(4), 503–507.

Cooper, L. F. (1948/1980). Time distortion in hypnosis: I. In E. L. Rossi (Ed.), *The collected papers of Milton H. Erickson* (Vol. II, pp. 221–230). New York: Irvington. (Reprinted from *The Bulletin, Georgetown University Medical Center,* 1948, *1*(6), 214–221.)

Cooper, L. F., & Erickson, M. H. (1950/1980). Time distortion in hypnosis: II. In E. L. Rossi (Ed.), *The collected papers of Milton H. Erickson* (Vol. II, pp. 231–265). New York: Irvington. (Reprinted from *The Bulletin, Georgetown University Medical Center,* 1950, *4*(6), 50–68.

Cooper, L. F., & Erickson, M. H. (1954). *Time distortion in hypnosis.* Baltimore: Williams & Wilkins.

Cooper, L. M. (1979). Hypnotic amnesia. In E. Fromm & R. E. Shor (Eds.), *Hypnosis: Developments in research and new pPerspectives* (pp. 305–349). Chicago: Aldine.

Corley, J. B. (1982). Ericksonian techniques and general medicine problems. In J. K. Zeig (Ed.), *Ericksonian approaches to hypnosis and psychotherapy* (pp. 287–291). New York: Brunner/Mazel.

Council, J. R., & Loge, D. (1988). Suggestibility and confidence in false perceptions: A pilot study. *British Journal of Experimental and Clinical Hypnosis, 5*(2), 95–98.

Council on Scientific Affairs (1985). Scientific status of refreshing recollection by the use of hypnosis: A council report. *Journal of the American Medical Association, 253,* 1918–1923.

Crawford, H. J., MacDonald, H., & Hilgard, E. R. (1979). Hypnotic deafness: A psychophysical study of responses to tone intensity as modified by hypnosis. *American Journal of Psychology, 92,* 193–214.

Cunningham, P. V., & Blum, G. S. (1982). Further evidence that hypnotically induced color blindness does not mimic congenital defects.

Journal of Abnormal Psychology, 91(2), 139–143.

de Shazer, S. (1985). *Keys to solution in brief therapy.* New York: W. W. Norton.

Dolan, Y. M. (1991). *Resolving sexual abuse: Solution-focused therapy and hypnosis for adult survivors.* New York: W. W. Norton.

Dywan, J., & Bowers, K. S. (1983). The use of hypnosis to enhance recall. *Science, 222,* 184–185.

Edgette, J. H. (1985). The utilization of Ericksonian principles of hypnotherapy with agoraphobics. In J. K. Zeig (Ed.), *Ericksonian psychotherapy: Vol. 2. Clinical applications* (pp. 286–291). New York: Brunner/Mazel.

Edgette, J. H. (1988). Dangerous to self and others: The management of acute psychosis using Ericksonian techniques of hypnosis and hypnotherapy. In S. R. Lankton & J. K. Zeig (Eds.), *Ericksonian monographs number 3: Treatment of special populations with Ericksonian approaches* (pp. 96–103). New York: Brunner/Mazel.

Edgette, J. S. (1989). Tempest in a teapot: Ethics and Ericksonian approaches. In S. R. Lankton (Ed.), *Ericksonian monographs number 5: Ericksonian hypnosis: Application, preparation, and research* (pp. 105–116). New York: Brunner/Mazel.

Edgette, J. S. (1991). A marriage of Ericksonian and psychodynamic therapy in the treatment of emotionally disturbed adolescents. In S. R. Lankton, S. G. Gilligan, & J. K. Zeig (Eds.), *Ericksonian monographs number 8: Views on Ericksonian brief therapy, process and action* (pp. 36–52). New York: Brunner/Mazel.

Edgette, J. S. (1994). "Ironic" therapy: Utilizing unconscious conflict in single-session hynotherapy. In S. R. Lankton & K. K. Erickson (Eds.), *Ericksonian monographs number 9: The essence of a single-session success* (pp. 75–80). New York: Brunner/Mazel.

Edgette, J. S., & Edgette, J. H. (1991). Ericksonian therapy and clinical hypnosis. *Primijenjena psihologija,* Vol. 12, *1-2,* 55–59. Zagreb.

Edgette, J. S., & Edgette, J. H. (1993). Doing more effective hypnotherapy: Deciding which interventions, for what clients, when. Workshop, *Third Eastern Conference on Ericksonian Hypnosis and Psychotherapy: Tools for Transforming Personal Experience*©, Philadelphia, PA.

Edmonston, W. E., (1986). Hypnosis and social suggestibility. *The Behavioral and Brain Sciences, 9*(3), 470–471.

Erickson, E. M. (1941/1980). Discussion: Critical comments on Hibler's presentation of his works on negative afterimages of hypnotically induced hallucinated colors. In E. L. Rossi (Ed.), *The collected papers of Milton H. Erickson on hypnosis. Vol. II. Hypnotic alteration of sensory, perceptual, and psychophysical processes.* New York:

Irvington, 11–17. (Reprinted from *Journal of Experimental Psychology*, 1941, *29*, 164–170)

Erickson, M. H. (1933/1980). The investigation of a specific amnesia. In E. L. Rossi (Ed.), *The collected papers of Milton H. Erickson on hypnosis. Vol. III. Hypnotic investigation of psychodynamic processes.* New York: Irvington, 38–44. (Reprinted from *The British Journal of Medical Psychology*, 1933, Vol. XIII, Part II)

Erickson, M. H. (1934/1980). A brief survey of hypnotism. In E. L. Rossi (Ed.), *The collected papers of Milton H. Erickson on hypnosis. Vol. III. Hypnotic investigation of psychodynamic processes.* New York: Irvington, 3–12. (Reprinted with permission from the *Medical Record* for December 5, 1934)

Erickson, M. H. (1938/1980). A study of clinical and experimental findings in hypnotic deafness: Experimental findings with a conditional response technique. In E. L. Rossi (Ed.), *The collected papers of Milton H. Erickson on hypnosis. Vol. II. Hypnotic alteration of sensory, perceptual, and psychophysical processes.* New York: Irvington, 100–113. (Revised and reprinted from a report given before the American Psychiatric Association at St. Louis, 1936; reprinted from *The Journal of General Psychology*, 1938, *19*, 151–161)

Erickson, M. H. (1939/1980). The applications of hypnosis to psychiatry. In E. L. Rossi (Ed.), *The collected papers of Milton H. Erickson on hypnosis. Vol. IV. Innovative hypnotherapy.* New York: Irvington, 3–13. (Reprinted from the *Medical Record*, 1939, 60–65)

Erickson, M. H. (1941/1980). Hypnosis: A general review. In E. L. Rossi (Ed.), *The collected papers of Milton H. Erickson on hypnosis. Vol. III. Hypnotic investigation of psychodynamic processes.* New York: Irvington, 13–20. (Reprinted fom *Diseases of the Nervous System*, Vol. II, No. I)

Erickson, M. H. (1943/1980). Experimentally elicited salivary and related responses to hypnotic visual hallucinations confirmed by personality reaction. In. E. L. Rossi (Ed.), *The collected papers of Milton H. Erickson on hypnosis. Vol. II. Hypnotic alteration of sensory, perceptual, and psychophysical processes.* New York: Irvington, 175–178. (Reprinted from *Psychosomatic Medicine*, April, 1943, *5*, 185–187)

Erickson, M. H. (1944a/1980). An experimental investigation of the hypnotic subject's apparent ability to become unaware of stimuli. In E. L. Rossi (Ed.), *The collected papers of Milton H. Erickson on hypnosis. Vol. II. Hypnotic alteration of sensory, perceptual, and psychophysical processes.* New York: Irvington, 233–250. (Reprinted from *The Journal of General Psychology*, 1944, *31*, 191–212)

Erickson, M. H. (1944b/1980). Hypnosis in medicine. In E. L. Rossi (Ed.),

The collected papers of Milton H. Erickson on hypnosis. Vol. IV. Innovative hypnotherapy. New York: Irvington, 14–27. (Reprinted from *The Medical Clinics of North America,* 1944)

Erickson, M. H. (1952/1980) Deep hypnosis and its induction. In E. L. Rossi (Ed.), *The collected papers of Milton H. Erickson on hypnosis. Vol. I. The nature of hypnosis and suggestion.* New York: Irvington, 139–167. (Reprinted from *Experimental Hypnosis,* 1952, pp. 70–114)

Erickson, M. H. (1954a/1980). Hypnotism. In E. L. Rossi (Ed.), *The collected papers of Milton H. Erickson on hypnosis. Vol. III. Hypnotic investigation of psychodynamic processes.* New York: Irvington, 21–25. (Reprinted from *Encyclopedia Britannica,* 14th edition, 1954)

Erickson, M. H. (1954b/1980). Pseudo-orientation in time as a hypnotherapeutic procedure. In E. L. Rossi (Ed.), *The collected papers of Milton H. Erickson on hypnosis. Vol. IV. Innovative hypnotherapy.* New York: Irvington, 397–423. (Reprinted from the *Journal of Clinical and Experimental Hypnosis,* 1954, 261–283)

Erickson, M. H. (1954c/1980). The clinical and therapeutic applications of time distortion. In E. L. Rossi (Ed.), *The collected papers of Milton H. Erickson on hypnosis. Vol. II. Hypnotic alteration of sensory, perceptual, and psychophysical processes.* New York: Irvington, 266–290. (Written with L. Cooper. In *Time Distortion in Hypnosis.* Baltimore: Williams and Wilkins, 1954. Reprinted with permission of the publisher)

Erickson, M. H. (1956/1980). The reorganization of unconscious thinking without conscious awareness: Two cases with intellectualized resistance against hypnosis. In E. L. Rossi (Ed.), *The collected papers of Milton H. Erickson on hypnosis. Vol. IV. Innovative hypnotherapy.* New York: Irvington, 439–443. (Unpublished manuscript, 1956)

Erickson, M. H. (1958/1980). Naturalistic techniques of hypnosis. In E. L. Rossi (Ed.), *The collected papers of Milton H. Erickson on hypnosis. Vol. I. The nature of hypnosis and suggestion.* New York: Irvington, 168–176. (Reprinted from the *American Journal of Clinical Hypnosis, I,* 3–5)

Erickson, M. H. (1959/1980). The basis of hypnosis: Panel discussion on hypnosis. In E. L. Rossi (Ed.), *The collected papers of Milton H. Erickson on hypnosis. Vol. III. Hypnotic investigation of psychodynamic processes.* New York: Irvington, 26–33. (Reprinted from *Northwest Medicine,* October, 1959)

Erickson, M. H. (1961/1980). Historical note on the hand levitation and other ideomotor techniques. In E. L. Rossi (Ed.), *The collected papers of Milton H. Erickson on hypnosis. Vol. II. Hypnotic alteration of sensory, perceptual, and psychophysical processes.* New York:

Irvington, 135–138. (Reprinted from the *American Journal of Clinical Hypnosis*, 1961, *3*, 196–199)

Erickson, M. H. (1965). The use of symptoms as an integral part of therapy. *American Journal of Clinical Hypnosis, 8*, 57–65.

Erickson, M. H. (1966/1980). Hypnosis: Its renascence as a treatment modality. In E. L. Rossi (Ed.), *The collected papers of Milton H. Erickson on hypnosis. Vol. IV. Innovative hypnotherapy.* New York: Irvington, 52–75. (Reprinted in *The American Journal of Clinical Hypnosis*, 1970, *13*, 71–89, with permission of the original publishers: Merck, Sharp, & Dohme, *Trends in Psychiatry*, 1966, *3*(3), 3–43)

Erickson, M. H. (1967/1989). Hypnosis. In S. R. Lankton (Ed.), *Ericksonian monographs number 5: Ericksonian hypnosis: Application, preparation and research.* New York: Brunner/Mazel, 1–6. (Reprinted with permission from the *Encyclopedia Britannica*, 14th edition)

Erickson, M. H. (1979/1980). The February man: Facilitating new identity in hypnotherapy. In E. L. Rossi (Ed.), *The collected papers of Milton H. Erickson on hypnosis. Vol. IV. Innovative hypnotherapy.* New York: Irvington, 525–542. (Reprinted from *Hypnotherapy: An Exploratory Casebook*, 1979, Chapter 10)

Erickson, M. H. (1980a). An introduction to the study and application of hypnosis for pain control. In E. L. Rossi (Ed.), *The collected papers of Milton H. Erickson on hypnosis. Vol. IV. Innovative hypnotherapy.* New York: Irvington, 237–245.

Erickson, M. H. (1980b). Clinical and experimental observations on hypnotic amnesia: Introduction to an unpublished paper. In E. L. Rossi (Ed.), *The collected papers of Milton H. Erickson on hypnosis. Vol. III. Hypnotic investigation of psychodynamic processes.* New York: Irvington, 53–57. (Unpublished manuscript, circa 1950s)

Erickson, M. H. (1980c). Age regression: Two unpublished fragments of a student's study. In E. L. Rossi (Ed.), *The collected papers of Milton H. Erickson on hypnosis. Vol. III. Hypnotic investigation of psychodynamic processes.* New York: Irvington, 104–111. (Written between 1924 and 1931)

Erickson, M. H. (1980d). A brief survey of hypnotism. In E. L. Rossi (Ed.), *The collected papers of Milton H. Erickson on hypnosis. Vol. III. Hypnotic investigation of psychodynamic processes.* New York: Irvington, 3–12.

Erickson, M. H. (1980e). An introduction to the study and application of hypnosis for pain control. In E. L. Rossi (Ed.), *The collected papers of Milton H. Erickson on hypnosis. Vol. IV. Innovative hypnotherapy.* New York: Irvington, 237–245. (Reprinted from *Proceedings of the International Congress for Hypnosis and Psychoso-*

matic Medicine, edited by J. Lassner, Springer-Verlag, Berlin, Heidelberg, New York)

Erickson, M. (1980f). *The collected papers of Milton H. Erickson on hypnosis*. Edited by Ernest Lawrence Rossi.
   Vol. I: *The nature of hypnosis and suggestion.*
   Vol. II: *Hypnotic alteration of sensory, perceptual, and psychophysical processes.*
   Vol. III: *Hypnotic investigation of psychodynamic processes.*
   Vol. IV: *Innovative hypnotherapy.*
   New York: Irvington.

Erickson, M. H., & Cooper, L. F. (1954/1980). The clinical and therapeutic applications of time distortion. In E. L. Rossi (Ed.), *The collected papers of Milton H. Erickson on hypnosis. Vol. II. Hypnotic alteration of sensory, perceptual, and psychophysical processes.* New York: Irvington, 266–290. (Reprinted from L. F. Cooper & M. H. Erickson, 1954, *Time distortion in hypnosis*. Baltimore: Williams & Wilkins)

Erickson, M., & Erickson, E. (1938/1980). The hypnotic induction of hallucinatory color vision followed by pseudonegative afterimages. In E. L. Rossi (Ed.), *The collected papers of Milton H. Erickson on hypnosis. Vol. II. Hypnotic alteration of sensory, perceptual, and psychophysical processes.* New York: Irvington, 5–10. (Reprinted from *Journal of Psychology, 22*, 581–588).

Erickson, M. H., & Erickson, E. M. (1941/1980). Concerning the nature and character of posthypnotic behavior. In E. L. Rossi (Ed.), *The collected papers of Milton H. Erickson on hypnosis. Vol. I. The nature of hypnosis and suggestion.* New York: Irvington, 381–411. (Reprinted from *The Journal of Genetic Psychology*, 1941, *24*, 95–133)

Erickson, M. H., & Erickson, E. M. (1958/1980). Further considerations of time distortion: Subjective time condensation as distinct from time expansion. In E. L. Rossi (Ed.), *The collected papers of Milton H. Erickson on hypnosis. Vol. II. Hypnotic alteration of sensory, perceptual, and psychophysical processes.* New York: Irvington, 291–298. (Reprinted with permission from *The American Journal of Clinical Hypnosis*, October 1958, *I*, 83–89)

Erickson, M. H., & Kubie, L. S. (1938/1980). The use of automatic drawing in the interpretation and relief of a state of acute obsessional depression. In E. L. Rossi (Ed.), *The collected papers of Milton H. Erickson on hypnosis. Vol. III. Hypnotic investigation of psychodynamic processes.* New York: Irvington, 158–176. (Reprinted from *The Psychoanalytic Quarterly*, October 1938, Vol. VII, No. 4)

Erickson, M. H., & Kubie, L. S. (1940/1980). The translation of the cryptic automatic writing of one hypnotic subject by another in a trance-like dissociated state. In E. L. Rossi (Ed.), *The collected papers of Milton H. Erickson on hypnosis. Vol. III. Hypnotic investigation of psychodynamic processes.* New York: Irvington, 177–187. (Reprinted from *The Psychoanalytic Quarterly*, January 1940, Vol. IX, No. 1)

Erickson, M. H., & Lustig, H. S. (1975). *The artistry of Milton H. Erickson, M.D.* (Video tape recording). Distributed by Herbert S. Lustig, M.D., LTD., Box 261, Haverford, PA 19041, USA.

Erickson, M. H., & Rossi, E. L. (1974/1980). Varieties of hypnotic amnesia. In E. L. Rossi (Ed.), *The collected papers of Milton H. Erickson on hypnosis. Vol. III. Hypnotic investigation of psychodynamic processes.* New York: Irvington, 71–90. (Reprinted from the *American Journal of Clinical Hypnosis*, 1974, *16*)

Erickson, M. H., & Rossi, E. L. (1975/1980). Varieties of double bind. In E. L. Rossi (Ed.), *The collected papers of Milton H. Erickson on hypnosis. Vol. II. Hypnotic alteration of sensory, perceptual, and psychophysical processes.* New York: Irvington, 412–429. (Reprinted from the *American Journal of Clinical Hypnosis*, 1975, *17*, 143–157)

Erickson, M. H., & Rossi, E. L. (1979). *Hypnotherapy: An exploratory casebook.* New York: John Wiley & Sons.

Erickson, M. H., & Rossi, E. L. (1980a). Indirect forms of suggestion in hand levitation. In E. L. Rossi, (Ed.), *The collected papers of Milton H. Erickson on hypnosis. Vol. I. The nature of hypnosis and suggestion.* New York: Irvington, 478–490. (Previously unpublished paper written with E. L. Rossi, 1976–1978)

Erickson, M. H., & Rossi, E. L. (1980b). Self-exploration in the hypnotic state: Facilitating unconscious processes and objective thinking. In E. L. Rossi (Ed.), *The collected papers of Milton H. Erickson on hypnosis. Vol. IV. Innovative hypnotherapy.* New York: Irvington, 393–396.

Erickson, M. H., & Rossi, E. L. (1981). *Experiencing hypnosis: Therapeutic approaches to altered states.* New York: Irvington.

Erickson, M., Rossi, E., & Rossi, S. (1976). *Hypnotic realities.* New York: Irvington.

Esdaile, J. (1846). *Mesmerism in India and its practical application in surgery and medicine.* London: Longmans, Brown, Green and Longmans.

Evans, F. J. (1979). Contextual forgetting: Posthypnotic source amnesia. *Journal of Abnormal Psychology*, *88*(5), 556–563.

Evans, F. J., & Staats, J. M. (1989). Suggested posthypnotic amnesia in four diagnostic groups of hospitalized psychiatric patients. *American Journal of Clinical Hypnosis*, *32*(1), 27–33.

Fishman, H. C., & Rosman, B. L. (Eds.). (1986). *Evolving model for family change.* New York: The Guilford Press.

Frecaia, N. F. (1982). Misconceptions concerning the clinical use of hypnosis in dentistry. *Journal of the American Society of Psychosomatic Dentistry and Medicine, 29*(2), 64–70.

Friction, J. R., & Roth, P. (1985). The effects of direct and indirect hypnotic suggestions for analgesia in high and low susceptible subjects. *American Journal of Clinical Hypnosis, 27*(4), 226–231.

Friday, P. J., & Kubal, W. S. (1990). Magnetic resonance imaging: Improved patient tolerance utilizing medical hypnosis. *American Journal of Clinical Hypnosis, 33*(2), 80–84.

Fromm, Erich. (1955). *The sane society.* Greenwich, CT: Fawcett Publications.

Fromm, Erich. (1956). *The art of loving.* New York: Harper and Row.

Fromm, Erika. (1970). Age regression with unexpected reappearance of repressed childhood language. *The International Journal of Clinical and Experimental Hypnosis, 18,* 79–88.

Fromm, E., Brown, D. P., Hurt, S. W., Oberlander, J. Z., Boxer, A. M., & Pfeifer, G. (1981). The phenomena and characteristics of self-hypnosis. *The International Journal of Clinical and Experimental Hypnosis, 29*(3), 189–246.

Fromm, E., & Gardner, G. (1979). Ego psychology and hypnoanalysis: An integration of theory and technique. *Bulletin of the Menninger Clinic, 43*(5), 413–423.

Fromm, E., & Shor, R. E. (Eds.). (1979). *Hypnosis: Developments in research and new perspectives* (2nd ed.). New York: Aldine.

Gallagher, L. B. (1974). The use of hypnoanesthesia in tattoo removals: Age progression studies in the selection of candidates for cosmetic surgery. *Journal of the American Institute of Hypnosis, 15*(1), 18–20.

Gallway, T. (1981). *Inner game of golf.* New York: Random House.

Gilligan, S. G. (1987). *Therapeutic trances: The cooperation principle in Ericksonian hypnotherapy.* New York: Brunner/Mazel.

Gilligan, S. G. (1988a). Psychosomatic healing in Ericksonian hypnotherapy. *Hypnose und kognition, 5,* 25–33.

Gilligan, S. G. (1988b). Symptom phenomena as trance phenomena. In J. K. Zeig & S. R. Lankton (Eds.), *Developing Ericksonian therapy: State of the art.* New York: Brunner/Mazel.

Gilligan, S. G. (1990). Coevaluation of primary process in brief therapy. In J. K. Zeig & S. G. Gilligan (Eds.), *Brief therapy: Myths, methods, and metaphors.* New York: Brunner/Mazel.

Gravitz, M. A. (1988). Early uses of hypnosis as surgical anesthesia. *American Journal of Clinical Hypnosis, 30*(3), 201–208.

Gross, M. (1982). Hypnoanalytic age regression based on Piaget's cognitive developments theory. *Medical Hypnoanalysis, 3*(2), 73–77.

Gustavson, J. L., & Weight, D. G. (1981). Hypnotherapy for a phobia of slugs: A case report. *Journal of Clinical Hypnosis, 23*(4), 258–262.

Haley, J. (1963). *Strategies in psychotherapy.* New York: Grune & Stratton.

Haley, J. (1973). *Uncommon therapy: The psychiatric techniques of Milton H. Erickson, M.D.* New York: W. W. Norton.

Haley, J. (1976). *Problem solving therapy.* San Francisco: Jossey-Bass.

Hammond, D. C. (1993, Fall). False memories, misrepresentations and ritual abuse. *Psychological Hypnosis,* 2–11.

Harriman, P. L. (1942). Hypnotic induction of color vision anomalies: II. Results on two other tests of color blindness. *Journal of General Psychology, 27,* 81–92.

Hart, B. B. (1985). Type of suggestion and hypnotizability in clinical work. *British Journal of Experimental and Clinical Hypnosis, 2*(2), 89–93.

Harvey, M. A., & Sipprelle, C. N. (1978). Color blindness, perceptual interference, and hypnosis. *American Journal of Clinical Hypnosis, 20,* 189–193.

Haule, J. R. (1986). Pierre Janet and dissociation: The first transference theory and its origins in hypnosis. *American Journal of Clinical Hypnosis, 29*(2), 86–94.

Havens, R. A. (1986). Posthypnotic predetermination of therapeutic progress. *American Journal of Clinical Hypnosis, 28*(4), 258–262.

Havens, R. A. (1987). The future orientation of Milton H. Erickson. In S. R. Lankton (Ed.), *Ericksonian monographs number 2: Central themes and principles of Ericksonian therapy.* New York: Brunner/Mazel.

Hilgard, E. R. (1973). A neodissociation interpretation of pain reduction in hypnosis. *Psychological Review, 80*(5), 403–419.

Hilgard, E. R. (1974). Sequelae to hypnosis. *The International Journal of Clinical and Experimental Hypnosis, 22*(4), 281–298.

Hilgard, E. R. (1977). *Divided consciousness: Multiple controls in human thought and action.* New York: Wiley.

Hilgard, E. R. (1979). Divided consciousness in hypnosis: The implications of the hidden observer. In E. Fromm & R. E. Shor (Eds.), *Hypnosis: Developments in research and new perspectives.* New York: Aldine.

Hilgard, E. R. (1987). Research advances in hypnosis: Issues and methods. *The International Journal of Clinical and Experimental Hypnosis, 35*(4), 248–264.

Hilgard, E. R., & Hilgard, J. R. (1975). *Hypnosis in the relief of pain.* Los Altos, CA: William Kaufmann, Inc.

Hilgard, E. R., & Hilgard, J. R. (1983). *Hypnosis in the relief of pain, revised edition.* Los Altos, CA: William Kaufmann, Inc.

Hilgard, E. R., & Hilgard, J. R. (1994). *Hypnosis in the relief of pain, revised edition.* New York: Brunner/Mazel. (Reprinted from 1983 edition, published by William Kaufmann, Inc., Los Altos, CA)

Hilgard, J. R., & LeBaron, B. (1984). *Hypnosis in the treatment of pain and anxiety in children with cancer: A clinical and quantitative investigation.* Los Altos, CA: William Kaufmann, Inc.

Hilgard, J. R., & LeBaron, S. (1982). Relief of anxiety and pain in children and adolescents with cancer: Quantitative measures and clinical observations. *International Journal of Clinical and Experimental Hypnosis, 30,* 417–442.

Hilgard, E. R., Morgan, A. H., & Macdonald, H. (1975). Pain and dissociation in the cold pressor test: A study of hypnotic analgesia with "hidden reports" through automatic keypressing and automatic talking. *Journal of Abnormal Psychology, 84,* 280–289.

Hull, C. L. (1933). *Hypnosis and suggestibility: An experimental approach.* New York: Appleton-Century-Croft.

Hynes, J. V. (1982). Hypnotic treatment of five adult cases of trichotillomania. *Australian Journal of Clinical and Experimental Hypnosis, 10*(2), 109–116.

Jackson, J. A. (1978). The use of hypnosis for analgesia in upper gastrointestinal endoscopy. *Australian Journal of Clinical and Experimental Hypnosis, 6*(1), 27–33.

Jackson, J. A., & Middleton, W. R. J. (1978). The use of hypnosis for analgesia in upper gastrointestinal endoscopy. *Australian Journal of Clinical and Experimental Hypnosis, 6*(1), 27–33.

Jones, B., & Spanos, N. P. (1982). Suggestions for altered auditory sensitivity, the negative subject effect and hypnotic susceptibility: A signal detection analysis. *Journal of Personality and Social Psychology, 43,* 637–647.

Kampman, R., & Kauppila, A. (1978). Severe vaginismus as the cause of unconsummated marriage: A case report of hypnoanalytic treatment. *Psychiatria-Fennica,* 179–181.

Kershaw, C. D. (1992). *The couple's hypnotic dance: Creating Ericksonian strategies in marital therapy.* New York: Brunner/Mazel.

Kihlstrom, J. F. (1979). Hypnosis and psychopathology: Retrospect and prospect. *Journal of Abnormal Psychology, 88*(5), 459–473.

Kihlstrom, J. F. (1985). Hypnosis. *Annual Review of Psychology, 36,* 385–418.

Kihlstrom, K. M., Evans, F. J., Orne, E. C., & Orne, M. T. (1980). Attempting to breach posthypnotic amnesia. *Journal of Abnormal Psychology, 89*(5), 603–616.

Knox, V. J., Crutchfield, L., & Hilgard E. R. (1975). The nature of task interference in hypnotic dissociation: An investigation of automatic behavior. *The International Journal of Clinical and Experimental Hypnosis, 23,* 305–323.

Knox, V. J., Morgan, A. H., & Hilgard, E. R. (1974). Pain and suffering in ischemia: The paradox of hypnotically suggested anesthesia as contradicted by reports from the "hidden observer." *Archives of General Psychology, 30*(6), 840–847.

Koe, G. G. Hypnotic treatment of sleep terror disorder: A case report. *American Journal of Clinical Hypnosis, 32*(1), 36–39.

Kohen, D. P., Olness, K. N., Colwell, S. O., & Hieimel, A. (1984). The use of relaxation-mental imagery (self-hypnosis) in the management of 505 pediatric behavioral encounters. *Developmental and Behavioral Pediatrics, 5*(1), 21–25.

Kroger, W. S. (1963). *Clinical and experimental hypnosis* (2nd edition). Philadelphia: J. B. Lippincott.

Lankton. S. R. (1982). The occurrence and use of trance phenomena in non-hypnotic therapies. In J. K. Zeig (Ed.), *Ericksonian approaches to hypnosis and psychotherapy.* New York: Brunner/Mazel.

Lankton, S. R. (Ed.). (1985). *Ericksonian monographs number 1: Elements and dimensions of an Ericksonian approach.* New York: Brunner/Mazel.

Lankton, S. R., & Lankton, C. H. (1983). *The answer within: A clinical framework of Erickson hypnotherapy.* New York: Brunner/Mazel.

Lankton, S. R., & Lankton, C. H. (1986). *Enchantment and intervention in family therapy: Training in Ericksonian approaches.* New York: Brunner/Mazel.

Laurence, J-R, Nadon, R., Nogrady, H., & Perry, C. (1986). Duality dissociation and memory creation in highly hypnotizable subjects. *The International Journal of Clinical and Experimental Hypnosis, 34*(4), 295–310.

Laurence, J-R, & Perry, C. (1983). Hypnotically created memory among highly hypnotizable subjects. *Science, 222,* 523–524.

Lehman, R. E. (1978). Brief hypnotherapy of neurodermatitis: A case with four-year followup. *American Journal of Clinical Hypnosis, 21*(1), 48–51.

Lewis, B. J. (1979). Treatment of a schizoid personality using hypnooperant therapy. *American Journal of Clinical Hypnosis, 22*(1), 42–46.

Loftus, E. F. (1993). The reality of repressed memories. *American Psychologist, 48,* 518–537.

Loftus, E. F., & Yapko, M. D. (1995). Psychotherapy and the recovery of repressed memories. In T. Ney (Ed.), *Allegations in child sexual abuse cases: Assessment and management.* New York: Brunner/Mazel.

Luria, A. R. (1973). *The working brain.* New York: Basic Books.

Lynn, S. J., Neufeld, V., & Maré, C. (1992). Direct versus indirect suggestions: A conceptual and methodological review. *The International Journal of Clinical and Experimental Hypnosis, 41*(2), 124–152.

MacHovec, F. J. (1985). Treatment variables and the use of hypnosis in the brief therapy of post-traumatic stress disorders. *The International Journal of Clinical and Experimental Hypnosis, 33*(1), 6–14.

Madanes, C. (1981). *Strategic family therapy.* San Francisco: Jossey-Bass.

Malone, M. D., Kurtz, R. M., & Strube, M. J. (1989). The effects of hypnotic suggestion on pain report. *American Journal of Clinical Hypnosis, 31*(4), 221–230.

Matheson, G. (1979). Modification of depressed symptoms through post-hypnotic suggestion. *American Journal of Clinical Hypnosis, 22*(1), 61–64.

McConkey, K. M., Glisky, M. L., & Kihlstrom, J. F. (1989). Individual differences among hypnotic virtuosos: A case comparison. *Australian Journal of Clinical and Experimental Hypnosis, 17*(2), 131–140.

McConkey, K. M., Sheehan, P. W., & Cross, D. G. (1980). Post-hypnotic amnesia: Seeing is not remembering. *British Journal of Social and Clinical Psychology, 19*, 99–107.

McCue, E. C., & McCur, P. A. (1988). Hypnosis in the elucidation of hysterical aphonia: A case report. *American Journal of Clinical Hypnosis, 30*(3), 178–182.

Messerschmidt, R. A. (1927–1928). A quantitative investigation of the alleged independent operation of conscious and subconscious processes. *Journal of Abnormal and Social Psychology, 22*, 325–340.

Miller, M. F., Barabosz, A. F., & Barabosz, M. (1991). Effects of active alert and relaxation hypnotic inductions on cold processor pain. *Journal of Abnormal Psychology, 100*(2), 223–226.

Millette, C. (1988). Using subparts in a case of multiple personality. In S. R. Lankton (Ed.), *Ericksonian monographs number 3: Treatment of special populations with Ericksonian approaches* (pp. 104–119). New York: Brunner/Mazel.

Mills, J., & Crowley, R. (1986). *Therapeutic metaphors for children and the child within.* New York: Brunner/Mazel.

Mills, J., & Crowley, R. (1988). A multidimensional approach to the utilization of therapeutic metaphors for children and adolescents. In J. K. Zeig & S. R. Lankton (Eds.), *Developing Ericksonian therapy: State of the art* (pp. 302–326).

Minuchin, S. (1974). *Families and family therapy.* Cambridge, MA: Harvard University Press.

Mon, C. T. (1982). Ericksonian approaches to general practice. In J. K. Zeig (Ed.), *Ericksonian approaches to hypnosis and psychotherapy* (pp. 292–298). New York: Brunner/Mazel.

Murray-Jobsis, J. (1991). An exploratory study of hypnotic capacity of schizophrenic and borderline patients in a clinical setting. *Ameri-*

can Journal of Clinical Hypnosis, 33(3), 150–160.

Nace, E. P., Orne, M. T., & Hammer, A. G. (1974). Posthypnotic amnesias as an active psychic process. *Archives of General Psychiatry, 31,* 257–260.

Nash, M. (1987). What, if anything, is regressed about hypnotic age regression? A review of the empirical literature. *Psychological Bulletin, 102,* 42–52.

O'Hanlon, W. H. (1987). *Taproots: Underlying principles of Milton Erickson's therapy and hypnosis.* New York: W. W. Norton & Company.

O'Hanlon, W. H., & Martin, M. (1992). *Solution-oriented hypnosis: An Ericksonian approach.* New York: W. W. Norton.

Olson, H. A. (1984). Hypnosis in the treatment of pain. *Individual Psychology Journal of Adlerian Theory, Research and Practice, 40*(4), 412–423.

Orman, D. J. (1991). Reframing of an addiction via hypnotherapy: A case presentation. *American Journal of Clinical Hypnosis, 33*(4), 263–271.

Orne, M. T. (1959). The nature of hypnosis: Artifact and essence. *Journal of Abnormal Psychology, 58,* 277–299.

Orne, M. T. (1979). The use and misuse of hypnosis in court. *International Journal of Clinical and Experimental Hypnosis, 27,* 311–341.

Oystragh, P. (1988). Vaginismus: A case study. *Australian Journal of Clinical and Experimental Hypnosis, 16*(2), 147–152.

Perry, C., & Lawrence, J. R. (1983). Hypnosis, surgery and mind-body interaction: An historical evaluation. *Canadian Journal of Behavioral Science, 15*(4), 351–372.

Pickering, J. D. (1986). Use of age regression in a case of traumatization during late childhood and adolescence. *Australian Journal of Clinical and Experimental Hypnosis, 14*(2), 169–172.

Price, D. D., & Barber, J. (1987). An analysis of factors that contribute to the efficacy of hypnotic analgesia. *Journal of Abnormal Psychology, 96*(1), 46–51.

Price, R. (1986). Hypnotic age repression and the reparenting of self. *Transactional Analysis Journal, 16*(2), 120–127.

Protinsky, H. (1988). Hypnotic strategies in strategic marital therapy. *Journal of Strategic and Systematic Therapies, 7*(4), 29–34.

Putnam, W. H. (1979). Hypnosis and distortions in eyewitness memory. *The International Journal of Clinical and Experimental Hypnosis, 27,* 437–438.

Raikov, V. L. (1980). Age regression to infancy by adult subjects in deep hypnosis. *American Journal of Clinical Hypnosis, 22*(3), 156–163.

Rausch, V. (1980). Cholecystectomy with self-hypnosis. *American Jour-*

nal of Clinical Hypnosis, 22(3), 124–129.

Reiff, R., & Scheerer, M. (1959). *Memory and hypnotic age regression: Developmental aspects of cognitive function explored through hypnosis.* New York: International Universities Press.

Relinger, H. (1984). Hypnotic hypermnesia: A critical review. *American Journal of Clinical Hypnosis, 26*(3), 212–225.

Rigler, D. (1982). Ericksonian techniques in a pediatric hospital. In J. K. Zeig (Ed.), *Ericksonian approaches to hypnosis and psychotherapy* (pp. 201–209). New York: Brunner/Mazel.

Rosen, S. (1985). Hypnosis as an adjunct to chemotherapy in cancer. In J. K. Zeig (Ed.), *Ericksonian psychotherapy: Vol. 2, Clinical applications* (pp. 287–297). New York: Brunner/Mazel.

Rossi, E. (1971). Growth, change and transformation in dreams. *Journal of Humanistic Psychology, 11*, 147–169.

Rossi, E. (1972a). *Dreams and the growth of personality.* New York: Pergamon Press.

Rossi, E. (1972b). Self reflection in dreams. *Psychotherapy, 9*, 290–298.

Rossi, E. (1973a). The dream-protein hypothesis. *American Journal of Psychiatry, 130*, 1094–1097.

Rossi, E. (1973b). Psychological shocks and creative moments in psychotherapy. *American Journal of Clinical Hypnosis, 16*, 9–22.

Rossi, E. (1973c). Psychosynthesis and the new biology of dreams and psychotherapy. *American Journal of Psychotherapy, 27*, 34–41.

Rossi, E. L. (Ed.). (1980a). *The collected papers of Milton H. Erickson on hypnosis.*
Vol. I: *The nature of hypnosis and suggestion.*
Vol. II: *Hypnotic alteration of sensory, perceptual, and psychophysical processes.*
Vol. III: *Hypnotic investigation of psychodynamic processes.*
Vol. IV: *Innovative hypnotherapy.*
New York: Irvington.

Rossi, E. L. (Ed.). (1980b). Time distortion. In *The collected papers of Milton H. Erickson on hypnosis. Vol. II. Hypnotic alteration of sensory, perceptual, and psychophysical processes.* New York: Irvington, 219–220.

Rossi, E. L. (Ed.). (1980c). Psychophysiological processes. In *The collected papers of Milton H. Erickson on hypnosis. Vol. II. Hypnotic alteration of sensory, perceptual, and psychophysical processes.* New York: Irvington, 143–144.

Rossi, E. L. (Ed.). (1980d). Approaches to trance induction. In *The collected papers of Milton H. Erickson on hypnosis. Vol. I. The nature of hypnosis and suggestion.* New York: Irvington, 133–134.

Rossi, E. L., Ryan, M. O., & Sharp, F. A. (Eds.). (1983). *Healing in hypno-*

sis. I. The seminars, workshops and lectures of Milton H. Erickson. New York: Irvington.

Rossi,. E. L., & Ryan. M. O. (1985). *Life reframing in hypnosis. II. The seminars, workshops and lectures of Milton H. Erickson.* New York: Irvington.

Rossi, E. L., & Ryan, M. O. (Eds.). (1986). *Mind-body communication in hypnosis. III. The seminars, workshops and lectures of Milton H. Erickson.* New York: Irvington.

Rowen, R. (1981). Hypnotic age regression in the treatment of a self-destructive habit: Trichotillomania. *American Journal of Clinical Hypnosis, 23*(3), 195–197.

Sacerdote, P. (1982). Erickson's contribution to pain control in cancer. In J. K. Zeig (Ed.), *Ericksonian approaches to hypnosis and psychotherapy* (pp. 336–345). New York: Brunner/Mazel.

Sackeim, H. A., Nordlie, J. W., & Gur, R. C. (1979). A model of hysterical and hypnotic blindness: Cognition, motivation and awareness. *Journal of Abnormal Psychology, 88*(5), 474–489.

Sanders, G. S., & Simmons, W. L. (1983). Use of hypnosis to enhance eyewitness accuracy: Does it work? *Journal of Applied Psychology, 68*, 70–77.

Schwarz, R. (1993). Ericksonian approaches to resolving post-traumatic stress disorder. Workshop, *Third Eastern Conference on Ericksonian Hypnosis and Psychotherapy: Tools for Transforming Personal Experience©*, Philadelphia, PA.

Scott, D. L. (1975). Hypnosis in plastic surgery. *The American Journal of Clinical Hypnosis, 18*(2), 98–103.

Selvini Palazzoli, M., Boscolo, L., Cecchin, G., & Prata, G. (1978). *Paradox and counterparadox.* New York: Jason Aronson.

Sexton, R. O., & Maddock, R. C. (1979). Age regression and age progression in psychotic and neurotic depression. *American Journal of Clinical Hypnosis, 22*(1), 37–40.

Sheehan, P. W., & Tilden, J. (1983). Effects of suggestibility and hypnosis on accurate and distorted retrieval from memory. *Journal of Experimental Psychology: Learning, Memory, Cognition, 9*, 283–293.

Shor, R. E., & Orne, E. C. (1962). *Harvard Group Scales of Hypnotic Susceptibility.* Palo Alto, CA: Consulting Psychologists' Press.

Silva, M. N. (1990). "May the force be with you": hypnotherapy with a leukemic child. *Psychology in Private Practice, 8*(3), 49–54. Presented at 96th annual convention of the American Psychological Association: Hypnotherapy with children and adolescents [1988, Atlanta, Georgia].

Singh, R. (1989). Single-session treatment of refractory headache: Evaluation with three patients. *Australian Journal of Clinical and Experi-*

mental Hypnosis, 17(1), 99–105.

Spanos, N. P. (1982). A social psychological approach to hypnotic behavior. In G. Weary, H. L. Mirels (Eds.), *Integrations of clinical and social psychology.* New York: Oxford.

Spanos, N. P. (1986). More on the social psychology of hypnotic responding. *The Behavioral and Brain Sciences, 9*(3), 489–502.

Spiegel, D., & Rosenfeld, A. (1984). Spontaneous hypnotic age regression: Case report. *Journal of Clinical Psychiatry, 45,* 522–524.

Spiegel, H., & Spiegel, D. (1978). *Trance and treatment.* Washington, D.C.: American Psychiatric Press.

Spiegel, D., Bierre, P., & Rootenberg, J. (1989). Hypnotic alteration of somatosensory perception. *American Journal of Psychiatry, 146,* 749–754.

Spiegel, D., Cutcomb, S., Ren, C., & Pribram, K. (1985). Hypnotic hallucination alters evoked potentials. *Journal of Abnormal Psychology, 94*(3), 3249–3255.

Squire, L. R. (1987). *Memory and brain.* New York: Oxford University Press.

Stava, L. J., & Jaffa, M. (1988). Some operationalizations of the neodissociation concept and their relationship to hypnotic susceptibility. *Journal of Personality and Social Psychology, 54*(6), 989–996.

Stevenson, J. A. (1976). Effect of posthypnotic dissociation on the performance of interfering tasks. *Journal of Abnormal Psychology, 85,* 398–407.

Tart, C. T. (1978/1979). Quick and convenient assessment of hypnotic depth: Self-report scales. *American Journal of Clinical Hypnosis, 21*(2)(3), 186–205.

Tenebaum, S. J., Kurtz, R. M., & Bienias, J. L. (1990). Hypnotic susceptibility and experimental pain reduction. *American Journal of Clinical Hypnosis, 33*(1), 40–49.

Tilton, P. (1983). Pseudo-orientation in time in the treatment of agoraphobia. *American Journal of Clinical Hypnosis, 25*(4), 267–269.

Twerski, A. J., & Naar, R. (1976). Guilt clarification via age regression. *American Journal of Clinical Hypnosis, 18*(3), 204–206.

Unestähl, L-E. (1979). Hypnotic preparation of athletes. In G. Burrows, D. Collison, & L. Dennerstein (Eds.), *Hypnosis.* North-Holland: Elsevier.

Van Gorp, W. G., Meyer, R. G., & Dunbar, K. D. (1985). The efficacy of direct versus indirect hypnotic induction techniques on reduction of experimental pain. *The International Journal of Clinical and Experimental Hypnosis, 33*(4), 319–328.

Wagenfeld, J., & Carlson, W. A. (1979). Use of hypnosis in the alleviation of reading problems. *American Journal of Clinical Hypnosis,*

22(1), 51–53.

Walthan, R. G., Morris, D. M., Goebel, R. A., & Blass, N. H. (1987). Preoperative and intraoperative rehearsal in hypnoanesthesia for major surgery. *American Journal of Clinical Hypnosis, 29*(4), 238–240.

Warren, C. (1990). A program for self-hypnosis and age regression. *Individual Psychology, 46*(4), 503–507.

Weeks, G. R., & L'Abate, L. (1982). *Paradoxical psychotherapy: Theory and practice with individuals, couples, and families.* New York: Brunner/Mazel.

Weitzenhoffer, A. M. (1950). A note on the persistence of hypnotic suggestion. *Journal of Abnormal Social Psychology, 45,* 160–162.

Weitzenhoffer, A. M. (1961). Signal injection and objectification of hallucinatory experiences. A methodological note. *Perceptual and Motor Skills, 13,* 115–118.

Weitzenhoffer, A. M. (1963). "Credulity" and "skepticism" in hypnotic research: A critical examination of Sutcliff's thesis and evidence. Part I. *American Journal of Clinical Hypnosis, 6,* 137–162.

Weitzenhoffer, A. M. (1964). "Credulity" and "skepticism" in hypnotic research: A critical examination of Sutcliff's thesis and evidence. Part II. *American Journal of Clinical Hypnosis, 6,* 241–268.

Weitzenhoffer, A. M. (1989a). *The practice of hypnotism* (Vol. I). New York: John Wiley & Sons.

Weitzenhoffer, A. M. (1989b). *The practice of hypnotism* (Vol. II). New York: John Wiley & Sons.

Weitzenhoffer, A. M., & Hilgard, E. R. (1959). *Stanford Hypnotic Susceptibility Scale, Forms A and B.* Palo Alto, CA: Consulting Psychologists' Press.

Weitzenhoffer, A. M., & Hilgard, E. R. (1962). *Stanford Hypnotic Susceptibility Scale, Form C.* Palo Alto, CA: Consulting Psychologists' Press.

Weitzenhoffer, A. M., & Hilgard, E. R. (1967). *Revised Stanford Profile Scales of Hypnotic Susceptibility, Forms I and II.* Palo Alto, CA: Consulting Psychologists' Press.

Werner, W. E., Schauble, P. G., & Snudson, M. S. (1982). An argument for revival of hypnosis in obstetrics. *American Journal of Clinical Hypnosis, 24*(3), 149–171.

Wickramasekera, I. E. (1988). *Clinical behavioral medicine: Some concepts and procedures.* New York: Plenum Press.

Wicks, G. R. (1982). A rapid induction technique, mechanics and rationale. *Australian Journal of Clinical and Experimental Hypnosis, 10*(2), 117–119.

Wojcikiewicz, A., & Orlick, T. (1987). The effects of post-hypnotic suggestion and relaxation with suggestion on competitive fencing anxiety and performance. *International Journal of Sport Psychology, 18,* 303–313.

Wolpe, J., & Lazarus, A. (1966). *Behavioral therapy techniques.* New York: Pergamon Press.

Yapko, M. D. (Ed.). (1986). *Hypnotic and strategic interventions: Principles and practice.* New York: Irvington.

Yapko, M. D. (1990). *Trancework: An introduction to the practice of clinical hypnosis.* New York: Brunner/Mazel.

Yapko, M. D. (1994). Memories of the future: Regression and suggestion of abuse. In J. K. Zeig (Ed.), *Ericksonian methods: The essence of the story.* New York: Brunner/Mazel.

Zeig, J. K. (1974). Hypnotherapy techniques with psychotic inpatients. *American Journal of Clinical Hypnosis, 17,* 56–59.

Zeig. J. K. (1978). *Symbolic hypnotherapy* (video recording). Phoenix, AZ: The Milton H. Erickson Foundation, Inc.

Zeig, J. K. (1984). Hypnotic constellation. (Handout)

Zeig, J. K. (1985a). The clinical use of amnesia: Ericksonian methods. In J. K. Zeig (Ed.), *Ericksonian Psychotherapy, Vol. II: Structures.* New York: Brunner/Mazel.

Zeig, J. K (1985b). *Experiencing Erickson: An introduction to the man and his work.* New York: Brunner/Mazel.

Zeig, J. K. (1987). Therapeutic patterns of Ericksonian influence on communication. In J. K. Zeig (Ed.), *The evolution of psychotherapy* (pp. 392–412). New York: Brunner/Mazel.

Zeig, J. K. (1988a). Ericksonian Psychotherapy. Workshop sponsored by the Milton H. Erickson Institute of Philadelphia. Philadephia, PA.

Zeig, J. K. (1988b). An Ericksonian phenomenological approach to therapeutic hypnotic induction and symptom utilization. In J. K. Zeig & S. R. Lankton (Eds.), *Developing Ericksonian therapy: State of the art.* New York: Brunner/Mazel.

Zeig, J. K. (1990a). Ericksonian methods of pain control. Workshop sponsored by the Milton H. Erickson Institute of Philaelphia. Philadelphia, PA.

Zeig, J. K. (1990b). *The language of hypnosis: Microdynamic gift wrapping of possibilities.* Workshop Handout.

Zeig, J. K. (1990c). Seeding. In J. K. Zeig & S. G. Gilligan (Eds.), *Brief therapy: Myths, methods, and metaphors.* New York: Brunner/Mazel.

Zeig, J. K., & Lankton, S. R. (Eds.). (1988). *Developing Ericksonian therapy: State of the art.* New York: Brunner/Mazel.

Zeig, J. K., & Rennick, P. T. (1991). Ericksonian hypnotherapy: A communications approach to hypnosis. In S. J. Lynn & J. W. Rhue (Eds.), *Theories in hypnosis: Current models and perspectives.* New York: The Guilford Press.

Zelig, M., & Beidelman, W. B. (1981). The investigative use of hypnosis: A word of caution. *International Journal of Clinical and Experimental Hypnosis, 29*, 401–412.

Zelling, D. (1989). Hole in the soul. *Medical Hypnoanalysis Journal, 4*(3), 94–99.

NAME INDEX

SUBJECT INDEX

311